20,522

363.2

D   Dudley, William

Police Brutality

Police Brutality

Other books in the Current Controversies series:

The AIDS Crisis
Drug Trafficking
Energy Alternatives
Iraq
Women in the Military

Police Brutality

David L. Bender, *Publisher*
Bruno Leone, *Executive Editor*
Bonnie Szumski, *Managing Editor*
Carol Wekesser, *Senior Editor*

William Dudley, *Book Editor*

Cover photo: P.F. Bentley/Time Magazine

Library of Congress Cataloging-in-Publication Data

Police brutality / William Dudley, book editor.
    p. cm. — (Current controversies)
  Includes bibliographical references and index.
  Summary: An anthology of various articles debating whether police brutality is a national crisis, what its causes are, how it can be stopped, and a case study of police brutality.
  ISBN 0-89908-580-6 (lib. bdg.) — ISBN 0-89908-586-5 (pbk.)
  1. Police—United States—Complaints against. [1. Police—Complaints against.] I. Dudley, William, 1964-   . II. Series.
HV8141.P564   1991
363.2'32—dc20   91-22818

Printed on
recycled paper

Contents

No: Police Brutality Is Not a National Crisis

Chapter 2: What Are the Causes of Police Brutality?

Chapter 3: How Can Police Brutality Be Stopped?

The Police Can Police Themselves

Civilians Must Police the Police

responsible for their actions. Only civilian review boards, comprised of members of the community who have the power to investigate and punish incidents of brutality, can stop police misconduct.

Foreword

By definition, controversies are "discussions of questions in which opposing opinions clash" (*Webster's Twentieth Century Dictionary Unabridged*). Few would deny that controversies are a pervasive part of the human condition and exist on virtually every level of human enterprise. Controversies transpire between individuals and among groups, within nations and between nations. Controversies supply the grist necessary for progress by providing challenges and challengers to the status quo. They also create atmospheres where strife and warfare can flourish. A world without controversies would be a peaceful world; but it also would be, by and large, static and prosaic.

The Series' Purpose

The purpose of the Current Controversies series is to explore many of the social, political, and economic controversies dominating the national and international scenes today. Titles selected for inclusion in the series are highly focused and specific. For example, from the larger category of criminal justice, Current Controversies deals with specific topics such as police brutality, gun control, white collar crime, and others. The debates in Current Controversies also are presented in a useful, timeless fashion. Articles and book excerpts included in each title are selected if they contribute valuable, long-range ideas to the overall debate. And wherever possible, current information is enhanced with historical documents and other relevant materials.

Thus, while individual titles are current in focus, every effort is made to ensure that they will not become quickly outdated. Books in the Current Controversies series will remain important resources for librarians, teachers, and students for many years.

In addition to keeping the titles focused and specific, great care is taken in the editorial format of each book in the series. Book introductions and chapter prefaces are offered to provide background material for readers. Chapters are organized around several key questions that are answered with diverse opinions representing all points on the political spectrum. Materials in each chapter include opinions in which authors clearly disagree as well as alternative opinions in which authors may agree on a broader issue but disagree on the possible solutions. In this way, the content of each volume in Current Controversies mirrors the mosaic of opinions encountered in society. Readers will quickly realize that there are many viable answers to these complex issues. By questioning each author's conclusions, students and casual readers can begin to develop the critical thinking skills so important to evaluating opinionated material.

Current Controversies is also ideal for controlled research. Each anthology in the series is composed of primary sources taken from a wide gamut of informational categories including periodicals, newspapers, books, United States and foreign government documents, and the publications of private and public organizations.

Readers will find factual support for reports, debates, and research papers covering all areas of important issues. In addition, an annotated table of contents, an index, a book and periodical bibliography, and a list of organizations to contact are included in each book to expedite further research.

Perhaps more than ever before in history, people are confronted with diverse and contradictory information. During the Persian Gulf War, for example, the public was not only treated to minute-to-minute coverage of the war, it was also inundated with critiques of the coverage and countless analyses of the factors motivating U.S. involvement. Being able to sort through the plethora of opinions accompanying today's major issues, and to draw one's own conclusions, can be a complicated and frustrating struggle. It is the editors' hope that Current Controversies will help readers with this struggle.

Introduction

In July 1991, a specially appointed commission called the Christopher Commission released its findings concerning brutality in the Los Angeles Police Department (LAPD). The commission, created in response to the videotaped and widely shown beating of motorist Rodney King on March 3, 1991, examined more than one million documents and interviewed hundreds of people, including police officers, private citizens, and criminal justice experts. The commission concluded that police brutality was a significant problem within the LAPD, arguing that a minority "problem group" of officers engaged in repetitive, unjustified use of force. To support its conclusions, the commission noted that over a period of four years, forty-four police officers were cited in at least six allegations of brutality, yet still received favorable performance reviews from the department.

Los Angeles is not alone in its problems with police brutality. Most major U.S. cities have had publicized incidents of alleged police brutality. For example, in New York City in August 1988, fifty-two people required medical attention after police violently enforced a curfew in a city park. In San Francisco seven protesters at a 1988 United Farm Workers demonstration were beaten; they eventually won a $24 million lawsuit. In Atlanta in March 1991, two black youths were beaten by police officers after a car chase; one fifteen-year old was killed.

Incidents like these have raised questions and sparked a national debate about police brutality.

Investigations such as that done by the Christopher Commission reveal that brutality is one manifestation of the often troubled relationship between the police and the community they are supposed to serve and protect. This relationship and differing conceptions concerning the proper role of police in society are the roots of much of the controversy over police brutality.

Two Views of the Police

Criminal justice professor Donald B. Walker has argued that Americans are divided between two fundamentally different views of the police officer's role in society. "One camp, fearful of crime and disorder, views the police as the last remaining force standing between them and the overwhelming chaos," he writes. Those who hold this view of police as a "thin blue line" against criminals are often quicker to defend the police against criticisms of brutality. The other view of police, according to Walker, perceives them "as brutal, oppressive agents of the state and tends to paint all police with the same brush." People who hold this view are more apt to believe all reports of police brutality and to view all police officers with suspicion.

Despite their seeming opposition, these two ways of viewing the police are similar in one crucial aspect. Both see the police and civilians as fundamentally opposed to each other and police brutality as almost inevitable. Perhaps a new middle ground between these views is necessary; one that tries to find ways of encouraging trust and cooperation between the two groups.

An analysis of police brutality thus becomes an examination of the obstacles to mutual trust and understanding between civilians and police. One major obstacle is that police are often separated from the community by the nature of their work. In the past, many police officers patrolled a particular neighborhood and became acquainted with most of its residents. Today the neighborhood patrol officer has been replaced by officers in squad cars who respond to emergency calls. They interact with community members only after crimes have been committed, not in an effort to prevent crime. Consequently, the civilians police most often come in contact with are people they are trying to arrest or confront. Their work thus leaves little room for normal human interaction with members of the community, and thus little opportunity for mutual understanding.

Hazards of Police Work

In addition, police work is often brutal and dehumanizing in a way few people outside the police force understand. About 80 percent of police work involves responding to accidents, injuries, medical emergencies, and other non-crime-related incidents. The other 20 percent involves dangerous, even life-threatening situations. Police routinely deal with people whose behaviors range from rude and disorderly to extremely dangerous. In 1989 in the U.S., 146 police officers were killed and 62, 172 were victims of assaults. Kent W. Perry, a police officer for almost twenty years, writes:

> I've been shot, punched, kicked, spat upon and cussed. As personally unsettling as all these things are, even more disheartening is the simple fact that for most police such occurrences are almost routine.

Police officers, according to criminal defense lawyer Kevin M. Doyle, must endure such abuse. They have few legal ways to respond. Doyle writes, "New York courts, for instance, pretend that cops are androids and hold that what would be punishable harassment if directed at a regular citizen should just roll off an officer's thick-skinned back." Such frustrations worsen police-community relations and are a contributing factor to brutality.

Mixed Messages

Police-community relations are also complicated by the mixed messages police receive from their superiors and from the general public. Street officers are told by their superiors to do what is necessary to get the job done, but not to get caught in acts of brutality. Politicians and the media build public support for "wars on crime," yet police are expected to use force only when absolutely necessary. Doyle argues that despite rules and laws against unnecessary force, the message many police officers implicitly receive is that "there are times when unnecessary force is necessary or, at least, to be expected and overlooked."

While few people state this position so openly, Mark H. Moore, criminal justice professor at Harvard University, writes that much of the U.S. public has a similar understanding of the police.

> If the police were going to do the hard job of dealing with crime and offenders, they had to be allowed to behave badly. This view was articulated by one police officer who explained to me: "If you're going to have to shovel society's [garbage], you ought to be indulged a little bit."
>
> The police eventually discover that this tacit deal with the community is . . . unreliable. . . . . When an incident occurs, as it inevitably will, . . . the public turns on the police.

Such mixed messages, Moore and others write, can create cynicism and a sense of isolation in many police departments. Police officers in many departments band together for support and understanding. One result of this group identity is the police "code of silence." Police officers face strong peer pressure not to report on each other in incidents of brutality, and to support each other in their dealings with uncooperative citizens. A Los Angeles police officer elaborates: "What do you do if you see your partner do something wrong? If you can't stop him from doing it, you're supposed to tell the watch commander. But if you squeal, no one will want to work with you." In a job where one's life can depend on the quick action of a fellow worker, such pressure is hard to ignore. The unwillingness of police to testify against each other makes it difficult to punish and discipline offenders. Feeling confident that other officers will not testify, some may be more inclined to continue acts of brutality.

Finally, police-community relations, including police brutality, are affected by many of the racial, ethnic, and economic divisions in U.S. society. For example, while only 40 percent of the population of Los Angeles is nonwhite, white officers make up 61 percent of the LAPD. Similar imbalances exist in other major U.S. cities with large nonwhite populations. Police officers often confront people who are not only of a different race, but of a different ethnic and economic background. These social factors, combined with the nature of police work, often foster feelings of racial prejudice and cultural misunderstanding. These feelings can reinforce any tendencies toward brutality the police officers may have. Sociologist James Marquart argues that "white officers don't understand a lot of things that go on in these areas. One way to deal with that is to use force. It goes across all cultural boundaries." The result is that police brutality is most common in minority communities. As writer Kerwin Brooks asserts, "Unlike other types of crime, the vast majority of police brutality cases are committed by white police officers against non-white victims. In almost all of these cases, racial epithets are part of the verbal onslaught victims suffer."

Journalist Salim Muwakkil has called brutality evidence of the "racist reality of U.S. law enforcement." His judgment was supported by the Christopher Commission's examination of the transcripts of computer messages Los Angeles police officers made while working. Among the messages found were: "If you encounter these negroes, shoot first and ask questions later," and "I almost got me a Mexican last night but he dropped the gun too damn quick." The commission also found that "a large number of witnesses complained that there is a general climate of hostility between the police and members of minority communities."

These factors are only part of the complexities surrounding the police brutality issue, complexities that are implicitly and explicitly dealt with in this volume. *Police Brutality: Current Controversies* is divided into three chapters which examine the extent of police brutality, its causes, and its prevention. Current and former police officers, criminal justice experts and professors, psychologists, journalists, and others present their theories about the complex issue of police brutality and the broader problem of the relationship between the police and the communities they serve.

Chapter 1

Is Police Brutality a National Crisis?

Police Brutality in the U.S.: An Overview

Eric Harrison

About the Author: *Eric Harrison is a staff writer for the* Los Angeles Times, *a daily newspaper.*

Editor's note: Incidents of police brutality are often difficult for the victim to prove. This is especially true of poor victims or those with criminal records, people who may not have the resources or support to make their stories heard. Rodney King, a black unemployed construction worker with a previous felony conviction, originally doubted whether anyone would believe his story of being beaten by Los Angeles police officers on March 3, 1991, according to his lawyer Steven Lerman. Fortunately for King the beating was captured on videotape and broadcast on national television. This tape sparked a national uproar in part because it lent credence to many other complaints of police brutality. A poll taken by Newsweek *after the Rodney King incident found 62 percent of those polled believed that police brutality was a significant problem for minority communities.*

Was the Rodney King incident an "aberration," as Los Angeles Police Chief Daryl Gates stated, or did it prove that brutality is common and widespread? The viewpoints in this chapter focus on this question and come to varying conclusions. In the following overview, Los Angeles Times *journalist Eric Harrison examines incidents of police misconduct in several cities, and notes the divergent opinions held by experts as to whether police brutality is common nationwide.*

John Davis, a white 46-year-old farmer in rural Mason County, Wash., has little in common with Los Angeles' Rodney G. King. But, in recent weeks, whenever he has watched the videotape of the beating King received at the hands of Los Angeles police officers, Davis has been carried back to a summer afternoon in 1985.

On that day Davis was beaten by sheriff's deputies, in the words of one witness, until he "looked like he had been dipped in a bucket of blood."

Davis and his 15-year-old nephew were driving a load of hay in a horse-drawn wagon down a public road when a sheriff's deputy ordered him to move over to let cars pass. The patrol car's loudspeaker frightened the horses, though, and Davis couldn't control them.

That was when the deputy drew his gun. When the farmer stepped down, he was beaten, kicked and shocked with an electric stun gun by the deputy and two others who arrived on the scene. They swarmed over him, Davis recalled. "It just escalated into more and greater excitement. Their adrenaline just kept building until the climax," he said.

The videotape of the King beating began airing several days before a federal appellate court awarded Davis a $375,000 settlement stemming from his beating. When he saw the tape, "boy howdy, I had the feelings come right back to me," Davis said. "There was the same energy in the air, I could see it. I'd just cringe to watch it."

> ## "Forty-one people died in New York in 1990 in police gunfire, the highest number since 1975."

But how emblematic was that disturbing videotaped scene? Did it truly, as the Davis and other cases suggest, pull back the covers from America's dirty little secret, a secret some suggest had never really been kept under wraps in certain neighborhoods?

While some activists and lawyers describe police brutality as "endemic," particularly in minority communities, most law enforcement officials and some legal authorities say it would be a mistake to conclude that the problem is getting worse nationwide. On the contrary, most see it as less severe today than 20 years ago.

No one can quantify the police brutality problem because no agency keeps national records, and comparing statistics from city to city is rendered meaningless by inconsistent record-keeping methods.

"It's almost impossible to speak about the problem except in an anecdotal, impressionistic manner," said Gerald M. Caplan, a George Washington University law school professor, who formerly headed the National Institute of Justice and served as general counsel of the District of Columbia police.

Fewer Civilians Killed

"The number of people killed by police has gone down from the mid-1970s to the mid-1980s in major cities," said Patrick V. Murphy, who rose from a beat patrolman in New York City to head police commissions in Detroit and New York and a similar post in Washington, D.C. He now directs the police policy board of the U.S. Conference of Mayors and will serve as a senior adviser to Mayor Tom Bradley's panel investigating the King incident. "I'm satisfied departments are much stricter about it [police brutality]," he said. "The FBI investigates these things, and it didn't 20 years ago. Lawsuits have increased dramatically, and liability forces mayors and city councils to get into it."

Samuel Walker, a criminal justice professor at the University of Nebraska, agrees that there has been improved management, higher personnel standards and better training since the 1960s. Furthermore, he said, about 30 of the nation's 50 largest cities have adopted some form of citizen review board to handle complaints against police officers, many since 1986.

"So L.A.," he said, "is out of step at this point."

But, acknowledging the lack of statistical evidence, he argues that police departments "lost momentum" in the late 1980s on curbing the use of excessive force. "Something happened out there," he said. "I can't prove that, but I believe it."

Federico Pereira was killed Feb. 5, 1991. A grand jury indicted five New York City police officers March 20 on charges of murder, manslaughter and assault in the choking and beating death of the 21-year-old car theft suspect.

One of the five officers indicted allegedly climbed onto the back of the prone and handcuffed Pereira and placed two hands around his neck, pulling his head back until his spine was bowed. Pereira died at a hospital soon after.

The officers, all of whom have pleaded not guilty, maintain that Pereira became violent when the officers tried to arrest him and that he repeatedly banged his head on the pavement while they attempted to restrain him.

But to Latino activists in New York, the Pereira case was another demonstration of rising police violence in their community. From 1986 to 1989, an average of seven Latinos a year were killed by police gunfire in the city, but in 1990, 23 were killed.

In all, 41 people died in New York in 1990 in police gunfire, the highest number since 1975 and an increase of 37% over the 30 fatal shootings of civilians by police in 1989.

Police officials contend that the rise in the number of fatal shootings reflects a harsh reality—the streets are getting meaner as the drug trade grows more violent and guns become increasingly prevalent. Thirty-three of the 41 civilians killed in New York, for example, were armed, according to official statistics.

"In most cities allegations of police misconduct are investigated by other police officers."

But critics of the department note that almost 75% of New York's police force is white—in a city where whites make up less than 50% of the population—and more than 40% of the officers live outside the city. Many of those who live in the suburbs, Latino activists contend, bring with them prejudices and phobias.

Part of the problem nationwide, said Walker, the University of Nebraska professor, may be racism. But he and others also think the war on drugs is to blame. "It sent a message to police officers that you can go out there and kick some butt, do whatever you need to do."

Murphy agreed. "There is no doubt that this war-on-drugs rhetoric is part of the problem—raiding all these crack houses, more guns on the street, cops getting automatics," he said. "It has cops so psyched up they think they are in combat."

Said Seattle attorney Timothy K. Ford: "What is the war on drugs? It's a war on people, and with a war, there's going to be collateral damage."

Miami Cases

In March 1991, two West Palm Beach police officers were indicted on charges of second degree murder and aggravated battery in the death of a man who was savagely beaten to death in November 1990 as he was walking home from a McDonald's restaurant.

Undercover officers Stephen Rollins and Glen Thurlow were driving down the street in a gold Cadillac, police say, when they stopped Robert R. Jewett, a 34-year-old plasterer. There are no witnesses to exactly what happened next. But within minutes, Jewett was dead from a beating in which his Adam's apple was crushed, nine ribs were broken and he was hit between the legs with nightsticks with such fury as to cause what one veteran medical examiner called "the most severe testicular damage I'd ever seen."

Both officers, who were suspended without pay, have been named in previous brutality complaints.

In South Florida, and particularly in Miami, the issue of police brutality has long haunted relations between police and the black community.

In what became a landmark event in Miami history, black insurance man Arthur McDuffie was riding a friend's motorcycle on the morning of Dec. 17, 1979, when, according to police, he flashed them an obscene gesture and sped away. After a short chase, McDuffie pulled over and up to 12 officers wielding heavy flashlights began to pummel him. He died four days later of a fractured skull.

Almost five months later, when four of the officers on trial for taking part in the beating, and then covering it up, were acquitted by an all-white jury, Miami erupted. In three days of vicious rioting, 18 persons were killed, hundreds were injured and blocks of Liberty City were sacked and torched.

During the 1980s, two other riots convulsed Miami, both touched off by shootings of black men by Latino police officers.

Law enforcement officials acknowledge that many officers are edgy and that tempers get short. But they argue that cops have a right to be that way.

Col. W.D. Teem, commander of the North Carolina Highway Patrol, said, "police officers are running scared" because "more and more people resist arrest. These men and women have to be careful. It's a sign of the times."

"What gets lost is we have to deal with a lot of society's rejects and misfits," said Ronnie Clackum, chief of the Clayton County Police Department in Georgia. "People call the police when there's no one else to call."

"The number of police brutality complaints have gone up since the Rodney King case first was publicized."

Clackum, who said he doesn't tolerate excessive force in his department, added that high-speed chases put officers on edge. "The adrenaline gets to flowing, and by the time someone sideswipes your car, officers get so caught up in the events and emotion that they overreact," he said.

But Brian Spears, an Atlanta lawyer, speaks of

the "spiraling effect" of police brutality, arguing that, in communities where the police have a reputation for using excessive force, suspects may flee or resist arrest precisely because they fear what will happen to them in police custody. "It [police brutality] breeds disrespect and mistrust and makes it likely that people who are taken into custody will act out of fear and run. Or fight."

A New York state investigative panel called for the appointment of a special prosecutor to look into the fatal police shooting of a black man on Long Island in 1984.

The state Commission of Investigation charged that local prosecutors had skewed evidence to favor the police account of the death of Ricky McCargo, 27, who was shot in a parking lot by a Nassau County detective. A Nassau County grand jury heard evidence in the case in 1984 and refused to hand up an indictment against the detective.

Several witnesses said McCargo was on his knees, begging for his life, when he was shot.

In a large number of excessive force cases, there are no outside witnesses. Determining the facts—both for the public and for juries—often is difficult, according to lawyers and civil rights organizations that deal with brutality issues.

Code of Silence

Even when other officers are present, corroboration often is difficult to get, say lawyers, because officers stick to the "code of silence" that bonds them. As Ralph Goldberg, an Atlanta lawyer, explained: "You don't rat on your partner."

In most cities allegations of police misconduct are investigated by other police officers, so there is widespread public suspicion that brutality or other misdeeds are covered up.

"In approximately 8,000 complaints investigated [in New York City] in 1987 and 1988, there was not a single instance of an officer coming forward with incriminating information about another officer," said Norman Siegel, executive director of the New York Civil Liberties *Union.*

John R. Dunne, assistant U.S. attorney general for civil rights, said criminal civil rights prosecutions for police misconduct are "among the most difficult under federal law. Almost always, the victims of police abuse have themselves committed some kind of law violation which has brought them to the attention of the police in the first place. Thus, their credibility is not always easy to establish."

"With the L.A. tapes, people are shocked, people who wouldn't have believed police brutality existed."

But some lawyers contend that frequently the only charge filed against brutality victims is resisting arrest. "I get a lot of guys coming in here with black eyes and bruises," said Lori Lefferts, assistant district attorney for Pima County (Tucson), Ariz. "They're being charged with resisting arrest to cover the officers' rear ends, but I've never seen any of these charges prosecuted."

Some lawyers think the nationwide publicity surrounding the Rodney King tape will make it easier to successfully prosecute police brutality cases.

"With the L.A. tapes, people are shocked, people who wouldn't have believed police brutality really existed," said Patty Bates, who works with brutality victims on behalf of Dallas' privately funded Community Relations Commission. "There's no way you can deny anymore that it's happening."

"It's one of those epiphanies," said Harvard law professor Alan Dershowitz. "It's one of those transforming events which will never allow the situation to be viewed the same."

Such visual evidence is producing quick action elsewhere. Charleston, S.C., policeman Julius Jeng was photographed kneeing a suspect who was being held by another officer. Police later released the suspect, Howard Sims, saying he had been mistaken for another man. Although no complaint was filed against the department, Jeng was temporarily suspended.

How Big a Problem?

Charles Friel, dean of the college of criminal justice at Sam Houston State University in Huntsville, questions whether the highly publicized police brutality cases are a good sample of reality.

"Hundreds, thousands of arrests are done competently," he said. "When you have an incident like L.A., and it gets in the media, it's like a magnet sucking up little filings. The incident becomes a lightning rod for other issues [such as racism]. You have to be careful to separate the facts from what's sensational."

Beatings such as that dealt to Rodney King are "not tolerated in the vast majority of police departments," said James J. Fyfe, a former New York City police lieutenant who has appeared as an expert witness in damage claims against the LAPD. Fyfe contends that Los Angeles stands apart from other departments in excessive use of force. "The reason," he said, "is accountability. The police answer to the chief, and he answers to no one.

"In New York, Chicago, Houston, Philadelphia and every other big city, except for Los Angeles, elected mayors appoint police chief executives," Fyfe said. "Regardless of their expertise in police administration, the chiefs of these big cities all serve at the pleasure of their mayors."

In Los Angeles, Police Chief Daryl F. Gates' job is protected by civil service procedures. He can only be dismissed for cause by the city's Police Commission, with the concurrence of the Civil Service Commission.

Many cities also rely on civilian review boards. They have varying degrees of independence, said the University of Nebraska's Walker, and most cities adopt them only after controversial incidents, such as shootings and beatings, spark public protests.

But in Chicago, New York and in some other cities that have review boards not wholly independent of the police department or city administration, critics contend that they are set up in such a way that they become little more than arms of the police department.

"Every single [review board] that exists still only has power to make recommendations to the police chief, so the single critical factor is the attitude of the police chief," Walker said. Also, in slightly more than half of the big cities that have them, the initial investigations are performed by police officers, not independent investigators.

Jay Miller, director of the American Civil Liberties Union of Illinois, said his office does not refer brutality victims to Chicago's Office of Professional Standards, which sustained only 190 of the 2,410 excessive force complaints filed with it in 1990. "We don't trust them," he said.

In addition, police critics complain that the agencies charged with investigating police misconduct frequently are not interested in determining whether a systematic problem exists. In many cities records of complaints filed against police officers are purged after a few years.

"You're going to see a lot of groups and individuals running around with camcorders."

For Denver City Councilman Hiawatha Davis, an advocate for changes in the internal investigations system in his city, the failure of police departments to keep records is evidence that the system is "severely flawed and totally compromised. They obviously don't have any information to evaluate trends. Without records, you can't do any analysis of the characteristics of complainants or the officers who have been complained about."

He added: "Ironically, the investigative nature of the police institution suggests that one of their primary activities would be record keeping. Police work thrives on bits and pieces of information gathered over a long period of time."

But Chuck Lepley, assistant district attorney in Denver who investigates police brutality complaints in his county, contends that independent civilian review might hamper the police. "If police officers feel they cannot trust the review process, they may just decide to let the guy go," he said.

"I think there's quite a few false reports of excessive force. The people who stand between violence and the public are the police. Sometimes in the process people don't want to cooperate, but the police are still expected to arrest them," he said.

More Complaints

In some places across the country, lawyers and civil rights organizations say the number of police brutality complaints have gone up since the Rodney King case first was publicized.

"People are coming out of the woodwork," said Joe Cook, executive director of the Dallas ACLU, whose office receives some 200 citizen complaints a year against the police. "Before, they thought it wouldn't do any good. Now they have hope someone will listen to them."

"Our calls have increased since the L.A. videotape," said Ellen Spears, interim director of the ACLU of Georgia. "People feel that maybe something can be done."

"You're going to see a lot of groups and individuals running around with camcorders," said Clackum, the Clayton County police chief in Georgia.

He may be right. In May 1990, well-known Miami attorney Ellis Rubin settled for $15,000 a police brutality case for a client whose mistreatment had been videotaped. Then he issued a call for blacks and other minorities to band together as "video vigilantes."

"I think people in neighborhoods where this brutality goes on should get together, buy a camera and then be there with it when police do a round-up or raid a crack house," he said. "I think that could put an end to this."

Is Police Brutality a National Crisis?

Yes: Police Brutality Is a National Crisis

Police Brutality Is a National Crisis
Police Brutality Is a Serious Problem
Police Brutality Is Common in the U.S.
Police Brutality Against Blacks Is a National Crisis
Police Brutality Against Juveniles Is a Serious Problem
Police Brutality Against the Poor Is a National Crisis

Police Brutality Is a National Crisis

NAACP

About the Author: *The NAACP is the oldest and largest civil rights organization in the nation. The following viewpoint is taken from a statement by its Washington bureau director Wade Henderson, and was presented in a congressional hearing on police brutality on April 17, 1991.*

The brutal beating of Rodney King by officers of the Los Angeles Police Department has brought much-needed public focus to the problem of police brutality nationwide. The NAACP [National Association for the Advancement of Colored People] has a longstanding interest in the problem of police violence—the use of excessive and often deadly force, by police officers "under color of law." For too long, African Americans and other racial minorities have been among the special targets of police abuse. Rather than being the beneficiaries of the equal protection of the law, too often innocent black people—including many of our youngsters—find themselves the victims of the abuse of authority and law.

Some police officers, for example, make plain their fear or contempt of black people while on patrol in black communities or when they observe African Americans in the predominantly "white areas" of our cities and towns. This is usually done through simple harassment or verbal abuse directed at an individual because of the color of his skin, although the real reason may be masked by a pretext.

The NAACP case of *Murphy v. City of Reynoldsburg* is an excellent example of this problem. *Murphy* is a civil case about racially motivated po-

The NAACP, statement before the U.S. House of Representatives Subcommittee on Civil and Constitutional Rights, April 17, 1991. Public Domain.

lice misconduct in Reynoldsburg, Ohio. A special unit within the Reynoldsburg Police Department called itself the "S.N.A.T." squad, and took it upon itself to harass blacks found passing through town. It was later discovered that S.N.A.T. is an acronym for "Special Nigger Arrest Team."

Blacks were followed for no reason until some minor infraction was found. They were then stopped, searched and subjected to thorough computer checks for any outstanding traffic tickets, or other matters, from any jurisdiction covered by the computer. On some occasions, it appears that drugs were planted on the suspects during these manufactured searches. The NAACP is assisting in litigating the case on behalf of an individual on whom drugs were planted.

Another common complaint from many black people is that white policemen, in particular—whether because of racial fears, animosities, or other factors—frequently overreact in a given circumstance. They use excessive force in situations which require deliberate, careful and even-handed policing. The result is often severe injury or death for the victim of this abuse.

> ## "For too long, African Americans and other racial minorities have been among the special targets of police abuse."

The local NAACP branch is often called upon to investigate complaints by African Americans of excessive violence by police officers. In the course of our work, we have gathered disturbing evidence of patently illegal law enforcement practices, which in the African American community, have become an intrinsic part of our daily lives. The elimination of illegal police killings against minority citizens remains, in particular, a priority of the

NAACP. . . .

Rock and bottle throwing incidents have begun again in the black community! The President of the Tampa Branch of the NAACP said the organization has made a move to call in the Department of Justice and the FBI to investigate the problem. The time was April 1987.

Brutality in Tampa, Florida

These actions were prompted after another black man died while in the custody of officers of the Tampa Police Department. In less than five months, five men died in Tampa police custody. While the officers involved in the incidents were white, four of the dead men were black and one was Cuban-born. NAACP President Henry Carley was reported to have said, "The black community is demanding that we do something besides meet and form task forces and we're going to respond in order to protect our people."

These incidents followed a severe beating inflicted upon New York Mets pitcher Dwight Gooden by members of the Tampa Police Department in December 1986.

Following the disturbances, the Greater Tampa Chamber of Commerce established a biracial commission to study police practices, employment, housing and other issues. Subsequently, the commission hired the Police Foundation, a nonprofit research group headquartered in Washington, D.C., to review Tampa's police practices. The Police Foundation's report paints a troubling portrait of relations between the black community and police in Florida's third largest city.

The report suggests police officials failed to see a growing gap between the department and the black community that erupted after the February 1987 death of 23-year-old Melvin Hair, killed by a white officer responding to a report that Hair was threatening his family with a knife. Hair's death touched off two nights of violence in Tampa.

Race relations were a primary focus of the study. Twenty-five people—city officials and blacks and whites who had observed officers interacting with the public—were interviewed to gauge police-community relations.

The most frequent complaint encountered among black members of the Tampa community was an apparent lack of discipline among all ranks of the Tampa Police Department. This view was repeatedly cited by members of the NAACP. The view among those interviewed was that the internal investigative processes used by the Tampa Police Department are ineffective, and designed to protect the officer, not the citizen.

"In less than five months, five men died in Tampa police custody."

A second theme that ran through many interviews was that Tampa police officers seemed particularly intent on pure law enforcement, rather than on delivery of a city service to the black community. This manifested itself in several ways; the most eloquent was in a statement by a black professional who remarked:

> The police [in Tampa] hurt themselves by being too willing to take enforcement action. The police here tend not to understand the environment in which they work. There's too much discretion, which leads to arrogance and abuse of power. Quite simply, there is an arrogance of power, and there has been for quite some time.

A recurring complaint voiced by many NAACP members focused on police accountability. How is it that the police can investigate themselves in cases in which deadly force is used? Police detectives investigate all deaths or the significant use of force by officers and forward their findings to the State Attorney to determine whether any laws were violated.

Many of those interviewed alluded to a pervasive prejudice among the officers, supervisors, and management of the Tampa Police Department. Many recounted stories—undoubtedly referred by black former police officers—about sergeants at roll call reading general information such as "pick up a nigger female, age . . .". Others recounted bitter complaints from black former officers concerning the way they were treated by their white supervisors. Much of the general nature of these complaints was supported by whites who have had exposure to the Tampa Police Department:

> Racial epithets are common[ly] used at [roll] calls, written in the bathrooms. If a white officer and black officer are together and the white officer uses nigger or boy, and [the black officer] reports that, it's always [ignored]. Nothing is done to them [the white officer]. Consequently, they aren't going to change. If they can call somebody nigger right in front of a black officer and the black officer's word isn't heeded, then the attitude is not going to change.

The Police Foundation report made 36 recommendations to the Tampa Police Department. As a general matter, the Police Foundation report was well received. The NAACP President said he considered the report a "good sign that the department welcomed the review."

In February 1990 the Foundation conducted its first audit of the implementation of its recommendations to the Tampa Police Department. It reported a stunning turnaround.

Tampa's city administration and the police department acted on nearly all of the Foundation's original 36 recommendations, which ranged from the revision of training lessons to the development of community outreach programs. The result is that police officers are now better prepared to deal with volatile situations, especially in minority neighborhoods. Department actions include an increased emphasis on recruiting—and retaining—minority officers, a training agenda that stresses racial sensitivity, and an ongoing dialogue with citizens.

Unrequited Anger

But for every success in combating police abuse such as that of Prince Georges County or Tampa, there are other communities that are seething with unrequited anger. . . .

In early December of 1990, a little-noticed story appeared in the *Houston Chronicle*. It announced that the last of four grand juries that had investigated ex-policeman Scott Tschirhart's killing of Byron Gillum, a Houston security guard, had disbanded. Houston Fire Marshall Eddie Corral, who was grand jury foreman, said jurors who initially were curious about the controversial case eventually "lost interest."

The expiration of the grand jury's term marked a quiet end to a case that touched off a storm of public protest. Although for the Texas State Conference of the NAACP, the memory lingers on.

The facts of Gillum's death are as profoundly disturbing as they are bizarre. What is frightening about Byron Gillum's death is that it could have happened to anyone.

On November 15, 1989, Officer Tschirhart pulled over 24-year-old Byron Gillum near the main campus of the University of Houston. Officer Tschirhart said he became suspicious when Gillum slowed to 10 mph after spotting the officer's patrol car behind him. He stopped Gillum when he saw he was not wearing a seat belt.

"For every success in combating police abuse such as that of . . . Tampa, there are other communities that are seething with unrequited anger."

Tschirhart said Gillum "seemed very agitated" as he approached him. He said Gillum insinuated "I was stopping him just to harass him," by telling the officer that he should be chasing "real criminals." Byron Gillum waited in his car for 13 minutes while the officer checked for pending charges against him. When the dispatcher reported finding no warrants against Gillum, Tschirhart responded: "Please say you have something on Gillum . . . bad attitude."

Returning to Gillum's car, Tschirhart said that

he spotted a pistol that he had not seen earlier, wedged between the car's bucket seats. Tschirhart said that he had twice ordered Gillum to get out and not touch the gun, but that Gillum had reached for the weapon.

Officer Tschirhart opened fire and continued firing as Byron Gillum lunged through the open window on the passenger's side of his car and attempted to flee for his life. Eight bullets from Tschirhart's 10mm automatic pistol struck Gillum—four in the back!

Officer Tschirhart contended he merely followed his police training, which called for officers to shoot to kill to defend themselves, and to keep firing until the person posing the threat goes down. He said he feared that Byron Gillum might be armed, but in reality, Gillum was unarmed.

A Pattern of Killing

Byron Gillum was the third black person slain by Officer Tschirhart, who is white. Gillum's death inflamed relations between the black community and the Houston Police Department, since it followed on the heels of the controversial police slaying of another black citizen, Ida Lee Shaw Delaney. Ms. Delaney, 50, was shot to death on October 31, 1989 by Alex Gonzales, an off-duty police officer, in an incident on Houston's Southwest Freeway. Officer Gonzales was convicted of voluntary manslaughter and given a seven-year sentence.

Then-Police Chief Lee P. Brown fired Tschirhart, a police officer for 7½ years, for violating the department's rule that prohibits shooting at a fleeing suspect unless the lives of officers or others are in danger. Tschirhart appealed his dismissal, and under state law, his case went to binding arbitration. Meanwhile, two Harris County grand juries returned "no bill of indictment" against Officer Tschirhart, and a third decided to take no action after reviewing his case.

Arbitrator Charles J. Morris, a Southern Methodist University law professor, held that Officer Tschirhart's ineptitude led to the shooting death of Byron Gillum and upheld his dismissal. Tschirhart "should have had a better understanding" of why a young black man like Gillum, who thought he had done nothing wrong, would tell a white officer "he should be going after 'real criminals.'"

Officer Tschirhart's "conduct in firing those last five shots was grossly irresponsible, even though he may have fired spontaneously, without conscious thought," wrote Professor Morris. "He was apparently obsessed with firing his weapon at the suspect until he dropped. He obviously gave no thought to protecting the suspect's life."

Ironically, Officer Tschirhart's involvement in three fatal shootings did not give him an exceptionally unusual record for using deadly force according to Don Smyth, Chief of the Civil Rights Division in the Harris County District Attorney's Office, who presented a statistical study of police shooting during the appeal of Officer Tschirhart's dismissal. A statistical analysis presented earlier by noted criminologist Lawrence W. Sherman showed that during the time Officer Tschirhart was in the HPD, he was the only officer involved in three fatal shootings. Sherman said Tschirhart displayed "a propensity to kill people."

"A culture of violence and disregard for human life may permeate . . . many . . . police departments."

Prompted by the death of Byron Gillum and the comments of Lawrence Sherman, Smyth's study of all shootings by local law enforcement officers in the county covered the period from July 1979, when the Civil Rights Division was formed, and mid-August 1990. The study showed that during this period, a total of 26 officers were responsible for the injury or death of at least three persons. Three of the officers, like Scott Tschirhart, were involved in three fatal shootings, and one was involved in four such killings.

What these statistics may demonstrate is that a culture of violence and disregard for human life may permeate, not only the Houston Police Department, but also many other police departments which are not sufficiently sensitized to its responsibilities to protect all its citizenry. . . .

The Death of Alfred Sanders

On December 29, 1987, in Laurelton, Queens, Alfred Sanders, a thirty-nine (39) year-old black man, was killed in a fusillade of bullets fired by white police officers. There have been several similar police shootings against minority persons in New York in recent years. Accordingly, the Jamaica Branch of the NAACP and the Laurelton Federation of Block Associations expressed grave concern about yet another shooting death.

Representatives of these organizations urged Governor Mario Cuomo to appoint a Special Prosecutor in the case of Alfred Sanders. Although he refused, the Governor directed his "Special Screening Committee" (for Special Prosecutor cases) to continue to monitor developments in the case. The grand jury looking into this matter under the direction of Queens District Attorney John Santucci produced no bill of indictment. At the conclusion of the grand jury proceeding, Santucci remarked: "The grand jury obviously concluded that the police officers acted reasonably in defense of their own lives."

Dr. Benjamin L. Hooks, Chief Executive Officer of the NAACP, and Hazel Dukes, President of the National NAACP and President of the New York State Conference of NAACP Branches, immediately authorized the NAACP to conduct a parallel investigation of the Sanders shooting. In its initial stage, the NAACP investigation involved monitoring the grand jury proceedings and assisting the Jamaica Branch with its independent inquiry into the incident.

A meeting arranged by NAACP lawyers was held with District Attorney John Santucci and his prosecutors who investigated the shooting death. Mr. Santucci declined to release several reports and other evidence that had been presented to the grand jury; however, there was an open and frank discussion about the facts in the Sanders case.

On December 29, 1987, Alfred Sanders attempted to see his son at the home of his former companion, Elease Watson, the mother of the child. According to a message over the police department's "911" line, Watson called the police at approximately 6:47 p.m. claiming that there was a "man outside with a gun." She called again a few minutes later with a similar message, adding, "I have a protective order."

According to police records, at 7:04 p.m., an anti-crime unit picked up the call and responded to the scene in a "marked" vehicle. At 7:10 p.m., the marked unit called for back-up, stating that there was "an erratic male on the scene reaching into his pocket." Witnesses pointed out later that Sanders had complied with the police officers' demand that he remove his hands from his pockets. According to witnesses, Sanders withdrew a wallet, which he threw onto the hood of the unmarked police car, and a folded piece of paper.

"The problem of police brutality is pervasive, deep-rooted and alarming."

Police records indicate that at approximately 7:13 p.m., the second unit on the scene called for an Emergency Services Unit and demanded that a police sergeant be sent to the scene. Both the sergeant and the Emergency Services Unit were equipped with proper protective devices.

However, before these units arrived with the appropriate protective devices, Sanders had already been killed.

The shooting occurred at approximately 7:18 p.m., after Sanders had moved out beyond the gate surrounding Watson's residence, and while the officers were in the street. According to the District Attorney, the four officers on the scene had moved in sequence with Sanders' movements. All four officers had their guns drawn. Witnesses reported that Sanders yelled racial and taunting remarks at the officers.

The officers indicated that Sanders possessed a knife that he first held to himself. Moments later, he had allegedly pointed it towards the officers and lunged. The knife was described as a "007-type knife."

According to the District Attorney, six witnesses before the grand jury testified that they saw a knife; four others testified that there was no knife. One witness testified that he (or she) heard police say: "Put the knife down." A knife recovered by police officers and examined by lab technicians in the police department bore no fingerprints, fibers, or evidence that would identify the owner or corroborate their claim that the knife was in the possession of Sanders.

In total, eleven bullets were fired at Sanders by two of the officers. The other two officers declined to shoot. Sanders sustained ten bullet wounds in the location of his abdomen, chest, left arm, and left leg. His body fell to the middle of the street where he died.

There were numerous witnesses, neighbors of Elease Watson, and friends and relatives of Alfred Sanders. Some of these witnesses remembered that Sanders had been beaten badly by police officers in the summer of 1987. At that time, he had broken the windows of Watson's residence and had demanded to see his son. Later, Watson obtained a protective order. They viewed Sanders as sick but "non-threatening.". . .

A National Problem

The ongoing survey of NAACP branches demonstrates that the problem of police brutality is pervasive, deep-rooted and alarming. The national problem of police brutality cries out for a federal response.

It has been reported that the Department of Justice has received almost 8,000 complaints of criminal civil rights violations by police officers each year in the past five year period. Regrettably, this represents but a fraction of the police abuse cases. For example, we know that in 1990 in Los Angeles alone, over 2,500 complaints of police abuse were recorded by the Police Misconduct Lawyer Referral Service. The fact that complaints to the Department of Justice have declined by 20 percent since 1981 does not square with the apparent rise in police abuse incidents nationally.

There is a paucity of thorough investigation by the Department of Justice in response to complaints of police abuse. Only a bare minimum number of cases is actually presented to the grand jury. For example, it has been suggested that as few as 50 of 3,000 cases per year are presented to the grand jury, which represents approximately one-half of one percent. Further, there is a shortage of human and financial resources allocated to the difficult task of investigating and prosecuting criminal civil rights violations.

"The national problem of police brutality cries out for a federal response."

Attorney General Thornburgh's recent commitment to investigate all complaints of police brutality nationwide, in the last six years, is commendable. However, it has been suggested that old cases would not be reopened, which if correct, raises serious questions about the purpose of this new investigation.

However, in addition to the points already stated, there is a fundamental issue involving the scope of existing federal authority to address the problem of police brutality.

Admittedly, the Department of Justice has existing authority to certainly do more than they have done. For example, under 18 U.S.C. Sections 241 and 242, the Department has the power to file criminal civil rights charges against local police officers who willfully violate federally protected civil rights and/or who engage in conspiracies to violate these rights. However, it is generally accepted that these statutes are vague, poorly drafted, and actually make it difficult to bring successful federal civil rights prosecutions.

Moreover, the Department lacks the important authority to undertake "pattern and practice" lawsuits where the problem of police abuse is especially widespread in a community. Establishing the statutory authority needed to address this aspect of the problem should be a high priority.

Recommendations

In addition to enhanced statutory authority to prosecute civil rights violations, especially for the Department of Justice in the area of pattern and practice litigation, the NAACP supports the following additional recommendations:

• making the disbursement of federal funds to local enforcement agencies contingent upon aggressive enforcement of departmental policies prohibiting excessive force by local police officers;

• granting more authority to the local offices of the U.S. Attorney to initiate prosecutions in police misconduct cases;

• expanding remedies under 42 U.S.C. Section 1983 to make punitive damages available to victims of police abuse and to provide for injunctive relief to prevent egregious conduct by police officers in the future; this is particularly important where the police practice is known to cause death (e.g., the use of the choke-hold); and

• providing supplemental funding for training and technical assistance generally for local police units.

Police Brutality Is a Serious Problem

Michael Novick

About the Author: *Michael Novick is a writer for* The Guardian, *a leftist New York weekly newspaper.*

The maiming of Rodney King in a brutal beating by Los Angeles police, videotaped by an eyewitness, has served to cast a spotlight on a national problem. For decades, racist violence perpetrated by law enforcement personnel has been covered up. After brief efforts at reform in the late 1970s—which focused primarily on police spying and corruption and only secondarily on the use of deadly force—police departments nationwide in the Reagan-Bush era were given a free hand.

Armed with militaristic weapons and tactics, provided with marching orders to carry out a "war on drugs" and a "war on crime," the country's 12,000 police departments have interpreted recent legislative and judicial changes as a mandate to abandon restraint. The result has been a widening of the use of violence and deadly force, of which the King incident was part.

In order to contend with the violence, it is necessary to understand the underlying causes. In New York, five police officers were indicted in March 1991 for murder after a young Latino man found sleeping in a stolen automobile was beaten and choked to death. Three other officers were indicted in a separate incident for the unprovoked pistol-whipping of two men at whom they shouted anti-gay slurs. Several subsequently publicized cases of New York police brutality against Asian-Americans have been the subject of cover-ups, but at least one victim, Guo Qing Zhong, who was beaten unconscious after a traffic stop, is suing the department for damages.

Renewed attention has also been focused on the case of José Sanchez, killed by police in a drug raid early in 1990. An autopsy showed that despite the police story that he was shot only once in the chest, there were at least 16 bullet holes in his body, including five wounds to the back and four to the head.

"For decades, racist violence perpetrated by law enforcement personnel has been covered up."

In Chicago, complaints of brutality and misconduct against the police took a big jump in 1990, and 16 officers were dismissed for violating standards on the use of force. The firings followed a still-growing scandal of over more than 200 cases of domestic violence by police officers, and complaints by officers' wives that their calls to the Chicago Police Department for assistance were often discounted. The Daley administration moved to deny public access to monthly summaries of all police misconduct suits filed against the city.

A grand jury in Washington indicted two District police officers for incidents in which they broke one man's jaw and beat up two other men waiting for a bus. One officer is on administrative leave; the other got bumped from the force.

In Atlanta, a Clayton County officer was charged with battery and dismissed for the beating of a handcuffed drunk-driving suspect after a chase. An Atlanta officer was suspended for using excessive force on the passenger in the same incident. Investigations are continuing.

In Denver, the kicking and beating by police of a 15-year-old while he was face down on the ground in custody is being investigated by the department and the FBI [Federal Bureau of In-

Michael Novick, "L.A. Case Triggers Look into Police Brutality," *The Guardian,* April 10, 1991. Reprinted with permission.

vestigation]. Police brutality was the focus of a town meeting. . . .

Other police brutality cases have resulted in criminal prosecutions or large civil damages settlements recently in Memphis, Miami and San Francisco. In Texas, the *Dallas News* reported that more than 2,000 federal investigations, twice as many as for any other state, were conducted of civil rights violations by police officers in the 1984-89 period.

The violations included beatings, killings and coerced confessions. In Little Rock, Ark., a mentally retarded Black man on Death Row, Bobby Lee Fairchild, is seeking to overturn his conviction for murder that was based on a confession extracted through torture. At least one former deputy has come forward to testify that Fairchild was beaten and that the Fulton County sheriff routinely condoned the use of torture. In San Diego, police killed a record 12 people and wounded 16 others in 1990.

Clearly, violence on this scale is no aberration. Questions remain, however, as to its underlying causes. For the progressive movement, the point is to determine those causes and expose them to public scrutiny and condemnation.

The Klan Connection

The surge in police violence is beginning to highlight again the presence of organized white supremacist groups among law enforcement and corrections personnel. In Los Angeles in the wake of the beating of Rodney King, a Black policewoman has come forward to report the racist treatment she received while assigned to the Foothill Division, where the officers involved in the beating were stationed. Janine Bouey reported that she found a Ku Klux Klan calling card on her car in the station's lot, and that a Black male officer had a similar card placed in his locker in a controlled-access area of the station.

Similar harassment has taken place in other police departments in the area. In San Bernardino, Calif., Black officers received threatening messages from the "Aryan Police Officers'

Association," in a case investigated but never solved by the FBI. In the Los Angeles Sheriff's Department, a deputy, dismissed from the force for burning a cross inside the county jail with a makeshift blowtorch in order to intimidate Black prisoners, was reinstated by the elected sheriff. On New Year's Eve, the same deputy shot and killed a Mexican national who was shooting a handgun in the air in celebration of the holiday.

"The surge in police violence is beginning to highlight again the presence of organized white supremacist groups among law enforcement . . . personnel."

White supremacist groups have also been uncovered in police departments in other parts of California and in other states, often in connection with brutality against people of color. In Glendale, Calif., police were caught using a racist silhouette of a Black man for target practice. In Richmond, Calif., a police "fraternal" group calling itself the Cowboys included the brother-in-law of the local Klan leader; the group circulated a letter lauding the killing of "black bucks." In Louisville, Ky., a group called KOPS (Klan Order of Police) was uncovered after a veteran officer was caught using the National Crime Information Computer for KKK business. In Tarrant County, Texas, a reserve officer, a dispatcher and a jailer were dismissed after their membership in the Klan was revealed.

The operation of organized racist groups within police departments is symptomatic of the unchallenged racism within their ranks that often finds expression in beatings and shootings. President George Bush, who in campaigning for the presidency against Willie Horton in 1988 helped legitimize racism, actually stepped up his "anti-crime" rhetoric in the wake of the Rodney King beating. Although Bush proclaimed that the tape of King's beating made him "sick," he had earlier declared Los Angeles Chief Daryl Gates an "All-American hero," and on March 5, 1991 told a gathering of law enforcement personnel in Washington that the police should "take back the streets and liberate our neighborhoods from the tyranny of fear. . . . The national will that freed Kuwait can free [our] cities from crime."

Ron Wilkins, an African-American organizer in Los Angeles, attributes the beating of King to such domestic consequences of Bush's New World Order. "It's the same old racism," he says. The United States already imprisons Black males at four times the rate of South Africa and has the highest incarceration rate in the world, yet Bush claims Congress is "soft on crime." Lee Rawls, an assistant attorney general, says the administration expects the U.S. victory in the Gulf to boost its efforts to expand the federal death penalty, limit appeals by convicts and allow evidence illegally seized by the police to be used in court. And the Supreme Court ruled in March 1991 that police coercion of confessions would not taint the prosecution of those forced to incriminate themselves.

Political Weapon

In addition to the role of organized white supremacist groups and of a racist federal policy sanctioning a "gloves-off" approach to law enforcement, a third factor driving the recent steady growth in police violence has been conscious political repression. In San Francisco, United Farm Workers Vice President Dolores Huerta won a massive settlement in a suit against police who destroyed her spleen in a brutal beating while she was participating in a demonstration against Bush. Brutality against San Francisco anti-war protesters was captured on videotape during the protests against the Gulf war and is being used in a demonstrators' suit against the California Highway Patrol. Some anti-racist organizers speculate that the increase in police violence in Black and Hispanic communities may be related to both a general marginalization of those communities over the past decade and an attempt to intimidate communities in the early stages of grass-roots organizing against deteriorating economic and social conditions.

"Police brutality and excessive force is systemic."

Repression through police violence has also become more focused. In Los Angeles, Bill Gandall, a veteran of the Abraham Lincoln Brigade who was attacked by federal police during an anti-war demonstration at the Westwood Federal Building, Jan. 16, 1991, died March 23 in the hospital where he was taken for his injuries. Los Angeles sheriffs have conducted a virtual vendetta against ACT UP-Los Angeles activists, who have targeted the county supervisors for civil disobedience. The deputies have repeatedly been accused of using excessive force in making arrests of AIDS demonstrators.

Anti-abortion demonstrators have also filed several suits and complaints of police brutality. Police in Richmond, Va., won such a suit brought by Operation Rescue protesters. In Los Angeles, Operation Rescue spokespeople, bitter over the police use of "pain compliance holds" in dragging them away from clinics, joined in the calls for Gates' resignation after the King beating. . . .

Despite the evidence that police brutality and excessive force is systemic, however, opposition to such violence has tended to be localized, sporadic and reactive. Demands for justice in particular cases are often centered around the families of victims and do not even link up with similar cases in the same area. . . .

The King case, with its connections up the chain of command, with the president and the governor of California lining up in defense of Gates and the police, provides the left with an opening to combat police racism and violence at the national level.

Police Brutality Is Common in the U.S.

Revolutionary Worker

About the Author: Revolutionary Worker *is published by the Revolutionary Communist Party.*

Everybody's seen the videotape. It's seven minutes long, but it seems like an hour. White pigs, lots of them, surround a Black man lying on the ground. They beat him in the back, in the legs, in the groin, in the face and head—over and over. Rodney King tries to get up, get away, ward off their brutality. They beat him and kick him some more. Another cop gives him electric shocks with a Taser gun. It's a vicious pogrom by a uniformed lynch mob—brutal and cowardly.

Every new revelation about the lynching adds new outrages. The nurse at the hospital where Rodney King was treated heard the cops taunting him: "We played a little hard ball tonight, and you lost." The pigs gloated, "We hit a few home runs."

After the beating, one of the cops sent a message over their computer saying, "I haven't beaten anyone this bad in a long time." Another cop replied, "Oh not again."

Rodney King's condition is serious. The cops fractured his skull in nine places, broke his leg, gave him a concussion, and caused nerve damage and possible brain damage. Doctors say the electric shocks they gave him were like heart attacks.

Basic people around the country, especially Black people, saw the videotape and knew right away: Everything about the beating of Rodney

Adapted from the *Revolutionary Worker*, "The Everyday Reality of Pig Brutality," March 31, 1991. Reprinted with permission. Subheads and inserts have been added by Greenhaven editors.

King is typical, standard police procedure! This is the way the rulers of this country and their system does the people all the time—and it has been that way for hundreds of years. The USA is, and always has been, a racist country. Black people have been victims of the Man's violence from the time they were brought over in slave ships to the KKK [Ku Klux Klan] lynchings to today when the police consider any Black person on the street an automatic "suspect." The LAPD [Los Angeles Police Department] videotape peeled back the thin, phony cover of "equality" in this country and sharply exposed a view of the *daily reality of police brutality* for oppressed people. The only thing different about this police beating was that the pigs were caught red-handed on videotape—and now millions of people in this country and worldwide have had a chance to see what the real deal is for Black people in AmeriKKKa. As one Black youth said . . . "It's like a view where everybody can see how we're being treated."

"Everything about the beating of Rodney King is typical, standard police procedure!"

LAPD's Gestapo Chief Daryl Gates claims that the beating of Rodney King was an "aberration"—an unusual occurrence, something not typical of the police force. This is a big-time lie. Is it an "aberration" that a big gang of LAPD cops assaulted a person of color? No. The pigs are trained and taught that it is their "duty" and "right" to brutalize the people. The "swarm technique" is an approved tactic in the LAPD. Police everywhere use chokeholds that kill people. On the night of Rodney King's beating there were 27 pigs on the scene. *Not one of the cops on the scene made the slightest move to stop this lynching.* Isn't it clear the beating was standard police procedure? Is it an "aberration" that the LAPD lied about what they did, claiming that the victim was "on PCP," "resisted arrest" and "attacked them"?

No. The cops lie *every single time they maim or kill someone.* Before the videotape came out, the cops who lied about Rodney King in their police reports had no worry that *any* of their fellow pigs on the scene would contradict their story. Making up accusations, planting guns and drugs, claiming that the victim made a "suspicious move"—using such justifications to beat or kill people is standard police procedure.

Is it just a "problem with the LAPD"? No way! True, the LAPD is notorious for being brutal racists. Their Chief Gates makes racist statements all the time—*that's a big part of why he is a hero to rank-and-file cops everywhere.* But there were at least two other police agencies who were on the scene—the California Highway Patrol and L.A. School District police. *The L.A. School District police!* What does this show about the treatment dished out to the youth in the public schools?

And what about the police atrocities that go on in every city and town of this country, every single day? Five New York City cops were charged in the death of Federico Pereira in February 1990. Witnesses said that the cops handcuffed Pereira's hands behind his back and also tied one leg behind his back. Then with the victim on the ground, the cops beat him, sat on him, and yanked his head up. He choked to death. The cops then lied that the victim was on "cocaine" and threatened witnesses. Activists against police brutality in every city receive hundreds of complaints each month.

"All this is why the people call the cops pigs."

Why have people all around the country responded to the assault on Rodney King with massive outrage and anger and their own stories about the time the cops went after them or people they knew? It's exactly because the LAPD beating was typical of what happens to Black people, other people of color, and even many white people—all the time, everywhere in the USA.

All this is why the people call the cops pigs. What *is* unusual about the Rodney King incident is that this time there is undeniable proof. And the videotape is so powerful an indictment that the powers and their media have not been able to suppress it. They in fact have had to go on the defensive to minimize the damage to their whole system. There is deep and serious anger among the people. This has forced even George Bush, a close friend of Gates, to come out on national TV and shed a few crocodile tears about what happened.

Police Brutality and Iraq

The storm over the LAPD atrocity is happening in the middle of the U.S.'s big festival of shame—their blood-soaked celebration of the devastation of a relatively small, poor Third World country. There are many links between the LAPD beating of Rodney King and the U.S. military's rape of Iraq. Two days *after* the Rodney King beating, Commander-in-Chief Bush stood before a meeting of high-level cops and law enforcement officials and said, "The kind of moral force and national will that freed Kuwait City from abuse can free America's cities from crime." He called Chief Gates an "all-American hero." The people know what this means. "Crime in the cities" is a racist buzzword that the powers use to justify police attacks and clampdowns against the basic people. Just like the U.S. used "aggression" as an excuse to drop massive amounts of bombs on the people of Iraq.

The mauling of Iraq represented the kind of odds that the U.S. imperialist bullies like—a big, powerful and rich country against a smaller, weaker, poor country. It's the same kind of cowardly odds that racist lynchers like—a whole gang of pigs against a lone person of color. The LAPD's "swarm technique" is a homefront version of the murderous bombing of fleeing Iraqi soldiers on the highway in Kuwait.

The LAPD used the latest police technology. They shocked their victim with the electric Taser gun, used new side-handled batons to inflict maximum damage, circled a helicopter overhead to provide lighting and communicated with each other over computers. They were like the U.S. pilots dropping their "smart" bombs and carrying out high-tech mass murder from a safe distance.

The lynching of Rodney King was a way for the pigs to join in the "thrill of victory." Pumped-up cops laughed and joked while they almost killed him. They were getting "their licks" in.

These links got sharply focused when Daryl Gates' supporters staged a media event at the LAPD headquarters to back their chief—they decorated the whole place with yellow ribbons. People who should know better but were sucked into wearing yellow ribbons and saying "support the troops" should think long and hard about this. They should consider deeply what kind of horrible crimes they are supporting—here and around the world—by displaying the blood-soaked yellow.

Under Siege

The strong and widespread outrage at the Rodney King beating is forcing the powers into some maneuvers. Several weeks after it happened, Bush said that what he saw on the videotape was "sickening"—almost the exact same thing Gates said.

"There is opportunity now to deeply expose the ugly nature of the beast and step up the fight against it."

What is *truly* sickening is watching these major criminals lie. Does Bush really expect people to believe that he didn't know what was happening under his friend Daryl Gates' command? And what about his call to apply what the U.S. did to Iraq to "America's cities"?! Those on top of this

system know full well what they pay their pig enforcers to do in the streets. Murder and brutality is their stock in trade.

And who can believe that these big criminals are at all sorry about what happened to Rodney King? Chief Gates has continued to portray Rodney King as a "criminal" and even said that he hoped the incident would "turn around" Rodney's life. Even when they are trying to put up a front, these oppressors can't help but say racist shit! . . .

What are these plans? The powers have big schemes to clamp down with a police state atmosphere—to lock down and lock up those at the bottom in this country for whom this system has nothing to offer but misery and despair. They have actual programs in the works—like Operation Cul-de-Sac in Los Angeles—to turn *whole* neighborhoods into Nazi-style ghettos where police will have absolute control over people's lives. That's the kind of "war on crime" that Bush is calling for.

The powers are going full speed ahead with these plans. That's why they hope to come out of the Gates controversy by convincing as many people as possible that "reasonable officials" are "cleaning up the problems" in the LAPD and other police departments. They hope to get over on the people the lie that what happened to Rodney King was an "aberration"—not a slice of daily reality for millions of oppressed people.

But the people can see through their plans. There is opportunity now to deeply expose the ugly nature of the beast and step up the fight against it. The basic people who have always known what life under pig rule in this country means, and the many who have gotten a jarring look at this reality for the first time, can unite their anger and outrage to build a powerful struggle—to oppose not only the Chief Pig and his racists on the beat but the whole fascist clampdown.

Police Brutality Against Blacks Is a National Crisis

Les Payne

About the Author: *Les Payne is an award-winning journalist and assistant managing editor for* Newsday, *a daily New York newspaper. He writes a syndicated column.*

America got a two-minute videotaped look at a not uncommon scene of Los Angeles cops arresting a black man for speeding.

White traffic violators are handled differently.

What distinguishes this arrest from scores of other black cases in the City of Angels is not the violence, but the videotaping.

No fewer than a trio of policemen took turns clubbing and kicking the unarmed black motorist as a dozen others milled about. It recalled nothing so much as an old-fashioned lynching bee, where the more cold-blooded of the racist pack strike, while the voyeurs stroke their bellies as the victim writhes in pain.

The savagery of Los Angeles' finest loosed embarrassment, if not horror, among viewers watching the videotape on national television. Flash a light on any group of rats on attack and the squeamish will recoil from the bloody tangle of claws and fangs.

Such police etiquette against blacks and other minorities is almost a daily occurrence in Los Angeles, according to Karol Heppe, executive director of the Police Misconduct Lawyers Referral Service.

"The difference this time is that there was somebody there to videotape it," she was quoted as saying. "That's the only difference."

Los Angeles is not alone. Police brutality against blacks is as American as the Ku Klux Klan, occurring, no doubt, at this very hour. Almost every riot of the 1960s was sparked by uniformed storm troopers committing unwarranted street violence against African-Americans. The victims of police revolvers, truncheons and jackboots are piled to the sky: martyrs like Arthur MacDuffie of Miami, Michael Stewart and Eleanor Bumpurs of New York City, ad infinitum, ad nauseam.

The present orgy of cop brutality began after Rodney Glen King, a 25-year-old unemployed construction worker, was ordered from his 1988 Hyundai. Police claim, but King denies, that the chase had reached 115 mph on a freeway. Media accounts say King "appeared to be acting funny, but not violent—laughing and pointing up to the LAPD helicopter that was (overhead)."

Los Angeles police reportedly overruled the California Highway Patrol for battering rights to the unresisting black man. Already lying on the ground, King was shot with a Taser stun gun by a police officer bent on delivering the electrical shock.

> **"Police brutality against blacks is as American as the Ku Klux Klan, occurring, no doubt, at this very hour."**

Their victim sufficiently subdued, surrounded and outnumbered, the cowardly officers erupted into a routine frenzy of wild clubbing, kicking and gnashing of teeth. After a terrifying beating, King lay still during a brief lull interrupted by a cop stomping his boots on the victim's bloody head.

King was later hogtied, with handcuffs around his wrists and ankles, then taken away in an ambulance.

"I was scared. I was scared for my life," King was quoted as saying. "So I laid down real calmly and took it like a man." Hospitalized while under arrest, he suffered eye damage, multiple contusions, scars and a broken ankle.

"They shocked me," King recalled, "paused for a minute and then they struck me across the face real hard with a billyclub. They beat where it hurt in my ankles, they beat my whole body where it hurt. It hurts real bad."

Police Silence

Police tradition, at this point, calls for the cops who gathered to torture to band together and lie. King was written up for resisting arrest and considered for aggravated assault. Arrested Sunday night, King was not released until Wednesday.

Only the videotape prevented the badly mauled King from being slapped with further criminal charges. It also got the officers suspended, allegedly. Despite the horror the videotape stirred in viewers, it will take a miracle to get these cops convicted on any charges or thrown off the force. They acted with the tacit approval of Police Chief Daryl F. Gates, if not of the dominant society.

Meanwhile, there is a gathering of rage out there among African-Americans who truly suffer from such widespread injustice. Should it continue to go unpunished, it might well explode— and one day soon.

Police Brutality Against Juveniles Is a Serious Problem

Earl Shorris

About the Author: *Earl Shorris is a writer whose books include* Under the Fifth Sun: A Novel of Pancho Villa.

After the meeting of the *comunidad de base* the priest said, "Let's take the long way home." It was early evening. There were children in the streets of the parish. The priest greeted them with a smile or a pat on the head. "Hola, mijo." In the black sky above us we saw a helicopter. The severe white light of its hunting eye appeared suddenly, laying bare the spaces between the adobe and stucco houses east of the dead, dry riverbed. Our voices were obliterated by the stuttering bark of the engine.

We continued through the parish. The helicopter moved away. We heard music, someone singing, perhaps a radio. As we passed a one-room store, a man came hurrying toward us. The man and the priest greeted each other. We all stood in the light that came through the screened entrance to the store. "There are police at the church," the man said.

"How many?"

"Two cars, Father, maybe more."

"Are they going on the property?"

"I think so."

"We'd better hurry," the priest said. "Somehow they seem to know when I'm not there."

By the time we got back to the Dolores Mission the police had gone, but in the yard behind the chain link fence the gang members were still agitated. "They were here, they came inside the fence," the gangsters said. "The police said, 'Fuck TMC,' and we said, 'Fuck the po-lice.'"

"They said, 'All your homeboys from TMC nothing but pussies.'"

"We say, 'Beat us down, go ahead; we got a lot of witnesses.'"

"That one with the mustache, he say, 'We'll get you later, we'll fuck you up.'"

All evening the police cars prowled the street in front of the mission. It was part of the policy of "strict, high-profile enforcement," known officially as Operation Hammer. The gangsters were nervous; sooner or later they would have to leave the church property, walk down the contorted streets past the barrackslike buildings of the projects and go home. Then, they said, the police would pick them up, take them to a nearby factory area which was deserted at night, and "beat them down."

"The police would pick them up, . . . and 'beat them down.'"

They were little more than children, but each of them seemed to have a history in the dark or in the privacy of the station house. I had first heard of their problems with the police from the young Jesuit priest, Gregory J. Boyle, who ran the mission. We had been talking about the *comunidades de base*, or base communities, and the other organizing techniques he had learned in Bolivia. One of the aims of the *comunidades*, he said, was to stop the murderous gang wars that make Aliso-Pico, an area in the poorest parish in Los Angeles, one of the most dangerous.

The priest had chosen not to go along with the consensus, which was that the gangsters had to be "squashed." He started an alternative school for dropouts, virtually all of whom were gangsters. But the school is a problem because it is located on the top floor of the Dolores Mission Catholic Elementary School, and the idea of boys in the school with gang caps, tattoos and big rags hanging out of their pockets upsets the parents. Boyle made the old white stucco buildings of the mission, which had been declared a sanctuary for undocumented workers and their families, into a place where gangsters, too, could gather to watch television or lift weights or just "kick back." He gave the gangsters summer jobs at minimum wage. In return, he insisted that they live by his rules when they were on church property: no weapons, no drugs, no alcohol. Slowly they came to trust him, so that when he demanded an end to the use of Molotov cocktails by the gangs, they changed the rules of war.

Now they come to him for help in finding jobs, and he, not a lawyer, is the one they telephone when the police allow them the one call after they have been arrested. He speaks to them, whether in Spanish or in the argot of the gang. He knows what it means to "dis the hood" or "tag" a place or "cross out." He knows the meaning of "pleito" (problem) and "placa" (name or insignia), and he understands what can happen when a boy has been taunted by the police to the point where he ties the blue war rag on his head and gets drunk and begins to dance with rage.

The gangsters call him G-Dog, a gang name; they have even awarded him the honorific Loc (from *loco*, crazy). But the use of the church by the gangsters and the willingness of the priest to consider them human, to say that he loves them, have caused problems in the community: "I get this all the time," he said. " 'Uno de tus hijos, one of your kids'—and then fill in the blank— 'spray-painted my door, stole a bike from my kid, stole all my four tires of my car. Uno de tus hijos . . . '" His work has also caused a serious conflict between the police and the church. "There are," the priest said, "people who want to kick me out of this parish."

The methods of the police are calumny and harassment. If there is a dance at the mission, the police will suddenly invade the property, putting all the gangsters up against the wall. If the police see a gangster in a car, they will stop the car, tear it apart looking for dope, and when they find nothing, ticket the kid for having a broken headlight. In community meetings and casual contacts with members of the parish, the police speak against the priest. It is not respectable to consider the gangsters human.

When I asked him if the stories I had been told of police brutality and harassment were a matter of policy or merely isolated instances, he said, "Talk to the gangsters yourself."

The Meeting

Twelve gangs operate in Aliso-Pico: The Mob Crew, known as TMC; the East LA Dukes; East Coast Crips (the one black gang); Al Capone; and Clarence Street Locos are the largest. G-Dog arranged for me to meet with members of several of the gangs in a small room in the mission. I sat in a straight chair; the gangsters lounged on broken-down couches or sat on the floor. It was a curious meeting, an extraordinary display of manners by a group of adolescents. They spoke in turn, softly, explaining the language of the gang whenever they sensed that I might be lost. All were Chicano but one, a well-spoken black, handsome enough to be an actor and as self-possessed as a member of Skull and Bones at Yale, who said after the meeting that he was from the East Coast Crips, a branch of the countywide gang, which is allied with TMC.

"He hit me with the billy club under my arm."

This is what he and the others said. They asked that neither their names nor their gang names be used for fear of retaliation by the police.

They stopped us at the park, CRASH [Community Resources Against Street Hoodlums, a police antigang unit]. I was walking away. He seen me; he was passing by. He jumped over the fence. He hit me here in my face. He picked me up. He grabbed my chains, threw them in the trash. He got me by my balls, started squeezing my balls and threw me on the ground. He put me in the car, took me to the police station. The cop's name is Shepherd. It happened in April of this year. I'm 16. It was at night, about 8:30 or 9. We were in the park kicking back. They took me to the Glass House [Parker Center County Jail]. They took pictures of what they did to me [after his mother had lodged a complaint]; then they sent me a letter saying they can't do nothing.

———

We were in the store. A cop came in and hit us. Hit him [another boy sitting across the room] in the face. He hit me with the billy club under my arm. He knocked out all the [potato] chips. He bombed on him, made him fly through all the chips. Pah, he hit him like that, and I laughed, and he said, "Put your stuff down." I put it down, slow. Pah! He hit me in my jaw. I said, "Oh, man!" I stepped back. He got me from my back, put me down on the floor.

———

They know me already, because all the time they hit me. My mom goes up to the police station complaining, and they say they can't do nothing about it. I'm 15.

———

Once I was coming out of my house. There's an archway. We were hanging there. I came out of the house. I stopped to talk to my friend. We were riding off. They were just picking up anybody, anybody they see, beating them up and taking them to the police station. They stopped, just like that, and started beating us up. They hit my homeboy in the head. Cut him up, about six stitches in his head. Came after me, Boom! Hit me in my stomach. I fell. Then two other cops come, and one cop started hitting me in the head. Pah! About three times. They took us to the station, checked us out. We don't have nothing. They let us go. It was last year; I was 15.

———

I was in the station all day, until the night [brought in as a murder suspect; someone else was later arrested and charged with the crime].

They were saying, "We got people saying it was you." And I was like, "If you got so much proof, just take me in." They started beating me up when I said that. They say, "You can't tell me what my job is." You know, socking me, slapping me in the face. This one, he said, "I'm crazy," and he jump up on the table, and he start kicking me in my face. They beat me up, then the sergeant came in. They made me sit on my hands while they asked me a question, because, you know, I was blocking them every time they hit me. They made me sit on my hands, and they started slapping me in the head. I was 15.

Handcuffing and Beating

The guy who just left here, they took him to his house, and they told his mom, "You let your son do this and that." And she say, "No, no," you know. White light! They socked her, and he went crazy, you know. "What did you do that to my mom?" And then they started beating him down, and his mom was like, "No, no." And they socked her again and they handcuffed her to the staircase. And then they were beating him up, and they took his mom too for interfering.

———

Once, we were coming back from the store. It was closed. And this cop and a lady cop stopped us. They hit my homeboy; they were beating him down. He had a beanie. This cop took out his gum from his mouth and picked up the beanie and put the gum on my homeboy's head and smashed it down with the beanie.

"If you say you want a lawyer, they'll kick ass."

It's like another gang beating up our friends. One time, we were in the park, they hurt our friend bad, they like almost broke his ribs. They chased us out of the park, and they catch our friend—he's in jail right now—and they have him in the alley where no one can see them, and they beat him down. They beat him *down*. He couldn't even walk. We had to carry him out. They shocked him in the ear with the shocker. You know how many volts that got! We took him to his house and call the ambulance. We told them our friend got beat up, you know. They called the cops, who came and told us, "You guys get out of here before we beat you up." We left, and they let him sit right there.

If you say you want a lawyer, they'll kick ass.

"What did you say? You want to press charges against me?" They'll take you somewhere, they'll take you to the factories and beat the shit out of you. Everybody's scared of the factories. Once they see the factories, they know what's gonna happen.

The Housing [police employed by the L.A. Housing Authority, less well trained than the metropolitan police] caught my homeboy in the archway right here and they had him on his knees, with the gun in his mouth. He was crying "You better not move. You better not say nothing." He was already crying. He thought they were gonna shoot him. He was upset. Afterward, he came to us, he was upset, he was going off. They're just a gang, but they're legal.

High-profile Enforcement

Capt. Bob Medina, whose Hollenbeck Station command includes Aliso-Pico, denies that any of his officers have harassed the gangsters or used excessive force, although he said the police policy is "strict, high-profile enforcement." Community activists say that Medina, who is relatively new in his job, is not a good captain, that he will not accept complaints. Medina spent five and a half years in the Police Department's Internal Affairs Office investigating illegal acts by police officers. He said, "I sent one of the guys I went to the academy with to the joint." He says he will investigate every complaint, that he knows how to do it. He claimed that he was not hostile to Father Boyle's work with the gangsters. "By and large, I think he's doing the right thing," Medina said, then added, "I think he might be off

base in keeping information from us."

But the gangsters tell another story. When the boy with the beanie was later arrested for shooting at police cars from a rooftop, the police who were interrogating him told him G-Dog was "no damn good." When the boy defended the priest, saying, "He's the only one who cares about us," the police beat him. The boy told the priest they beat him for two hours until he confessed to the shooting. Then they read him his Miranda rights.

"The policy of the police . . . to 'squash' the gangsters is not the answer."

The gangsters named several of the police officers who regularly harass or beat them: Officers Shepherd, Martinez, Kellor and Aguila (or Avila). A member of the Neighborhood Watch community action group, Carmen Lima, said the police think all children are criminals. She described several incidents, including one she observed from her apartment window, in which children who did not appear to be gang members were handcuffed and made to kneel for as long as half an hour while Housing Police, who are not under Captain Medina's command, held guns to their heads. Her own son, who is 19 years old, works full time and has never been a gang member, has suffered the same kind of humiliation.

On the east side of Los Angeles anyone can get caught up in the wars. Since the White Fence and Tortilla Flats gangs came into existence during the Depression, the Mexicans and Mexican-Americans, known as Zoot Suiters, Pachucos, Cholos or Chicanos, have been fighting one another with sticks, fists, knives and sometimes guns. That is the internecine war. A second war is fought by police, who attack the gangsters with insults, billy clubs, flashlights, cattleprods, fists and guns.

Neither of the wars is legal; both have spread

into the general community. The gangsters sell drugs, commit other crimes and sometimes shoot bystanders during their battles. The pattern of police brutality predates the Zoot Suit Riots of the World War II era. Ruben Salazar, the newsman who was shot to death by a Los Angeles County deputy sheriff in 1969, wrote often in the *Los Angeles Times* describing the harassment and beating of Mexican-Americans by police and sheriff's deputies. Those abuses continue, according to the Latino Community Justice Center, with much of the police violence directed against people who are extremely vulnerable because they cannot speak English. The gangsters speak English, but they are also helpless. They have no allies in the establishment world. They are outlaws by choice, living by a highly articulated moral code based on fraternity and territoriality, a code that permits them to sell hard drugs but not to use them. Like that of the deceit-loving Dobus, about whom Ruth Benedict wrote, the gangsters' code seems ironic, a mirror image of our own.

At the end of the night, when G-Dog was closing down the mission, and the homeless, undocumented workers and families who also find sanctuary there were going to bed, the gangsters became calm. Instead of tales of war, they began talking about going home. They asked the priest or me to give them a ride, to spare them the beating the police had promised that night. They were afraid, and I understood then what Gregory Boyle meant when he said he loved them because he had seen them when they were most vulnerable.

Urban Guerrillas

For G-Dog the situation is becoming increasingly difficult, reminiscent of the double bind priests in Latin America have found themselves in. He opposes illegal acts by the gangsters yet he is close to them, he loves them. On the other hand, he wants to defend the members of his parish against violence and crime, but he knows that the policy of the police, which is to "squash" the gangsters, is not the answer.

In response to repression the gangsters have become urban guerrillas, not revolutionaries but members of a negative society. Their neighborhood, across the river from white Los Angeles, has become a banana republic, a murderous, anarchic place where helicopters seek out children in the night and black-gloved police squeeze them until they explode with rage. To the gangsters, it is the never-ending war of class and race made quick. They know what the police intend for them, what "strict, high-profile enforcement" means, but they cannot escape. Inside the cage the underdogs tear one another to pieces.

Police Brutality Against the Poor Is a National Crisis

Gregory J. Boyle

About the Author: *Gregory J. Boyle is pastor of Dolores Mission Church in Boyle Heights, Los Angeles, California.*

Most citizens viewing the tape of Rodney G. King being beaten by police officers were stunned and uncomprehending. Most citizens, that is, but the urban poor. To the members of my parish, a community of working poor and people of color east of downtown Los Angeles, George Holliday's video played like a grisly home movie, evoking grim memories of common and unchecked police brutality.

Police Chief Daryl Gates cautions us not to judge an entire department on one incident, but the inner-city poor know that the only thing isolated about this incident was the chance way in which it was captured on tape. Most people of color can recall such an incident happening to them or to a family member or neighbor. We are less than honest and commit a grave error if we insist that what happened to Rodney G. King was isolated and an exceptional case. The poor know better.

We need not wait for further, well-placed home video cameras to see that low-intensity warfare is being waged against low-income minorities. We need only listen to the voices of the poor; they can testify that they are dehumanized, disparaged and despised by the police. They are always suspect and seldom afforded the same courtesy or pledge of service and protection as residents of, say, Hancock Park. In fact, they expect the opposite: They have learned to fear the kind of abuse that befell King. Such brutality and the frightful attitude from which it is born are part of the air that the poor breathe.

No internal affairs investigation will right the wrongful attitude pervasive among Los Angeles police officers whose beat is the inner city. Well-publicized cases of police brutality, even judgments by juries, have not brought a change in attitude, much less behavior.

It has become hackneyed to underscore the difficult and frustrating nature of law enforcement in our city today. It is true that the job is more risky and complicated than it has ever been. No one would want to tie the hands of police officers and prevent them from doing the job they have been given. Among the urban poor, however, the police have routinely assumed duties not theirs. They often find citizens guilty of crimes and proceed to impose a sentence on the spot, whatever punishment they see fit. Perhaps it is because they have lost faith in the justice system that they insist on doling out justice themselves. Rodney King was tried, found guilty and punished all within minutes. The taxpayers saved a lot of money.

"The pattern of police abuse is discernible if we know to look in the right places."

To characterize the King incident as atypical and an aberration is to further insult and discredit the experience of minorities and the urban poor. The pattern of police abuse is discernible if we know to look in the right places. Time and again, people in my community have gone to the police to report unprofessional (to say the least) conduct by officers: rudeness, harassment, intimidation and physical abuse, from being "roughed up" to beatings. Time and again, they have been turned away.

Gregory J. Boyle, "Defenseless, the Poor Are Also Voiceless," *Los Angeles Times*, March 11, 1991. Reprinted with permission.

It is the sincere hope of the inner-city poor that law enforcement's pattern of excessive force and the degrading attitude that undergirds it will change and stop altogether. The great frustration of the poor is that they expend more energy just to be heard than they spend working together with the police to find solutions to the unsettling alienation that exists between them.

Rodney King is out of police custody now, free to nurse his wounds and heal his memory. Minorities and poor city-dwellers look forward to the same kind of healing of their own collective memory. They long to be listened to and hope that their experience will be valued. They know better than anyone that the first step to improved relations with the police is simply to be heard with respect.

Is Police Brutality a National Crisis?

No: Police Brutality Is Not a National Crisis

Police Brutality Is Not a National Crisis
Police Brutality Is Declining
Police Brutality Is Exaggerated
The Extent of Police Brutality Is Difficult to Measure
Police Officers Are Heroes
Criminals, Not Police, Are the Real National Crisis

Police Brutality Is Not a National Crisis

Edwin J. Delattre

About the Author: *Edwin J. Delattre is Olin Scholar in Applied Ethics at Boston University and former president of St. John's College in Annapolis, Maryland and Sante Fe, New Mexico. He is the author of* Character and Cops: Ethics in Policing.

Most of us have now seen the videotape of Los Angeles Police Department officers ruthlessly beating Rodney Glenn King: While he lay helpless, four policemen struck him 56 times with clubs that resemble baseball bats, shot him with a stun gun, fractured his skull in nine places and broke his leg.

It didn't stop there. We have also heard or read transcripts of radio communications in which some of these police referred to a domestic dispute as "right out of 'Gorillas in the Mist.'" In the aftermath of the King beating, some laughed over it, and one officer said, "I haven't beaten anyone this bad for a long time." The incident—which President Bush declared "made me sick"—has, in short, become too familiar to the American people. It has also, predictably, led to a widespread assumption that such behavior is commonplace in Los Angeles and other cities.

But how typical was that behavior? Why did these men go so terribly wrong? What can be done to stop such vicious things from happening?

In fact, the Los Angeles incident is not representative of most of the metropolitan police forces around the country. It is not necessarily even representative of Los Angeles, though the

Edwin J. Delattre, "Cops Who Pound More than a Beat," *The Washington Post Weekly Edition*, April 8-14, 1991. Reprinted with permission.

city's willingness to quickly settle lawsuits alleging police brutality hints at the seriousness of the problem there.

During the past 16 years, as a visitor and counselor, I have spent nights with police on duty throughout America. I have seen and heard violence inflicted on innocent victims countless times. In the company of patrol and command personnel, I have witnessed the suffering of women battered by husbands and boyfriends, children burned and broken by parents, grandparents beaten by their children and grandchildren, pedestrians maimed by drunken drivers, teachers raped by students, and innocent strangers—from the homeless to the advantaged—savaged by the predators of our streets.

I have never, though, personally witnessed anything resembling such depravity by police, although I have studied cases of police brutality that ended in murder. (Having said that, I should also note that when people like myself show up at arrest scenes, the violence tends to stop.)

"The Los Angeles incident is not representative of most of the metropolitan police forces around the country."

Still, it is important to remember that Los Angeles is set apart from many other police forces by several things. In particular, the LAPD is sometimes described as a paramilitary department in its manner of leadership and its policies on the use of "pain" as a coercive instrument in at least some situations involving demonstrators. Baltimore County, by contrast, prohibits pain as an instrument of compliance in dealing with nonviolent demonstrators. If demonstrators resist in Baltimore County, they are taken away on a stretcher. (Some techniques of pain—finger pressers, choke holds and wrist binders—are more and more rejected by U.S. jurisdictions.)

The contrast is huge, and as a result, the public's idea of the role of police varies radically from community to community. Most important, perhaps, police behavior tells a community how the police themselves envision the public they serve.

Even such profound differences in the accepted practices of a police department, though, cannot explain how such an ugly thing as the beating of Rodney King could have happened in Los Angeles.

As we look for additional explanations, one is surely a failure of leadership within the force. Students of the police, and police behavior, know that this is the most dangerous failing of all in policing. In Los Angeles, the behavior of the sergeant at the scene revealed the full collapse of responsible supervision in the field. In addition, there was staggering cowardice in the behavior of the officers who either bowed to peer pressure or—as their union representatives now insist—were just following orders. This is no more an acceptable excuse in America than it was at Nuremberg.

Why the sergeant lacked the judgment and courage to control his officers is unclear, but such profound failures of supervision—and of integrity, judgment and professional competence—cannot be accounted for simply by racism. Neither can they be attributed entirely to deficiencies in police training, nor to a shortage of "sensitivity" training of police in the customs and values of minority groups. But when police go this wrong, they are completely out of touch with the ideals of justice, freedom and professionalism. The only remedies, then, are highly professional supervision—from the top down—and peer pressure. Sometimes, this can be achieved only by sustained and candid communication with the community about their needs and desires.

No Wish to Hurt People

In the first course I ever taught in ethics for police in 1975, one of my police-officer students said to me, "You know, Mr. Delattre, most cops don't like to hurt people." In the years since, I

have learned how right he was.

I have seen police officers injured because they limited their use of force against wildly violent individuals, and I have seen them refrain from using deadly force even in life-threatening situations. Many police feel anguish after using fully justified force; few take pleasure in it, let alone react with glee. Some of my police friends have been shot in the line of duty. It is only a matter of fortune that none of them is among the 1,514 American police who were killed feloniously or died in the line of duty between 1980 and 1989 or the many who have been killed since.

"I have seen police officers injured because they limited their use of force against wildly violent individuals."

Even so, most police around the country do not have a bunker mentality. They go on forces knowing what they'll have to put up with; they like their jobs and are ready and able to stand the pressure.

But not always.

It is also true that some police adjust badly to the stresses of policing. They are ground down by danger, resentment of criminals who prosper, perceived failure of social service and criminal justice agencies, and the daunting repetitiveness of their work. Some drift toward despair over the violence, suffering, hopelessness, ignorance and self-destructive behavior they encounter day after day. Some are ineffective—even dangerous—because they become cynical, convinced of public ingratitude and convinced that policing is a daily battle of "us against them."

One particular danger is the "noble cause" phenomenon I've described to my students. The reasoning is something like this: We're the good guys, and the U.S. Constitution doesn't always apply to us. We're right, so anything we do is right. Sometimes, we may need to mete out punishment because the criminal justice system won't. Furthermore, the public will approve.

The notion that the ends justify the means, of course, is corrosive. Once you go beyond the law in one way, you might go beyond the law in other ways too. It is precisely this that gives rise to the sort of environment that would lead not just to the Los Angeles beating, but to the casual racism and brutality of the computer messages the cops sent one another in the case.

Danger of Corruption

Another danger is having a bunch of bad eggs in a department. An egregious—and celebrated—example of this occurred in Miami, after the Mariel boatlift from Cuba and riots in the city. The Miami city government then resolved to hire 200 new officers immediately, all of them to be residents of the city. This was all done so fast that a lot of police who didn't belong in uniform were suddenly patrolling the streets. As anyone who followed the worst of this Miami vice knows, a great many of these police recruits signed up just to get better access to the drug trade.

More commonly, though, some police departments are undermined by the sort of problems that can be found in any large institution: consumption of illegal drugs by their members, unchecked alcoholism and financial corruption.

All these problems are aggravated by insufficient budgets for thorough background investigation of applicants; abbreviated training, lax supervision and inappropriate assignments of personnel; assignment of officers in the same precinct or unit for too long; legal constraints against disciplining personnel and the threat of lawsuits; adversarial relations between management and unions; failure of moral leadership at various ranks; insufficient cooperation with the public and their civic and religious institutions; political interference; and poor lines of communication with federal agencies that can help root out unlawful behavior.

No broad-scale investigation of police brutality in the United States can possibly address or remedy all these problems. Indeed, nothing can make policing—or any other human endeavor—perfect.

But if police and federal agencies keep in mind that brutality always signals disrespect for limits of law and policy, and they look for the broader signs of such disrespect—financial corruption, drug consumption, sloppy and indulgent supervision—they are likely to uncover some of the breeding grounds of brutality. They may help to prevent brutality before it starts, and also to curb it where it exists. Many departments have longstanding traditions against excessive force. Senior officers frequently tell their junior colleagues, "We don't do that here.". . .

***

"Many departments have longstanding traditions against excessive force."

***

Throughout America, the horror felt by both police and general public over the treatment of Rodney King provides us with a rare opportunity to pursue the common good together. If we seize upon this moment to advance police and citizen cooperation rather than to draw farther apart, we may forge a future where even secret video and audio tapes routinely show us more of the best and less of the worst in human nature.

Police Brutality Is Declining

Ted Gest

About the Author: *Ted Gest is a staff writer for* U.S. News & World Report, *a weekly news magazine.*

Judging from the attention, police brutality is a contagion that could soon rival the urban riots of the 1960s. President Bush joined those denouncing the March 3, 1991, videotaped bludgeoning of Rodney King, savagely beaten by white Los Angeles officers after he was pulled over for speeding. At almost the same time, five officers in New York City were charged with murder for strangling a car thief after they found him asleep in a stolen car, and an officer in suburban Atlanta was thrown off the force just days after he roughed up a motorist following a traffic incident. In Washington, D.C., the Justice Department mounted a crash effort to review its file of 15,000 brutality accusations, some of which have sat for six years, as Congress convened hearings. The nation, warned Michigan Rep. John Conyers, was facing "a crisis of confidence in law enforcement."

Is the country truly experiencing a pandemic of police lawlessness? It is clear that indefensible brutalities—most of them inflicted on powerless minority victims—still take place too frequently in inner cities. Yet in most cities, abuse by officers seems less prevalent than in earlier eras. Judging by the number of complaints filed with civil-liberties groups and police departments—a good, though imperfect, measure of police-community relations—police brutality has declined in recent years in New York City, Chicago, New Orleans and even Los Angeles.

Moreover, even though some cities have shown a rise in complaints, police use of "excessive force" remains comparatively rare. In Kansas City, Mo., a representative urban area, a police force of about 1,100 officers provoked 108 complaints of excessive or unnecessary force during 1990, although the department received almost 500,000 calls for assistance and made 13,934 arrests. Even the notorious Los Angeles Police Department faces an average of just 18 brutality lawsuits for every 1,000 officers, according to the *Los Angeles Times.*

"In most cities, abuse by officers seems less prevalent than in earlier eras."

Much has been learned in the last generation about how to curb police abuse—and many departments have tried to apply those lessons. The problem is that some police agencies haven't been vigilant enough about weeding out the relatively small number of repeat offenders who are responsible for much, if not most, police abuse. In Los Angeles, two of the four officers indicted in the King beating had suspension records; one had been removed for 66 days in 1987 for beating and kicking a suspect. In a Miami incident that ultimately sparked disturbances in December 1990, several of a group of six policemen allegedly beat Leonardo Mercado, a Puerto Rican drug dealer, to death. All had remained on patrol duty despite the fact that five of the six had previously shown up on the Miami Police Department's "early-warning list" for their violent behavior and three had been counseled for stress in the months before the incident. Among them they had "forcibly controlled" suspects a total of 38 times in three years. All were cleared of civil rights violations charges.

It's not that there isn't great incentive for cities to act against abusive cops. Beyond the human toll, police brutality is expensive. Los Angeles paid $8 million in 1990 to settle civil claims, and localities from Dade County, Fla. to San Diego shelled out millions of dollars to victims during the 1980s. That doesn't include the cost of riots set off by police-citizen conflicts. Four riots in Miami over the past decade, started after police killed blacks under disputed circumstances, led to more than $100 million in damages.

Yet, the distressing truth is that brutality is likely to endure for these reasons:

The siege mentality. With drug traffickers heavily armed and more likely to fire away, many officers adopt an us-against-them mindset and a strict ethic against "ratting" on fellow officers. "If their authority is threatened, they retaliate with a kind of street justice," explains former New York cop William Walsh, a justice expert at Pennsylvania State University. Citizen demands for tough-guy law enforcers can subtly encourage intimidating tactics, too. In New York City, police recruits spend seven hours a day for eight days training with their weapons; by contrast, they devote 15 hours over five months to racial and cultural "sensitivity" training.

Failing Disciplinary Systems

Discipline lapses. A number of cities have created special boards to investigate charges of police misconduct, but many are hampered by budget woes and police unions. Flint Taylor, a Chicago lawyer who edits a newsletter on police misconduct, contends that "disciplinary systems across the country by and large are abject failures." While some brutality charges are baseless, discipline rates on the whole are virtually nil. In the Miami area, Metro-Dade officials have sustained 10 of 172 excessive-force complaints since 1988, resulting in only one cop's leaving the 2,457-officer force. The city of Miami reports a similar trend. One disquieting analysis by the *Detroit Free Press* found that the department reserves its lightest discipline for officers who assault citizens. Typically, police get fired for using cocaine, suspended for a month for smoking marijuana and reprimanded for showing carelessness or disrespect to a citizen. But the aver-

age penalty for assaulting a citizen is, literally, nothing.

"Much has been learned in the last generation about how to curb police abuse."

Missing evidence. Since most abuse occurs out of the public eye, the lack of independent eyewitnesses makes cases very difficult to prove. (Los Angeles's indictments within 10 days of the beating are extraordinary in the annals of brutality: Amateur filmmakers usually are not standing by.) Forced to choose between an officer and a victim who typically has a criminal past, juries and prosecutors usually side with the cop. Nationwide, the Justice Department presented just 2 percent of the most recent 15,000 brutality complaints to a grand jury. Local investigations are often less than thorough, too. In Chicago in 1988, civilian investigators backed an officer who said he killed a man who charged him. But investigators never checked an autopsy report that showed the victim had been shot in the back.

Legal loopholes. Not surprisingly, civil service regulations and union rules help protect abusive cops. Citizens Alert, a Chicago watchdog group, says the city's police union has forced adoption of a rule that bars investigators from consulting a cop's prior record during a probe. Meanwhile, the *Miami Herald* reports that the civil service board has retained most of the 24 troubled officers that the police chief *wanted* to fire since 1989, including one abusive cop who had shown up on the department's early-warning list 23 times in 10 years.

Despite the problems, the blueprint for reducing brutality seems clear. For starters, says Aleem Fakir of PULSE, a black Miami civic group, police departments "need to stop the fox from watching the henhouse and have more community civilian boards monitor them." Early-warning systems that automatically subject officers to investigations after several brutality accusations can help, as does reshaping a police force to reflect a city's ethnic makeup. The decline of brutality complaints in Houston and Philadelphia, for example, coincided with the reigns of black police chiefs who stressed programs that send cops out to cope both with crime and with social problems. In Atlanta, U.S. Rep. John Lewis, who as a civil-rights leader was bloodied by state troopers, insists that a white-on-black beating like the Los Angeles incident couldn't happen in his city because of the large percentage of black cops on the force.

Still, all such reforms can be virtually worthless unless the local police chief chooses to set and enforce a tone of tolerance of minorities and intolerance of abuse. Many police agencies, for example, have intensified formal training for recruits on how to handle charged incidents such as the aftermath of high-speed chases, but the training has little impact when field commanders feel free to ignore it. In the LAPD's case, the racist remarks and laughter of the cops who beat King suggest that Police Chief Daryl Gates's history of derogatory remarks about minorities created an open-season atmosphere among officers who worked the city's dangerous night beat.

"The blueprint for reducing brutality seems clear."

Ultimately, the combative nature of policing and the chronic tensions in inner cities will ensure the persistence of some brutality. But the growing and appropriate national revulsion over Rodney King's beating will make more than a few cops think twice before they exult about beating a suspect—or wield their nightsticks so freely.

Police Brutality Is Exaggerated

William F. Jasper

About the Author: *William F. Jasper is a senior editor of* The New American, *a magazine published by the John Birch Society, a conservative anticommunist organization.*

When George Holliday stepped out on his balcony with a video camera shortly after midnight on March 3rd, 1991, he had no way of knowing that what he was about to record would have national, even world, impact. Across the street from his home a high-speed chase had culminated with numerous police vehicles and over 20 officers of the Los Angeles Police Department converging on a white Hyundai driven (under the influence of alcohol) by one Rodney G. King—25, black, unemployed, on parole. What Holliday captured on tape—at least what the public has seen so far—is one of the most graphically brutal sequences ever shown on American television news: Three officers savagely kicking and clubbing a prostrate King while as many as two dozen more officers look on.

It has been aptly dubbed "America's Ugliest Home Video," and it has been broadcast on television stations worldwide again and again —and again. Charges of "media overkill" were justifiable only a couple of days after the shocking video came to light, by which time it had already been replayed dozens of times on most stations. But more than a month later the jolting scenes continued to play almost daily in most major television markets. An ugly act by a few that should have remained essentially a local Los Angeles incident, and a tape that should have served primarily as evidence to convict the wrongdoers, were transformed instead into a media event and a political vehicle to undermine law enforcement nationwide.

Ironically, the very videotape that exposed the flagrant abuse of King by Los Angeles police officers and guaranteed the victim his day in court, now, because of media saturation and sensationalism, stands to jeopardize justice not only in that case but in many others as well. Attorneys for the police defendants have charged that the hysteria engendered by the mega-coverage of the incident has made it impossible for their clients to get a fair trial. But if this plea doesn't work to the advantage of the offending officers, it is certain that other criminals will benefit from the crippling effect that the bad publicity is having on police work and our justice system.

"Every night we see the Rodney King videotape on every channel," said Los Angeles prosecuting attorney Steven Sowders in a *Los Angeles Times* interview. "We fear that every officer's credibility is being called into question . . . even in cases where the defendant is clearly guilty." The same *Times* article cited a current case in which a man arrested for felony assault on a police officer was released on a reduced misdemeanor charge because, as Deputy District Attorney Gil Garcetti put it: "I did not see that our case could go forward given the current atmosphere." The "current atmosphere" is a supercharged cauldron of hate that has been continuously fueled and stirred by local and outside agitators.

"An ugly act by a few . . . [has been] transformed instead into a media event and a political vehicle to undermine law enforcement."

Law enforcement across the nation, from rural, small town forces to major metropolitan departments, has felt the backlash. Most officers

1-14 William F. Jasper, "Keep Them Local, Keep Us Free," *The New American,* May 21, 1991. Reprinted with permission.

and police officials seem to agree that no other event in memory has come close to causing the widespread antipolice reaction of the LAPD/King affair. "I just saw [the video] again on Atlanta television last night, and I know that it will continue to give us a black eye in the community," says Corporal Richard McClarin, a veteran of the Fulton County (Georgia) Police Department and an instructor on firearms and deadly force at the county's police academy. "You see it on the street in the stares, hostile or fearful looks, taunts, comments. It hurts because it's not fair to the vast majority of officers, who are just as appalled as anyone [by the beating]."

David J. Stevens, chief of police of Bedminster Township, Pennsylvania (pop. 4,600), says even his five-man force, which has great community relations with the people of his rural jurisdiction, has been bruised by the King publicity. "We've never even had a police brutality suit in the history of our department," says Stevens, "but you go into a restaurant and someone makes a comment about police brutality or jokes about police 'batting practice.' Even though this will pass and I know virtually all the citizens around here support us, it is unreal how the repetitious playing of this video has implanted these doubts and fears in many people's minds."

Exploiting the Race Issue

Rodney King is black; the officers who did the thrashing are not. This in itself was all the proof needed by some, not only to declare the violent act itself to be racially motivated, but to declare the entire LAPD to be riddled with racism and to demand Chief Daryl Gates' resignation or dismissal. It should be noted that at his first press conference King and his attorney stated categorically that there was no evidence that this had been a racial incident. He had heard no racial slurs and had perceived no racial overtones before, during, or after the beating. That, of course, does not diminish the grievousness of the wrong or prove that racial prejudice wasn't a factor. Several of the crude comments and jokes by officers involved in the melee, recorded on

the patrol car computer transcripts, may indeed be racial in nature. But even if that is proven to be the case, it is still a long way from corroborating the charges of "systemic racism" leveled against the department by professional radicals like U.S. Representative John Conyers (D-MI).

"Criminals will benefit from the crippling effect that the bad publicity is having on police work."

Former LAPD Chief Ed Davis, now a state senator, challenges these charges with the following facts: "My police academy classmate and the mayor of Los Angeles for 18 years, Tom Bradley, is African-American. Direct control of the personnel and training bureaus in the LAPD was held, until his recent retirement, by an assistant chief of police, Jesse Brewer. . . . He happens to be African-American. During the three high-growth years, the internal-affairs division, which investigates charges of police misconduct, was directed by three different captains, two of whom are African-Americans. The percentage of African-American officers in the department exceeds the percentage of African-Americans in the city's population."

In addition, says Davis, for 18 years Bradley has appointed the police commissioners, who actually run the department, and with few exceptions they have been liberals. Some have been black. "I do not thus believe," Davis wrote in a *Times* opinion column, "there is any racially biased institutional prejudice within the LAPD." Lyman Doster, president of the Association of Black Law Enforcement Executives, agrees. So does former Assistant Police Chief Jesse Brewer, who retired as the highest ranking black officer in the department's history. To the contrary, says Brewer, under his tenure "anything that hinted at racism would be singled out, investigated and dealt with immediately."

Likewise, most police organizations representing ethnic minorities seem to endorse Chief Gates' assertion that the King beating was an "aberration." The Latino Peace Officers Association, the Oscar Joel Bryant Foundation (a black police group representing all of Southern California), the Association of Black Law Enforcement Executives, the California Oriental Peace Officers Association, the Hispanic Law Enforcement Administrators, and other minority groups joined other police organizations in placing a full-page advertisement in the *Los Angeles Times* that called on the people of Los Angeles to support the department and not blame all officers for the misdeeds of the few. The text of the ad read, in part, "We don't blame communities or a class or a group of people for the acts committed by individuals because we know everyone is responsible for his or her own actions. Those who attempt to blame an entire group are playing a fool's game and trying to dupe the public."

Indeed, says Ezola Foster, president of Black-Americans for Family Values, "that is exactly what has been going on. . . . I was just as filled with anger and outrage over the brutality against Mr. King as anyone," Mrs. Foster told *The New American*. But the current attack on Gates and the police department, she contends, "has nothing to do with the King beating, police brutality or departmental racism." It is, she says, a well-orchestrated, vicious campaign by left-wing political activists who have been vying for control of city politics for many years and who "have been exploiting this incident to inflame racial tensions for their political advantage."

"Another assault on local police that is seeing a revival is the call for . . . 'civilian review boards.'"

"The people of Los Angeles," says Mrs. Foster, "are in the midst of a fierce struggle over who will control the streets: The criminals and gangs and the political activists who support and champion them, or the representatives of lawful authority. . . . We have all of these 'non-profit' political groups here in the community—the ACLU [American Civil Liberties Union], NAACP [National Association for the Advancement of Colored People], Southern Christian Leadership Conference, Urban League, Mexican American Political Association, the Brotherhood Crusade—who receive millions of tax dollars and private donations that they have used to build their political power bases."

Foster cites the case of convicted murderer Jitu Sadiki as just one example in which activist groups coalesced around criminals who were victimizing minority communities. "This man," says Foster, "is a gang member who served six years in prison for second degree murder. The Brotherhood Crusade made him into a 'hero' after his release, and when he was arrested while breaking into a pawn shop all of these groups came to his aid, claiming he was the victim of police abuse.". . .

Federal Grab for Control

The most striking thing in the whole tragic Rodney King affair is how it has been blown into an issue of national proportions. Race, again, is the lightning rod. Jesse Jackson declared that the beating "exposed a national malady." U.S. Representative Don Edwards (D-CA), chairman of the House Judiciary Committee and a long-time critic of law enforcement, proclaimed that police brutality is "an epidemic" and announced that he would open national hearings on the federal response to this problem. Ira Glasser, executive director of the ACLU, charged that "this kind of abuse has been a feature of every time in our history," and called on Congress to enact new federal legislation to give the Justice Department the authority to file suits against police departments and department heads accused of brutality. The Congressional Black Caucus urged the FBI [Federal Bureau of Investigation] and the Justice Department to launch thorough investigations of the LAPD and other police departments to ferret out racism and brutality.

The federal government has already stepped

in. In response to the King videotape, Attorney General Thornburgh has launched a nationwide review of police brutality complaints filed with federal authorities over the past six years. Senator Joseph Biden (D-DE) has introduced federal legislation to create a national police corps. The *Los Angeles Times* has endorsed the police corps concept in its editorials on at least two occasions.

The advocates of federal intervention paint a grim picture of an America where local law enforcement has gone berserk and local police departments are dominated by rampaging racist goons or incompetent buffoons. If, as we have shown, evidence to back up charges of institutional racism in the LAPD is lacking, these sweeping charges against the entire system of American law enforcement are even more unfounded. They reveal a warped view of American society, just as proposals to interject the federal government into local police affairs reveal either an ignorance of our constitutional system and its separation of powers, or an intent to subvert the system. (Local police under local control are essential to maintaining our constitutional system of government and our liberties,) just as a national police is essential for the establishment of any tyranny.

During the 1960s the federal government launched the Law Enforcement Assistance Administration (LEAA) with the expressed intention of "assisting" local law enforcement. What local police officials discovered, though, was that along with the federal funds came federal regulations that were not only impairing law enforcement, but gradually turning local departments into mere administrative units of the federal government.

Thankfully, all funding for the agency was eliminated in 1981 and it went out of existence the following year. But now, in the wake of the furor over Rodney King, this type of dangerous federal intrusion is being revived. . . .

Another assault on local police that is seeing a revival is the call for the establishment of "civil-ian review boards" to monitor police abuse. This idea was invented by the Communist Party in the 1930s when it thought the country was ripe for revolution. According to Dr. Bella Dodd, a former member of the National Committee of the Communist Party who defected in 1948, the idea was to get the police out from under the control of elected officials and subject to the discipline of a "civilian" group that the Party could infiltrate and control. W. Cleon Skousen, a former member of the FBI and former chief of police for Salt Lake City, interviewed Dodd and questioned her concerning the communist plan for civilian review boards. According to Skousen, Dodd "stated that by this means [the communists] intended to mete out harsh and arbitrary punishment against the police until they were intimidated into a benumbed, neutralized, impotent and non-functioning agency."

Review Boards

That was exactly the result in those jurisdictions that implemented the communist-originated review boards. When the communist-inspired riots broke out in the 1960s the FBI was ordered to investigate. The FBI reported, "Where there is an outside civilian review board the restraint of police was so great that effective action against the rioters appeared to be impossible." The FBI found: "In one city with such an outside review board, police action was so ineffective that the police were ordered to . . . limit themselves to attempting to prevent the riot from spreading. In another such city the police frankly admitted the making of arrests was 'unfeasible' and mob action continued without deterrence."

It is no surprise that the Communist Party is still pushing this program. The Party's newspaper, the *People's Weekly World*, carried an article calling for the establishing of civilian review boards "to investigate complaints, discipline officers and oversee police activity, including recruitment and training."

The Extent of Police Brutality Is Difficult to Measure

Scott Armstrong and Daniel B. Wood

About the Authors: *Scott Armstrong and Daniel B. Wood are staff writers for* The Christian Science Monitor, *an international daily newspaper.*

In the spartan second-floor office, four phones log 50 calls a day. A student says she was punched by a policeman breaking up a campus party simply because she asked for his badge number. A mother tells of her teenage son who stole a car, but later surrendered to police quietly—only to be attacked by their German shepherd.

The complaints coming into the Police Misconduct Lawyer Referral Service, a local watchdog group, deal with allegations of police abuse in southern California. But they are similar to those logged with almost any legal-advocacy group in the country.

For years, such accounts have quietly trickled into law offices and police precincts. Now, in the wake of the videotaped beating of a black man by white police in Los Angeles, they lie at the heart of a searing national debate over police brutality in America.

In the days since the tape was shot and endlessly played, outrage over the incident has rocked the police and political establishment here, spurred a nationwide probe of police misconduct, and galvanized the civil rights movement as no other event in a quarter century.

The episode has also prompted the most extensive reappraisal of the nation's 600,000 men and women in blue since Frank Serpico blew the whistle on police corruption in New York in the 1960s. "Police misconduct is an American habit that has existed since the turn of the century," says Al Reiss, a Yale criminologist. "Nobody knew how prevalent it was then, nor do they now. But its power to sicken and sadden is shocking us anew."

Sharp differences exist over the extent of police brutality in America today. Some experts argue improved police training and more integrated departments have led to a decline in police violence. Others contend that lingering racism, meaner streets, and a society that demands tough treatment of criminals is fostering more baton tactics in many cities.

"I think we are better off than 20 years ago," says David Bayley, a police expert at the State University of New York at Albany.

"I think the situation is worse," counters Hubert Williams, president of the Police Foundation, a research group.

The problem is difficult to gauge because no comprehensive statistics exist. And the phenomenon involves an institution, the police, that is a closed culture, "almost monastic," in the words of one researcher.

"The problem is difficult to gauge because no comprehensive statistics exist."

What figures do exist reveal a contradictory and incomplete picture. In New York, the number of complaints filed against police—everything from charges of excessive force to ethnic slurs—dropped from 5,120 in 1986 to 3,515 in 1989.

Houston police have seen a 10 percent decline in each of the past three years. Even in Los

Angeles, police say the trend is down: from 1,813 in 1986 to 1,556 in 1990.

On the other hand, excessive-force complaints have risen recently in Chicago, while they have seesawed in Philadelphia.

Researchers say many who suffer police injustices don't file complaints, either because they fear the process or because they feel nothing will be done.

Handling Complaints

How police departments deal with complaints varies widely. Some take them by phone. Others require personal appearances to file sworn statements—a process that Jim Fyfe, a criminologist at American University, says can feel as if "you are walking into the shadow of the valley of death."

Some cities have set up offices outside police stations to receive complaints. Abuse investigations in a few cities are handled entirely by civilians. In most cases, the police do the probing internally, with the results frequently reviewed by a civilian board.

Even when complaints are filed, many critics contend nothing ever comes of them. They argue that a "code of silence" often takes over, in which one officer refuses to "rat" and may even corroborate a false story.

In New York in 1989, the civilian complaint review board—comprised of police and civilian investigators—found "substantiation" for 8 percent of the filed allegations of police misconduct. Also in 1989, the Los Angeles Police Department (LAPD) saw 1,800 complaints of misconduct result in 1,044 disciplinary actions ranging from six months suspension to verbal reprimand.

In Boston in 1990, 13 officers were fired and 37 suspended as a result of investigations into 472 complaints of police abuse.

"The majority of complaints filed with police departments are either unfounded or not sustained," says Darrel Stephens, head of the Police Executive Research Forum. He estimates that 5 to 10 percent of complaints result in disciplinary action.

Many of the complaints are false—"filed to get back at police," says Sgt. Dean Anderson, an LAPD watch commander. And allegations are difficult to prove: It often comes down to the officer's word against that of the person arrested.

Experts who believe police violence in America is declining cite several reasons: better training with additional doses of "cultural awareness"; higher education levels (50 percent of police are college trained today vs. 20 percent in 1960); and the integration of departments.

"I think the King case is an aberration," says Jerome Skolnick, of the University of California, Berkeley, referring to the March 3, 1991, beating, for which four police have been indicted. "I think the LAPD is an aberration."

Many blacks, among others, disagree. They see many forces contributing to a harsher climate in the squad car: enduring racial tensions; new cops who are less experienced (38 percent of LAPD officers have fewer than three years' service); greater firepower in the hands of criminals, which forces cops to react quicker.

Some suggest a clogged criminal-justice system encourages cops to mete out justice on the street. And the nation's prolonged war on drugs has put added pressure on police.

"Allegations are difficult to prove: It often comes down to the officer's word against that of the person arrested."

"Politicians don't want to take responsibility for the signals they are giving us," says Gerald Arenberg of the National Association of Chiefs of Police. "They are literally saying, 'go out there and bash their heads in.'"

Attorney General Richard Thornburgh, who has ordered a federal probe of police brutality complaints, counters: "There is nothing inconsistent between aggressive law enforcement and the observance of civil liberties."

Police Officers Are Heroes

David Kupelian

About the Author: *David Kupelian is managing editor of* New Dimensions, *a monthly magazine.*

In 1991, America's police are subject to greater scrutiny, second-guessing, and Monday-morning quarterbacking than at any other time in history. Their misdeeds and mistakes, real or alleged, are given saturation publicity. The videotaped beating of Rodney King was aired so many times that most Americans have its image etched permanently in their minds.

Yet, there are other videos that the public rarely sees. One month before the March 3, 1991 Rodney King beating, a Texas policeman, having routinely stopped a truck, was shot as he approached the driver. That video was shown on national TV for about one day. A week later a North Carolina state trooper was intentionally run over by a truck—also videotaped. It received very little air time. Is there a double standard here?

By sensationalizing and endlessly harping on several isolated incidents, the media, in conjunction with grandstanding politicians, have fostered a new and increasingly widespread perception of America's police as the enemy, rather than the protector, of decent society. Los Angeles is a city "under siege by occupying forces," claims Roland Coleman of the Southern California Civil Rights Coalition. Jesse Jackson practically accused the entire Los Angeles Police Department of being racist. Rep. John Conyers (D, Mich.) warns that the nation faces "a crisis of confidence in law enforcement." Responding to this intense political pressure, the U.S. Justice

David Kupelian, "The Most Stressful Job in America: Police Work in the 1990s," *New Dimensions*, August 1991. Reprinted with permission of *New Dimensions*, PO Box 811, Grant Pass, OR 97526-0069. Subscription rate: $23.97/yr.

Department has mounted a major effort to review its file of 15,000 cases of alleged brutality, some of which are six years old.

Did all this hysteria really result from three L.A. cops beating Rodney King?

Police brutality has always existed, and it *is* a problem today. But is it true, as current media reporting implies, that American law enforcement is increasingly populated by racists and bullies? "Any police brutality is a serious matter and deserves attention and correction," says former Attorney General Edwin Meese. "But you also have to maintain a perspective that these events are relatively rare." Meese faults the media for distorting the issue. "More and more of the police-beat reporters just do not understand what the police go through, as the older reporters did. Instead, they are young hot-shots fresh out of journalism school who want to make a name for themselves by castigating the police."

In fact, police brutality may actually be *less* prevalent today than it was twenty years ago. Civil liberties groups and police departments report *fewer* brutality complaints filed in recent years, not more. And while the FBI's Civil Rights Division reports 2,450 complaints involving law enforcement in 1989, during the same time period, 62,172 law enforcement officers were victims of assaults. . . .

> ## "Police brutality may actually be *less* prevalent today than it was twenty years ago."

"Every time you go out on duty you're going out there with a full deck of cards, and you have absolutely no idea how they are going to be dealt to you," muses Gary Steiner, an eight-year member of the Santa Monica Police Department in Los Angeles County. "Very often officers are put into situations where one minute everything is fine and the next second, literally, you are going to be killed unless you act.". . .

Every cop has his or her own personal horror

stories, nightmarish dramas into which the police willingly thrust themselves to play their valiant roles. Indeed, the only thing standing between average citizens and the hellish world of murder, drugs, and violent crime is a thinning blue line of beleaguered police men and women. Their task is formidable. Crime is up, way up. Police in New York City answered 4 million 911 calls in 1990 alone, up from 2.7 million in 1980. But the numbers tell only half the story.

"Isolated reports of police brutality are resulting in . . . mass condemnation of America's police force."

Criminals, many experts agree, are simply worse today than in previous eras. Vaguely reminiscent of the Biblical warning of an age when "the love of one for another will grow cold," a new, more violent, more death-embracing trance of hatred seems to have captivated armies of social outcasts, especially in the inner cities.

Whereas 20 years ago a fender bender might have resulted in an argument or fist fight, today it is not uncommon to hear reports of one driver shooting the other in cold blood, then coolly getting back into his car and driving off. . . .

Fueled by the lust of drug trafficking profits, tens of thousands of gang members have turned many of America's inner cities into Beiruts of gang warfare. "In the 1940s and 1950s, a single police officer could face down a crowd of two or three dozen young people," says Meese. "Just by his presence, he would restore order. If he asked them to move on, they would move. Today that isn't necessarily the case." Indeed, for many youths who have known nothing from the day they were born except violence and abuse, killing a cop is a badge of honor.

To fight back these incarnated demons of the underworld, police must play the role of combat soldier, referee, psychologist, urban negotiator, social worker, doctor, and older brother. To do all this, they must be supermen. "I will keep my private life unsullied as an example to all," reads the National Law Enforcement Code of Ethics, "maintain courageous calm in the face of danger, scorn, or ridicule, develop self-restraint and be constantly mindful of the welfare of others, honest in thought and deed in both my personal and official life." While there are some rotten apples, most cops try diligently to live up to their profession's call for Herculean strength and nobility. . . .

America's police force today finds itself in a war zone. As in the Vietnam War—a conflict in which America's young soldiers fought as bravely as in any war before or since, but who were not allowed to win—today's police, particularly in the nation's troubled inner cities, increasingly feel as though they, too, are fighting a war that they are not being allowed to win.

Whereas U.S. troops in Vietnam were hamstrung by confused and indecisive administration policies, today's domestic troops find their efforts being sabotaged by a judicial system overly concerned with the rights of the accused at the expense of the victim. In Vietnam, isolated reports of atrocities, such as at My Lai, led to the grossly unjust spectacle of American anti-war demonstrators condemning all U.S. soldiers. Today, isolated reports of police brutality are resulting in much the same thing: mass condemnation of America's police force. . . .

Need Support

For what they do, for what we pay them, police are the best employee value there is. And because cops are under such stress, Americans would do well to exercise a little compassion toward them. Cops have a difficult job to do, and that job becomes nearly impossible without the support of both the court system and the public. . . .

Public support provides the stability and faith that these men and women need in order to fight the good fight for the rest of us.

Criminals, Not Police, Are the Real National Crisis

Patrick J. Buchanan

About the Author: *Patrick J. Buchanan is a columnist who has served on the staffs of U.S. presidents Nixon and Reagan.*

Early March 3, 1991, the California Highway Patrol was in hot pursuit, at speeds over 100 mph, of one Rodney Glenn King, 25. When he cut off the expressway into the city, CHIPs called in the Los Angeles Police Department. When the boys caught up with Rodney—according to police—he refused to get out of the car. When he did, he pulled an officer to the ground.

Whereupon, Rodney got a lesson in driver's ed he will not soon forget. Using nightsticks like baseball bats, the Los Angeles cops beat him relentlessly as he lay on the ground feebly trying to crawl away. He was kicked or clubbed 30 times. Not a pretty sight.

Unfortunately for the LAPD, an amateur photographer caught the proceedings and the videotape made national TV, again and again.

As the cops were white and Rodney is black, reaction has been widespread and predictable. The social ambulance chasers say this proves the Los Angeles cops are racist, that blacks there are constantly victimized by brutal white cops. The ACLU [American Civil Liberties Union] compares the LAPD to the Crips and the Bloods: "A man was jumped and beaten Sunday night . . . beaten by a gang, not unlike many of the other gangs which terrorize our city. This

Patrick J. Buchanan, "Police Brutality and Popular Reaction," *Conservative Chronicle*, March 20, 1991. Reprinted by permission: Tribune Media Services.

gang has colors, has a tough-talking leader, carries guns and clubs and has the force of law on its side."

The Silent Majority? Though the beating was brutal and clearly excessive, my guess is that few will join the anguished protests.

Why not? Are we a racist nation that rejoices in "hate crimes"?

No, the answer is more complex.

In our polarized and violent society, most Americans have come to look upon the cops as "us," and upon Rodney, a convicted felon, as "them." He is the enemy in a war we are losing, badly; and we have come to believe the cops are our last line of defense.

If the police beat him brutally, many will say that even though the cops went too far, they are our troops. And Americans know in their hearts that had those cops been killed in that wild chase, or shot to death when Rodney got out of the car, neither the ACLU nor national TV would have hung around for the funeral.

"Cops are our last line of defense."

To understand why Americans seem sometimes "insensitive" to police misconduct, consider the statistics on race and crime, taken from Justice Department files, by Dr. William Wilbanks of Florida International University. Using the National Crime Survey of 135,000 people, and comparing one 36-month period in the late '70s with a similar period in the '80s, Dr. Wilbanks discovered:

Interracial crimes (less than 20 percent of all crimes) are declining; and the sharpest fall-off over the decade was in multiple offender white-on-black assaults and robberies, which fell by 64 percent (white-on-black rape is now a relative rarity in the United States).

For single-offender crimes, Wilbanks found that whites now choose black victims only 3 percent of the time. But black robbers, rapists and assailants choose white victims in 50 percent of their crimes.

Single-offender black-on-white crimes are almost 10 times as common as white on black. For gang crimes, black-on-white assaults are eight times as common as white on black, and robberies by gangs of black felons against individual white victims are an astonishing 60 times as common as the reverse.

Here is the real racism in America. Here is the real reason Middle America despises all that unctuous press commentary about how ours is a society where "white racism" is imbedded and "hate crimes" against poor and defenseless minorities are commonplace.

The Big Lie

People believe that to be a Big Lie because it is a Big Lie.

Why would many white folks not get exercised about Rodney's beating? Not because they don't like black folks. The same working-class people who dismiss Rodney's plight approve of black progress, cheer black athletes and applaud the black patriots of the Gulf War. They don't worry about Rodney because they know that if they were at risk, he wouldn't worry too much about them; but those cops might.

Few Americans are aware of Professor Wilbanks' statistics. Somehow, they are not newsworthy in a day when an antihomosexual crack by a college kid can make the front page as a pristine example of a hate crime. But most of us sense the numbers are right on.

Back around 1960, the press stopped identifying criminals and their victims by race. The stated purpose: avoid racial disharmony, avoid creating stereotypes. Fair enough.

"Single-offender black-on-white crimes are almost 10 times as common as white on black."

But why then does the press now wait for, seize on and exploit a Howard Beach or a Bensonhurst? Three reasons: Because white-on-black violence is emotionally explosive and socially divisive, hence good for TV ratings and news sales. Because such episodes enable social progressives to cast themselves in the role they play best—defender of the forgotten "victims" of society against a repressive, reactionary ruling class. And because such incidents fit perfectly the new media stereotype of a resurgent white racism on a rampage through America's persecuted black minority.

Too many have economic, psychological and political stakes in the Big Lie of Racist America to give it up.

But, there is real tragedy here, injustice here, and I don't mean for Rodney, but for the great law-abiding black majority. Because of our stark fear of black criminals, they are left behind by cab drivers and viewed with fear and suspicion by fellow citizens. They are watched more closely, frisked more freely, harassed more frequently by cops. That is a sad, sad situation. But the reason is not racism. The unfairness of it all lies in the terrible truth of those awful crime statistics.

Chapter 2

What Are the Causes of Police Brutality?

The Causes of Police Brutality: An Overview

Richard Lacayo

About the Author: *Richard Lacayo is a staff writer for* Time *magazine.*

Editor's note: The question of what causes police officers sworn to uphold and enforce the law to engage in violent and illegal brutality has interested people from many different fields, including criminal justice, psychology, and sociology. The viewpoints in this chapter give several theories from these and other perspectives. Their answers range from the stresses individual police officers experience in their work to their attitudes toward minorities.

The following overview by Time *journalist Richard Lacayo was written shortly after the March 3, 1991, Rodney King incident in which police officers were videotaped beating a Los Angeles motorist. It examines police brutality in Los Angeles and other U.S. cities and discusses different factors that are believed to cause brutality.*

To watch the videotape of Los Angeles policemen kicking and clubbing Rodney King was to suddenly explore a dark corner of American life. For many police officers who fear that the incident could undermine their image of cool professionalism, the case quickly became an occasion for dismay, soul searching and a measure of defensiveness. For many citizens, particularly blacks and other minorities, it brought back bitter memories of their own rough encounters with police. George Bush bluntly summarized the prevailing shock: "What I saw made me sick."

The sickening glare from that grisly scene has thrown light upon police brutality all across the country. Was the beating an aberration, as Los Angeles police chief Daryl Gates insists? Or did it affirm yet again that many cops resort to violence, and even deadly force, when no threat to their safety can justify it? Is racism so pervasive among police that the fight against crime all too often becomes a war on blacks? Has the criminal justice system, which permits too many criminals to go free after serving only token sentences or none at all, become so ineffectual that officers feel the need to play judge and jury on the spot? Has police work become so dangerous that even well-meaning officers can snap under the pressure?

Those questions became more urgent as evidence grew that the officers involved in King's beating might have expected their behavior to be winked at, at least in their own department. In tapes of radio calls and computer records of police communications on the night of the attack, some of the officers involved could be heard swapping racist jokes and boasting to other cops about the beating. Their lighthearted exchanges, which they knew were being recorded, sound nothing like the words of men who fear they have done something reprehensible—or even something out of the ordinary. Two nurses at Pacifica Hospital, where King was taken after the beating, testified to a grand jury that the officers who assaulted King showed up later at the hospital room to taunt him. One allegedly told the victim, "We played a little hardball tonight, and you lost.". . .

"Skull-drumming tactics have an enduring and dismal place in police history."

Los Angeles is far from the only place where police play hardball, dispensing curbside justice with disturbing regularity, especially in crime-plagued ghetto neighborhoods and to people whose only offense is the color of their skins. Those who live outside such areas can usually ignore that reality. Fed up with violent street crime, they are often content to send in the police force and demand that it do whatever is necessary while they look the other way. But the Los Angeles beating has shaken such head-in-the-sand attitudes. A spate of brutality cases that normally would have attracted little attention made national news:

• In New York City five officers were indicted on murder charges in the Feb. 5, 1991, death by suffocation of a 21-year-old Hispanic man suspected of car theft. The officers were accused of having hit, kicked and choked Federico Pereira while he lay face down and perhaps hog-tied—his wrists cuffed behind his back while another set of cuffs bound his hands to one ankle.

• In Memphis a black county sheriff was convicted . . . of violating civil rights laws in the June 1989 choking death of Michael Gates, 28, a black drug suspect. Gates' body was covered with bruises in the shape of shoe prints.

• In Plainfield, N.J., 50 people demonstrated outside police headquarters, charging that a policeman beat Uriah Hannah, a 14-year-old black. Hannah and his friends were playing with a remote-controlled toy car on a sidewalk near his home. A motorist stopped short at the spot where the boys were playing, and a police cruiser ran into the rear of his car. Hannah's parents, whose older son allegedly committed suicide in police custody last year, charged that the officer jumped from his car, accused the teenager of obstructing traffic and at one point tried to choke him. His parents were arrested when they tried to intervene.

Skull-drumming tactics have an enduring and dismal place in police history, not least in the U.S., where accusations of brutality commonly accompany charges of racism. Many of the ghetto riots of the 1960s were prompted by police incidents. More recently, Miami has suffered five street uprisings in 10 years, all ignited by episodes of perceived police brutality.

Spotty record keeping makes it hard to measure the frequency of police misconduct. Departments often refuse to disclose the number of complaints they receive. Citizens often bring their accusations to civil rights or police-watchdog groups, which complicates attempts to compile a comprehensive count. Allegations of misconduct can also multiply in the wake of reforms that make it easier for citizens to report abuses.

"As inner cities have degenerated into free-fire zones, many officers have become more aggressive."

In the end, many cases doubtless go unreported, especially in cities where complaints have to be filled out at the station house that is the home base of the very officers against whom the charge is being brought. "The general feeling out on the streets is that you can't get justice when a cop mistreats you," says Norman Siegel, executive director of the New York Civil Liberties Union. Many blacks believe, with considerable cause, that if the King beating had not been recorded, complaints about the case would have been discounted.

But while the experts cannot agree on whether abuses are up or down, few dispute that they are common—and sadly predictable. Even in the best of times, police work is dangerous and stressful, and an officer can face several life-or-death decisions during a single eight-hour watch. The pressures have mounted in recent years as crack has poured into the inner cities, giving rise to drug-dealing gangs armed with automatic weapons—and the hairtrigger temperament to use them.

In New York City, which has highly restrictive guidelines for when police may use their guns, the number of people shot by local cops soared in the past three years from 68 to 108. At the same time, police have been fired on by suspects in greater numbers every year since 1980. Though the number of officers killed nationally has fallen from 104 in 1980 to 66 in 1989, that is partly the result of wider use of bulletproof vests.

"It used to be that arrested suspects got right into the patrol car," sighs Boston policeman John Meade, who heads the department's bureau of professional standards. "Now they put up a fight. Weapons suddenly turn up. Just like that, everything explodes."

As inner cities have degenerated into free-fire zones, many officers have become more aggressive, if only in self-defense. Danger "is something you get used to," says Officer Dennis Rhodes, a 20-year veteran of the L.A.P.D., "but every time you check in for a shift, you don't really know if you're going to go home that night." Two weeks earlier, a suspected car thief pointed a 9-mm pistol at Rhodes' partner in the squad car, who then fired a shot at the gunman, forcing him to drop his weapon. "The whole incident took a minute and a half," says Rhodes, "and what raced through my mind was . . . the fact that I was going to get killed in the front seat of my car."

The temptation to administer street-corner sentences is sometimes reinforced by the frustration of knowing that many of those the police collar will get off on plea bargains or serve mockingly short sentences.

Beyond those factors, police have been saddled with a task for which they are singularly ill-equipped. Most authorities believe that urban street crime arises from a combination of poverty, poor education and a lack of opportunity in inner-city neighborhoods, problems that the police can do nothing about. Officers, who tend to be recruited from places far from the neighborhoods they will patrol, often have little in common with the citizens they must serve and protect. "The bulk of police forces are white males of the middle class," says Ron DeLord, head of the Combined Law Enforcement Associations of Texas. "Yet we send them into large urban centers that are black and Hispanic and poor, with no understanding of the cultural differences, to enforce white, middle-class moral laws. Doesn't that create a clash?"

Law-abiding residents of crime-infested neighborhoods are desperate for police protection. They, after all, are the ones most likely to fall victim to muggers or drive-by shooters. But they also want the police's use of force kept in check, especially in poor neighborhoods where everyone is apt to be treated like a suspect. Even though many police departments have abandoned the official use of so-called drug-dealer profiles, officers may continue to carry racial stereotypes in their heads. To them, virtually any young black male with a gold chain is a potential drug courier. Any well-dressed black man in an expensive car might be a big-time dealer.

As a result, middle-class blacks, including celebrities like actor Blair Underwood, one of the stars of *L.A. Law*, complain that they have been harassed, and worse, during simple encounters with the law. At the University of Massachusetts, Boston, the ACLU sponsored a conference that attracted 500 people to discuss the topic of police and local communities. "Over and over, black youngsters stood up and talked about how scary and demeaning it is to be stopped and searched," says ACLU state executive director John Roberts. "Even good kids now see police as the enemy. They shun cops."

"Hassled cops . . . often retreat into a bipolar outlook: us vs. them."

Hassled cops, in turn, often retreat into a bipolar outlook: us vs. them. "Police see the sorry side of it all," says Mark Clark, former president of the Houston Police Officers Association. "A policemen can start out bright-eyed and bushy-tailed, but it goes away quickly on the street. It takes a mature officer not to stereotype people." Immersion into the police culture can quickly strip away a rookie's idealism. Says Hubert Williams, president of the Police Foundation: "Many officers will say, the moment I graduated from the police academy my partner told me, 'Forget all that stuff they told you at the academy; this is the real world.'"

Many of the best cops are no longer willing to pay the physical and psychological costs. Take Paul Wyland, who is planning to quit the Washington force after 20 years. "How many dead bodies have you seen?" he asks. "I've lost count. I'm not burned out. But you look at yourself and you say, 'How long can I keep doing this and not get messed up?'" Partly because so many seasoned officers have retired, departments around the nation have found themselves seriously understaffed. Others have expanded too rapidly, filling their ranks with inexperienced—and sometimes poorly trained—officers. Because the L.A.P.D. grew from 6,282 to 8,382 in the past three years, 38% of its field officers and 36% of its sergeants have less than three years on the force.

"Episodes of police brutality are likely never to vanish entirely."

Experts on police psychology insist that most officers are attracted to police work by the opportunity to protect and serve. But a certain number of rotten apples, predisposed to brutality, make it through psychological testing that can be woefully inadequate. Ed Donovan, who runs a counseling service in Plymouth, Mass., for police suffering from stress, warns that police supervisors—and other officers—must be trained to be on the lookout for misfits as they move through the ranks. "Police are out there looking for troubled people," he says. "They ought to be able to spot troubled cops."

A few cities have revamped their training and supervision to make abuses less likely. Since 1988, all 2,400 police officers on the Metro-Dade county force have undergone violence-reduction training to school themselves in ways to defuse potentially violent situations and to avoid overreaction to typical confrontations.

Critics of the police say that legal-damage suits are a more useful deterrent to police brutality and that they would work even better if jury awards were paid out of individual officers' pockets instead of by city treasuries. While courts have decided that public employees are not individually liable for most of their actions on the job, taxpayer concern about the rising cost of lawsuits has revived the popularity of civilian review boards. Such panels are at work in 26 of the nation's 50 largest cities, up from 13 seven years ago. The boards save municipal dollars by providing complainants with an alternative to the courts. They can also help departments identify and weed out problem officers before they strike again. . . .

In the end, discipline must come from rank-and-file police with courage enough to break the so-called Blue Code, which prohibits one officer from ratting on another. A few encouraging signs exist that some officers are abandoning the tradition of blind loyalty to one another in misconduct cases. In Houston more than half of all complaints now come from other officers. During the King beating, two California highway-patrol officers reportedly took down the names of those involved from their breast-pocket name tags. They have since testified to investigators.

Episodes of police brutality are likely never to vanish entirely. But they could be significantly curtailed if more officers concluded that as long as their fellow police take the law into their own hands, there is no law at all.

Job-related Stress Can Cause Police Brutality

David Maraniss

About the Author: *David Maraniss is a staff writer for* The Washington Post. *This viewpoint is based on an interview with Russell Schmidt, a police officer in Austin, Texas.*

Senior Sgt. Russell Schmidt, Badge 393 in the Austin Police Department, is a muscular and mustachioed man of 41 who has worn the blue uniform for two decades: all his adult life. His colleagues say Schmidt is considered one of a kind, one tough cop. By his own account, that appears to be an understatement.

"I'm one of those guys that if something is going to happen, I'm going to be there," Schmidt says. "There are a lot of people who go through their entire career in the police department and never have to kick anyone or get shot at or split someone's head or have to bite someone or do any of those things. And I have done that on a continual basis during my career in the police department. . . . I cannot stand to ride around in the car for 10 hours and not catch anyone, or ride around and not do my job."

Since white officers from the Los Angeles Police Department were caught on videotape kicking and clubbing black motorist Rodney G. King after a car chase March 3, 1991, a national spotlight has focused once again on the abuse of nonwhite citizens by police.

The Los Angeles incident provoked a series of troubling questions about police brutality and how often and why it occurs. Sgt. Schmidt has no inside knowledge about the case. But for any-one interested in probing the mind of a white lawman who, by his own admission, has sometimes gone "overboard" in his treatment of blacks and Hispanics, he is a revealing study.

Twice during his career Schmidt has been suspended for excessive use of force. Both times he was cleared of major wrongdoing that would have prompted his dismissal. But there were other times, especially during the mid-1970s, Schmidt now acknowledges, when he used more force than necessary. He patrolled a black section of east Austin during those years, and so many complaints—and threats—were made against him because of the way he handled black suspects that the administration was compelled to transfer him.

Tight-lipped by nature, Schmidt distrusts politicians and rarely speaks with reporters on the police beat. But on a rainy April night, as he cruised his territory of nightclubs and residential streets, he let it all out, for the first time showing outsiders the world through his eyes. It is not a pretty sight.

A native of Kerrville, a small town in the Texas Hill Country, Schmidt joined the Austin police force in 1971 when there was such a need for young blood that "if you could walk and breathe, they'd hire you." After stints in uniform patrol, narcotics and homicide, he was promoted to senior sergeant, and for the past 3½ years has served as a line supervisor in charge of 10 units in a blue-collar and racially mixed quadrant of south Austin known in police argot as Frank Sector.

"Police mirror their environment."

This has been a tough year for him. First his former partner died of cancer. Then a close friend, Carlos Warren, a young officer with the Texas Department of Public Safety, was killed when he confronted three men in a car parked near Bergstrom Air Force Base. Unbeknownst to

Warren, the men were kidnappers, and one shot him as he approached the car. Schmidt arrived at the scene within minutes, in time to see his friend die.

"It irritates me," he says. "Carlos was a great kid. He got one story in the paper, one day, a little piece. And he's dead and gone and nobody knows his name anymore and this stuff in L.A. keeps going and going."

"No human being, no matter how sensitive or fair, can patrol the streets of an American city without undergoing a period of changing for the worse."

Another recent incident haunts Schmidt. It was a high-speed chase at the end of his last night shift in March. He was patrolling I-35 when he saw three souped-up Camaros heading south toward San Antonio. He was immediately suspicious. "It's an instinct, something you see hundreds of times: young Hispanic males, three different sets in three cars, all the types of cars we have stolen all the time. The type of individuals who steal cars: young, gang-type kids wearing baseball caps." Schmidt pulled behind the second car as it made a sudden exit off the expressway.

The chase was on. They reached speeds of 120 mph on a country road heading toward the town of Manchaca. The Camaro ran a truck off the road and Schmidt barely swerved in time to avoid hitting it. At the outskirts of Manchaca, Schmidt slowed down. They were approaching a dangerous curve that he assumed the suspect would fail to negotiate. He was right. The Camaro flipped over a guardrail and landed in a ditch. "The car was on fire," Schmidt says. "I pulled the kid out. His face was hamburger meat. I pulled him out and just like in the movies, when I got him out, the car blew."

Schmidt has been involved in several high-speed chases during his career. He says they scare him every time. And often change his behavior. He sees a connection between his last chase, all chases and what happened in Los Angeles.

"You get real, real frightened in the chase. And it's like you gotta vent that, and either you're at a level where you can vent it without hurting somebody—or you hurt somebody. Somebody gives you an excuse, you know, he'll swing at you, won't do what you tell him to do, he'll reach for something and do something he shouldn't do. He gets hurt.

"People don't understand that. I mean, here you are, you've got a wife and kids, and they're paying you to do a job, and this guy's making you drive faster than you should—maybe in L.A. it wasn't as fast as I drove the other night, but it was fast—in and out of traffic, and you can run over someone else or a lot of things, and you go through all that, and you get so . . . I mean it's an overwhelming feeling that you feel within you. And you get out and the guy's there and he wants to confront you. And when he does, you just take all the stops out. I've seen that happen."

Changing for the Worse

Schmidt has a saying about police work: "The dirt rubs both ways." By that he means that police mirror their environment. He believes that no human being, no matter how sensitive or fair, can patrol the streets of an American city without undergoing a period of changing for the worse. He struggles with conflicting feelings about that transformation, who is to blame for it, and how it can be avoided.

"It upsets me that we get a bad deal some of the time when we don't deserve it," he says. "But then again we do deserve it. We do some things we shouldn't do and I'm not quite sure there's an excuse for it. Like the L.A. thing, a lot of people want an excuse for this and an excuse for that—those guys were mean. They were just mean. Whether it is the environment or their training or whatever it is, I don't know, but you see people kill each other and ignore each other and let them die and abuse themselves and the whole system, and it hurts you. It's psychologically impossible to stay the way you should stay."

As Schmidt talks he is driving toward a rendezvous with detectives and uniformed officers who are hunting a drug dealer wanted on a capital murder warrant who is said to be hiding out at a house in Schmidt's sector.

The officers meet in a fast food store parking lot. They debate whether to approach the house now or in the early morning. Schmidt wants to go now, as does his former partner in homicide, Sgt. Bruce Boardman. They drive toward the house, coasting with lights out. As they approach, Schmidt is asked to describe what is running through his mind.

"One time when Bruce and I were working together we checked the computer to see how many search warrants we had done together," he says. "At the time it was around 500. That's more than 500 times confronting people who are potentially armed and aggressive. You get real tense inside. You get real hyped up. Your senses accelerate. When I was a patrolman or investigator I was more concerned with my personal safety. Now as a supervisor I have all these people I'm responsible for and it scares the heck out of me. I'm dealing with that emotion right now."

It turns out that the suspect had left town. The other officers are surprised to see Schmidt with a reporter. "I thought you hated the press," one says. They are further confused that Schmidt stands in a parking lot, with a tape recorder running, and tells a story about an incident where he was charged with police brutality.

"I can see the headline: 'Officer Confesses to Brutality,'" one jokes.

But Schmidt appears untroubled. He wants to tell his story.

An Incident of Brutality

"If they do a story on videos of police brutality in the state of Texas, you can see me on TV," he says. The incident took place April 23, 1978, along Town Lake. Mexican-American residents on Austin's East Side were protesting boat races along the lake. They claimed the boat races were for the enjoyment of rich Anglos and disturbed the weekend peace of their neighborhood. Leading the protest was East Side activist Paul Hernandez. A scuffle broke out when police ordered the protesters to move off the street.

"If they do a story on videos of police brutality in the state of Texas, you can see me on TV."

Schmidt was on the scene as a narcotics officer working the crowd for intelligence. As he tells the story, when the pushing and shoving started he came to the aid of a fellow officer.

"God sent me a nightstick. It came and landed at my feet," Schmidt recalls. "I drug Paul Hernandez off the back of a policeman. I think I hit him a couple of times. . . . I didn't do anything wrong. If I lost my temper and just pounded the crud out of someone for nothing, then I deserve whatever I get. But this guy had a policeman around the throat and was choking him. And I peeled him off and he kicked me, so I hit him with my nightstick a couple of times. . . . If you ever get a chance, look at the tape. It doesn't look that bad."

The tape shows a long-haired Schmidt beating Hernandez at least five times with a nightstick, at least twice near the neck or head.

Austin's police chief at the time, Frank Dyson, suspended Schmidt for five days without pay for unnecessarily hitting a demonstrator, a violation of articles under "Use of Nondeadly Force" in the General Orders of the Austin Police Department.

"I think he made a mistake," Dyson says of Schmidt. "I don't think it was a malicious mistake. If it had been malicious, I would have fired him." During the investigations it came out that Schmidt had been suspended once earlier for hitting a man who was handcuffed.

Schmidt says his fellow officers took up a collection for him after the boat race suspension and he actually made $52 extra that week. He wanted to fight the suspension, but his captain told him to go home and shut up. He says that for the next six weeks his family received threatening phone calls from people who said he was out to get Hispanics.

"That's what I have a hard time with," Schmidt says. "We come out here and we deal with people who break the law. We don't drive around and say, 'Okay, we're only going to get black guys' or 'We're only going to get brown people.' At that time there were only Hispanic people at that demonstration. So they say I picked him out and beat on him not because he was fighting a policeman or not because he was breaking the law but because he was Hispanic. It's so frustrating to me when they start that."

Police and Racism

There are police officers who are "not particularly fond" of different racial groups, Schmidt says. "That's part of society and the way it is. But I don't see any of them going out of their way to pick on certain groups because of their color. . . . You hear them use derogatory terms to describe them. But if someone was to say 'nigger' or 'meskin' or whatever term they want to use, that doesn't have anything to do with that particular race of people. It has to do with that particular individual. Those people that are black and live in the city of Austin that do not break the law and we do not come into contact with—they are people. Just people. And that's the way most of us look at them.

"But the scum of that particular race, if you want to call it that, we use derogatory terms and everybody uses them, and towards white people, too. We are not saying it because they are black but because of what they do and how they live their lives. You'll find people within our society that don't work, don't care about working. They deal dope, they steal. That's their job. That's what they do and that's the people we deal with most of the time. People have such a funny perspective when it comes to race. Or maybe I do. I

don't know. You cannot judge anyone by his color. You can judge someone by what he does in relationship with how you think he ought to act."

Among the 10 officers who work under Schmidt are four Hispanics and one black. "I don't even think of these people as black, Hispanic or white," he says. "I mean Robert or Hernando or Luis or any of those guys, when they come to my mind, I don't see color. I see a person."

Schmidt interrupts the conversation to check out the action in front of a series of nightclubs on Riverside Drive. He notes that one club is for blacks, one for Hispanics, one for undocumented aliens and another for whites. It was only a week earlier, he says, that he found himself in the middle of a fight outside the black nightclub, Prime Time. It involved several soldiers who had just returned from the Persian Gulf.

"I appreciate what those guys did for us, and I did everything I could do," says Schmidt. "This was their second day back from Saudi! They were fighting in the parking lot. Had this guy down on the ground and were kicking him in the head. We went up there and they jumped on me. I mean, grabbed hold of and hit me. It was a good fight there in the parking lot for a while. . . . We didn't stick anybody. No police brutality. They said we were picking on them because they were black. Those were the first words out of their mouths.

"I was not so much racially motivated when I would hit somebody. . . . I was frustrated."

"It's always that. Right! Find a white guy to hit on me and I'll pick on him. It wasn't like we were driving through looking for something. . . . That's common. And I mean common. Whenever you pick someone up: 'You're picking on me because I'm Hispanic,' or 'You're picking on me because I'm black.'"

Schmidt is asked whether he ever assumed that everyone who is Hispanic or black was suspicious.

"Ten years ago maybe. Or some period in my lifetime I can remember going through that as a policeman. Because all I ran into was that kind of guy. But you lose that. I mean it creeps up on you like anything else. You hit about the four- or five-year period right in there where you get real frustrated. You come out here riding a white horse. You're going to paint the whole ship, you know. You find after a while all you can do is chip some paint. And you blame it on all these things that don't have anything to do with it. I don't do that now." Schmidt has had no physical abuse complaints during his last three years as a sergeant.

Frustration

During his youth in Kerrville, Schmidt says, he did not have negative feelings toward blacks. "This is where I got a bad attitude toward them. In the police department. Because I went to east Austin and worked three and a half years and those people hate us. And they'd probably been abused before I got there. And jumped on and knocked on. And I got an attitude toward them then, but have since gotten rid of it."

Did he ever use excessive force in that period?

"Yes. When I got the chance. When it was legal. You would go overboard," he says. "Because of things you go through. It's an opportunity to vent all that pent-up anger that you have." He gives an example: "You went to an area and had to answer a disturbance call, and a big guy is there and you had to arrest him or he just tried to throw you out of the house, and you took out your nightstick and hit him in the head.

"You didn't hit him in the foot or the elbow or anywhere else, you hit him where you had to as hard as you could and as fast as you could, because you were going to get hurt. . . . You witness people dying, watch your friends get fired and

you get your nose broke, and you have all these things going on and they all relate to one race. And I worked in east Austin, so I didn't have anything else to relate to other than black people.

"So I would say I was not so much racially motivated when I would hit somebody. I would say I was frustrated. And I probably went overboard. I probably did. Because I was so upset with myself. I couldn't clean up the world. . . . You see the same things over and over and over and over again. . . . During that period I'd . . . go out of my way to look for a fight. Now maybe I'd talk my way out of it, where then I'd go, 'Hell, I'm going to fight him' and let it take its course. I don't think I was sadistic. . . . I had a reputation out there. They called me 'the Line,' as in 'Don't cross me.'"

Schmidt says he would like to find out what motivated the officers charged in the Los Angeles brutality case. "I would like to sit down and see where they're coming from," he says. "Because you don't take a human being and make him do that in one incident. Those guys have been through something. Those guys have had to deal with problems that they shouldn't have to deal with and haven't gotten any return on it. No telling what goes on in those guys' heads.". . .

"'You lose your perspective sometimes.'"

"I've had my ups and downs," he says. "You lose your perspective sometimes. The whole world is messed up. . . . I get upset with things. But I think it's the way I deal with this stuff. I rant and rave and then everything's okay. You can't carry it around with you all the time. You'd be an ugly, terrible person. You would explode. I mean the things that are imputed into my brain every day over a 20-year period of time, psychologically you couldn't handle it."

Racism Causes Police Brutality

Salim Muwakkil

About the Author: *Salim Muwakkil writes on African-American issues for* In These Times, *a socialist weekly newspaper.*

The videotaped beating of Rodney King by Los Angeles police has ignited a firestorm of condemnation and provoked a nationwide federal investigation into police brutality, but critics argue that the temporary spasm of public concern will do little to alter the racist reality of U.S. law enforcement.

Thanks to serendipity and a camcorder, an international audience witnessed the naked aggression of a U.S. police force just as the Bush administration's Desert Storm triumphalism had reached a crescendo. And on the domestic front, the videotape temporarily broke through the patriotic haze of a "won war" and forced people to consider whether black Americans' longstanding complaints of police brutality might be more than mere racial paranoia. Such doubts threatened to undermine the appeal of the Bush administration's prison- and police-oriented crime bill.

Realizing all of this and urged by black congressional leadership to take some action, Attorney General Dick Thornburgh announced in mid-March 1991 that the Justice Department will review all federal brutality charges filed for the last six years to determine if there are any patterns of police abuse. Such an investigation is unprecedented, but many observers familiar with the issue dismiss it as a publicity stunt designed to divert attention from the real issues. And even Thornburgh admits that no action—

except urging the development of more comprehensive training procedures—will be taken even if a systematic pattern of brutality is discovered.

"This FBI [Federal Bureau of Investigation] investigation won't make any difference at all, because the FBI supports the police, and, more importantly, it supports the racist mentality that is responsible for most of the brutality," explains Don Jackson, an organizer for a national campaign against police abuse. Jackson is a former police sergeant in Hawthorne, Calif., who gained nationwide fame in 1989 after appearing in a videotape as a victim of police abuse.

"Excessive police force against blacks has always been tolerated."

Despite the videotaped evidence supporting his case, Jackson says the offending officers are escaping prosecution. The former cop argues that racism pervades police culture so deeply that it will require a monumental national effort to change the status quo, and he doubts the country has the will for such an effort. Jackson's frustration is shared by many who find little interest in combating police brutality.

"This incident in Los Angeles, unfortunately, is nothing new," says Yussuf Naim Kly, an author and associate professor of international relations at the University of Regina. "The conditions of this culture have always encouraged the persecution of African-Americans. Part of being an American is to have imbibed that culture, and no matter how much we'd like it to be otherwise we cannot change present history."

Excessive police force against blacks has always been tolerated, Kly argues, because as a "formerly enslaved" minority, African-Americans are trapped, so to speak, in a cultural context specifically designed to inhibit their development and thus minimize the threat to white hegemony.

Salim Muwakkil, "The Racist Reality of Police Culture," *In These Times*, March 27-April 2, 1991. Reprinted with permission.

Anguish and anger over repeated abuse by white coercive authority has sparked the creation of black organizations from the National Afro-American League in 1890 to the Black Panther Party in 1966. Despite this ongoing grievance, official white America historically denied that a pattern of brutality exists. Most agencies that have been set up to investigate charges of brutality are heavily biased toward police departments. Redress for victims of police abuse is hard to come by. . . .

According to some observers familiar with the issue, many abusive police are emboldened by the [Bush] administration's paramilitary style of fighting crime. "We're giving away our rights—human and constitutional—to police under the guise of a war on drugs," cautions Louis Elisa, president of the Boston NAACP [National Association for the Advancement of Colored People] and a longtime critic of police tactics. "In the city of Boston, there is a real question of whether there is a war on drugs or on black people."

In general, the Bush administration seems intent on enhancing the enforcement and incarcerating powers of the criminal-justice system. This, despite the findings by a Washington, D.C.-based group called The Sentencing Project, that the U.S. already has the world's highest known rate of incarceration, and despite escalating complaints about the police's brutal and racist enforcement techniques. . . .

Just Crying Wolf

Had amateur photographer George Holliday not been on the scene with a video camera, Rodney King's extensive injuries would have been attributed to a slip on the pavement or, at best, to

him resisting arrest. If he had charged the police with abuse, the media would have regarded his story with extreme skepticism. After all, what's new about a young black man's complaint of police brutality?

But the videotape-fueled furor that now rages will mean little in the long run, notes Howard Saffold, a recently retired veteran of the Chicago Police Department and co-founder of the Afro-American Police League. "Black folks get mad and emotionally distraught when these incidents make a public impact, but then we soon forget about it and just go back to business as usual," he says.

> **"The nation's police departments have too much racist inertia to be changed by anything but the most persistent vigilance."**

Saffold, who also served as chief of security for the late Mayor Harold Washington, argues that the situation will not change as long as African-Americans fail to organize specifically around issues of police abuse. "We simply have to channel our sense of outrage into energy for the organization process," he says. "The nation's police departments have too much racist inertia to be changed by anything but the most persistent vigilance. We simply have to stay on the case and not be lulled into impotence by the roller-coaster effect of outrage at the most recent incident and then quiescence when the rage subsides. That changes absolutely nothing."

Group Psychology Explains Police Brutality

Janny Scott

About the Author: *Janny Scott is a medical writer for the* Los Angeles Times.

The sight of a handful of Los Angeles police officers beating an unarmed black man while nearly two dozen other uniformed officers stood by and failed to intervene may have shocked the public, but it comes as little surprise to experts in group behavior.

They say the beating of Rodney G. King is a case of "us versus them," typifying the tendency of tightly knit groups to divide the world into opposing camps, to devalue and dehumanize outsiders and, under certain conditions, to commit terrible violence against them.

In embattled groups such as the police or military, these tendencies are especially common, some psychologists say. Shared danger breeds intense loyalty and group identity. Over time, common values and common prejudices take root. Individualism fades.

Researchers see other patterns in group violence and the behavior of bystanders:

• The larger the group of attackers and the fewer the victims, the more savage the attack. One psychologist who studied lynchings found that large mobs not only shot and hanged their victims but left them "lacerated, mutilated, burned and flayed."

• The presence of multiple bystanders in an emergency appears to reduce the chance that any one of them will step in. The incident somehow seems less urgent, and individual responsibility less clear, than when just one person is looking on.

• A witness may be less likely to step in when the victim is black. Some psychologists have found that groups of white bystanders are slower to help blacks than whites, as though the desire to conform outweighs the urge to help.

Now, experts say, the shocking videotape of the March 3, 1991, incident in Lake View Terrace, made unnoticed by a civilian eyewitness and broadcast widely, offers society an important lesson in the evil that can emerge from the insidious comfort of groups.

"It's very difficult for societies to look at their faults and failures," said Ervin Staub, a social psychologist specializing in the roots of evil. "When there is something that makes it very difficult *not* to do it, that's a very important occurrence."

Four officers were indicted and pleaded not guilty to criminal charges of assault and use of excessive force in the King incident, which occurred after the 25-year-old Altadena man—on parole after a robbery conviction—was pulled over for speeding after a short chase.

"The sight of . . . Los Angeles police officers beating an unarmed black man . . . comes as little surprise to experts in group behavior."

But at least 27 uniformed officers from several agencies were present at various times during the beating—21 from the Los Angeles Police Department, four from the California Highway Patrol and two from the Los Angeles Unified School District. . . .

To Staub, a professor at the University of Massachusetts at Amherst, the beating raises two obvious questions: Why would police officers hit an unarmed man more than 50 times? And why would 23 other officers stand by and not intervene?

The answers, Staub suggests, may lie in the nature of certain groups, especially those that tend to shape their members' sense of self—often groups formed to do a job that is unusually demanding and dangerous, like law enforcement.

"Partly because they are doing something that is extremely demanding, they develop a strong 'us-them' orientation," Staub said. "'We as a group are special, we represent what is right . . . and we are willing to do what is required to do the right thing.'"

Forming groups is natural, psychologists say, and a strong group identity can build morale. Similarly, dividing the world into us and them is common, perhaps stemming from an infant's discovery of the difference between his caretakers and strangers.

Us vs. Them

But in some groups, members manipulate the sense of "us versus them" to bolster group spirit and divert attention from internal problems. A sense of identity forms from denigrating outsiders. Members especially devalue outsiders they view as hostile.

"Certain 'others' are defined even more as 'them,'" said Staub. "For example, people with whom the police are especially in conflict—because [to the police] they represent a lot of criminals, perhaps, and because they have set themselves in conflict with the police, right or wrong."

Under certain conditions, such attitudes can lead to violence, Staub contends.

Police officers risk their lives daily, but have little power or privilege. They are called names and sometimes abused—experiences that can lead to feelings of anger and powerlessness.

"One of the most basic ways to gain a feeling of power is to exercise power over another human being's body," said Staub. "That's a very elemental kind of power."

Staub is a Hungarian-born survivor of the Nazi Holocaust who attributes his survival to Raoul Wallenberg, the Swede who risked his life to save European Jews. He has done extensive research in altruism and published a book on the origins of genocide.

During the late 1960s, in a study of young children's behavior in emergencies, Staub noticed that their willingness to help increased until about the second grade, then leveled off and dropped significantly by the time they reached sixth grade.

"It seems to us that what may be happening is that kids learn social rules about appropriate behavior," Staub said. "And these rules inhibit them at a time when the circumstances really call for help."

In the course of Staub's study, he placed each child in a room with a task to complete. Suddenly, there would be a crash in an adjoining room and cries for help. The older children justified their inaction by saying they thought it would be wrong to leave their assigned task.

But when the researchers gave the children permission to go into the other room—to get more pencils, for example—they reacted differently. One child heard the crash, listened, waited, picked up each pencil and broke it, then ran into the adjoining room.

"It was a dramatic illustration of the way the social world would inhibit bystanders from responding," Staub said.

"The shocking videotape . . . offers . . . an important lesson in the evil that can emerge from the insidious comfort of groups."

The power of such social norms may be evident in the King beating, psychologists say. They cite extensive research suggesting that whatever the values of individual members, they will become more extreme in a group setting.

The most important principle is that people do what is "normative," or standard, in their group, one psychology professor said, adding: "If there is any single guide to predicting people's behavior, it's what they've done before in that kind of setting."

Researchers also cited certain long-observed principles of mob behavior—in particular, the emergence of a "collective mind" even in a heterogeneous crowd, and a lack of judgment, reasoning or critical thought.

They said the anonymity conferred by a crowd makes it possible for participants to abandon the sense of responsibility that normally controls individual behavior. Instincts and impulses can take over, rapidly infecting the entire group.

"There's a widely held view that groups can produce in some instances . . . a retreat from adult levels of thinking and experiencing to more primitive, infantile levels," said Steven E. Salmony, a North Carolina psychologist who has studied the Ku Klux Klan.

"The basic idea is an old one, that people get lost in a crowd," said Brian Mullen, an associate professor of psychology at Syracuse University. "But specifically what gets lost is . . . the self-regulation processes that guide and direct everyday, intentional behavior."

Not Paying Attention

Certain factors, including the wearing of uniforms, enhance that anonymity, says Mullen, who has studied accounts of lynchings over 150 years. Released from self-scrutiny, "people's behavior can quickly gravitate to the lowest common denominator."

According to Mullen, members of a group tend to focus on whatever is unusual or different, just as one's eye is drawn to one part of a picture and the rest blurs. A group's attention centers on the rare thing, the outsider.

"When a group of people are victimizing a lone victim, they are paying a great deal of attention to that lone victim," said Mullen. "They might notice the sounds that he makes or the dirt and blood on his clothing.

"But they don't recognize that I, John Smith, am a father and husband. I have a job where I am sworn to uphold these rules, and the behavior that I'm engaging in violates that person that I am."

But as early as the next morning, Mullen said, they wake up and say, "'How could I have done that?' When they examine their behavior in retrospect, they're now bringing this attentional focus to themselves. . . . It's simply that they were not paying attention."

"The anonymity conferred by a crowd makes it possible for participants to abandon [their] sense of responsibility."

Staub draws a slightly different picture of the evolution of group violence. He believes that group members move along a "continuum of destruction"—from prejudice and stereotyping to small acts of mistreatment to more violent acts.

People change because they justify their actions to themselves, he says. They persuade themselves that victims deserve to be harmed. They engage in "moral exclusion," deciding certain people are "not really human and that moral rules do not apply."

Bystanders move along that same continuum, Staub believes.

"If you stand by and observe somebody else harming another person, and you observe the person suffering and don't do anything, that's very painful," he said. "So what bystanders who remain passive tend to do [is] find reasons why this is right.

"People change as a result of their own actions. People who engage in helping behavior frequently become more helpful. People who engage in aggression that is not checked by others frequently become more aggressive."

For that reason, Staub and others believe that the evolution to group violence can be slowed or halted if bystanders and group members object. Otherwise, those involved will believe that their actions are acceptable.

Police Officers' Attitudes Toward Civilians Cause Police Brutality

Anthony V. Bouza

About the Author: *Anthony V. Bouza served twenty-four years in the New York City Police Department, becoming commander of police in the Bronx. He later served as chief of police in Minneapolis, Minnesota. The following is excerpted from his book,* The Police Mystique.

Cops work in a world shrouded with mystery and power, which attracts the attention of civilians in every quarter. The public's insatiable demand for movies and television programs dealing with cops attests to the subject's allure. The chill in the heart that accompanies the sight and sound of a police cruiser pulling you over is a reminder of the sense of awe cops inspire. Yet, with all the scrutiny and disclosure of police in the incalculable number of programs depicting them, it is more than fair to say that the actual world of cops continues to elude Hollywood. . . .

The real mission of the police, as defined in their charters, is to preserve the peace; protect life and property; detect and arrest offenders; prevent crime; and most important, to accomplish the task that gives the profession its name: enforce the law. . . .

It is said that the cop on the street exercises more power over our daily lives than the President of the United States. The President can press the button and create universal incineration, but this is a final and awful holocaust, not a daily intervention. Cops tell us when to stop and

when to go. They can question us or appear to ignore us. They can forbid or permit. They can snoop or overlook. Their options and scope are wider than is realized, yet, somehow, the citizen can sense the impending danger of a cop's arrival.

People instinctively recognize the power of the police in every encounter. This power has its expression in the visible gun; in the public image conveyed in countless dramatizations; in the hesitancy at approaching them; or in the tremor induced when they single any of us out. The caricature is of an impenetrable facade, made concrete by reflecting mirror glasses, behind which lurks a powerful, willful operative.

Cops have scores of encounters daily. Out of necessity, they tend to stereotype. They know much more about criminal law than most lawyers and readily develop a mastery of the handier sections. In the more subtle areas of law, they have a sound general feeling for the limits and know how to obtain the necessary help, whether from the desk officer at the station or the city's attorney later. It is important that the average person realize this, in order to avoid being stereotyped negatively. Failing the "attitude test" and being labeled "an asshole" (someone who fails to treat the cop with the proper measure of respect, or who is truculent or defiant or challenging) usually leads to problems. Cops don't take real or imagined assaults on their authority lightly. Their work is peculiar in that the greatest power and autonomy exist at the lowest rank level.

> **"Cops develop the sense that they can exercise power without too great a risk of being called . . . strictly into account for its use."**

Cops also know that, as preservers of the peace and protectors of life and property, they are called on to make countless decisions and judgments daily. The system, in order to accommodate the need for action, is notably understanding of the errors that are bound to occur. Thus cops develop the sense that they can exercise power without too great a risk of being called too strictly into account for its use. Observers have commented that there is more law at the end of a cop's nightstick than in any court of law or legal tome. . . .

Police Power and the Underclass

Police power assumes its most formidable aspect when cops deal with the underclass. This is the group they've been pressured, implicitly, to control. This message gets transmitted in code, as in "What are you doing about the vagrants, drunks, and bums harassing honest citizens downtown?" When cops deal with the poor (blacks, Hispanics, the homeless, and the street people), the rubber of power meets the road of abuse.

Society's problems center in the cities and their ghettos, where the underclass—the poor, ill-housed, malnourished, undereducated, unemployed, and spaced-out on drugs and alcohol—resides.

The ghetto is the volatile center of every chief's concern over long, hot summers. It is there that the excluded, disaffected, and angry reside, while getting daily messages about the lives they might be leading, from their omnipresent TV sets. It is there that a latent force lies, seemingly ready to be galvanized into furious action by a cop's mistake.

Street crime is the province of the poor, as both perpetrators and victims. The public, frightened by the specter of violence on its streets and television screens, pressures cops to erase it. The exasperation of the cops filters through, in the form of brutality, when they encounter addicts and obstreperous drunks, sociopaths, beggars, and other street types. This is the population the street cop most comes in contact with. The detectives and investigators get to handle the heavier cases and the weightier criminals. The obduracy of these criminals simi-

larly tempts the detectives and investigators to third-degree methods or other shortcuts. Ironically, because criminals have a lot to do with cops, they've hardened and come to realize the value of not cooperating in the effort to jail them. To a surprising degree, investigators rely on the help and cooperation of suspects, but this help becomes harder to obtain as the criminal's experience with cops deepens. In the main, it's the "gloms" (inexperienced or first-time suspects) who confess.

The white middle class—the overclass—rarely encounters the reality of police brutality, except for such events as the campus or peace protests of the 1970s or the civil rights actions of the 1960s. When it does confront police power—at a traffic light, for example—it vociferously makes its outrage known, not only at the scene (in such original attacks as "Why aren't you out capturing muggers and rapists, instead of harassing honest citizens?") but in follow-up calls and letters to police superiors, who will know how to make these cops squirm. Cops have learned to be wary of such problems.

"When cops deal with the poor . . . the rubber of power meets the road of abuse."

Cops deal with people who are in trouble or disarray and are most comfortable in that role. They are invited not to festivals or happy events, but to brawls. They observe the human animal's dark underside. Cops get called to control nasty instincts and to curb wicked appetites. They are summoned when things get out of hand. They fly from problem to problem, chasing the calls a crackling radio spews out. In order to deal with hurt children, blood, human misery, and anguish, they unconsciously grow calluses over their emotions. They become profoundly skeptical. Their temptation to cow those whose behavior they're trying to control into compliance often proves irresistible. Many of their coping strategies are hard for outsiders to understand. Civilians don't, and perhaps can't, understand cops. This is one of the most painful lessons learned by the entering recruit.

"It is not an accident that cops speak of . . . 'civilians' with a barely concealed scorn for the uninitiated."

Society grants the police a monopoly on the use of violence. Only they may bludgeon, subdue, Mace, or even kill legally. This exclusive right adds enormously to their powers to search, seize, detain, question, arrest, or investigate people they deem suspicious. The borders of action are laced with stretchable legal concepts like *reasonable suspicion, probable cause, questionable circumstances,* and *articulable grounds.* It doesn't take the skills of a sophist to construct a justification for aggressive actions within those parameters.

The study of the use of police power is usually described as an analysis of the need to limit or redirect the exercise of police discretion. The phrase conceals a very bitter struggle for control, between the chief and his or her need to direct the enterprise, the cop-on-the-street's determination to maximize his or her field of action, and the civilian's concern over abuses.

There is a push-pull nature to it all that outsiders rarely get a peek at. There is a struggle between the supervisor's need to control and direct a cop's actions on the street and that rugged individualist's stubborn fight to retain autonomy. One of the comic opera aspects of this invisible battle is the administration's imposition of endless restrictive regulations (of the well-known Mickey Mouse variety) that have nothing to do with performance (like the length of mustaches and the color and state of the uniform) but that lend a semblance of sovereignty over the process.

Another one of the hidden truths about policing is that, although the brass can decide the general thrust and direction, the slug in the trenches retains the power to work her or his will in countless ways. The result is that guidelines become rough limits, within which a great deal of independent action can be exercised.

The fight for control over the street cop's actions takes place within the impenetrable world occupied by both supervisors and patrol officers. However, the battle does not distract them from the need to sustain the separateness of their corps from tinkerers and prying eyes.

The mystery begins with the fabled insularity of the police. It is not an accident that cops speak of the "outside world" and of "civilians" with a barely concealed scorn for the uninitiated. The fact that they think of their precincts as embattled fortresses in alien lands reflects, at once, their problems with the minorities they've been sent to police and their resentment toward an overclass that has issued the *sub rosa* marching orders.

Insularity

Cops understand the straightforward charter responsibilities, which, although tough to discharge, are nevertheless unequivocal and direct. The problem arises from the hypocrisy they see in a society that insists that they control "them." *Them* refers to blacks, ghetto residents, the homeless, the poor, and all others who evoke a sense of fear or unease. These orders are implicit and indirect. The laws enabling control aren't there. The facilities to which "they" might be taken don't exist. The "offenses" of the group aren't crimes, but they do offend the overclass.

How did this separateness develop? Why are the police insulated from the surrounding world? How could an agency devoted to the public's protection and service be as profoundly alienated from the people as the police are? How is it possible that an organization that inspires as much fascination and scrutiny as the police can remain a mystery to a society that constantly examines this organization's daily workings? . . .

There are many good reasons for this continuous isolation of the police. Cops resist intrusion in various ways. They reveal what they must, when they must, and slip and slide or simply stonewall the public and the press the rest of the time. Those who study the police are put off by the long stretches of boredom that constitute such a large chunk of what is called *police work*. As the repositories of society's secrets and the wielders of power, cops have an understandable jealousy about protecting their turf. The probing media are usually resisted, often subtly, and are seen as the enemy. Cops are expert feigners of cooperation while in reality they do their best to deflect probes.

The depicters and moviemakers tend to focus their representations on juicier public-relations aspect of the job. Many cops wind up laughing up their sleeves at the ersatz images their manipulations manage to produce on the screen. Cops understand that the reality of their daily work is guided by complex and sometimes conflicting explicit and implicit messages that are more confusing than photogenic. What they see on the screen—an image they are happy to promote—is the heroism and terror that form an infinitesimal part of their lives. Still, they are flattered and pleased by the simplistic heroic visions being communicated to the public they serve. Cops use a coarse expression for this technique of evasion, which reveals their cynicism and hardheadedness; they call this "pissing in their pocket and telling them it's raining." Cops can manage to get a lot of folks to look up at the clouds, as they spin their webs with insouciant looks.

"Some cops . . . adopt the media's image and act out the impulses of such avenging angels as Clint Eastwood's 'Dirty Harry'."

Some cops, though, adopt the media's image and act out the impulses of such avenging angels as Clint Eastwood's "Dirty Harry" or Charles Bronson's character in *Death Wish*. The simplistic, idealistic view offered by these dispensers of perfect justice proves irresistibly tempting to some cops. The results are very often tragic, either for the cops or for their targets. Controlling these would-be heros may very possibly be a chief's greatest challenge. Turning Rambos into servants, rather than masters, of the law is a trickier business than might be expected. The theory that "we're the good guys, they're the bad guys, and anything we can do to get them has to be okay" dies hard.

Stability and Homogeneity

Police agencies are peopled, overwhelmingly, by cops, even in inside or clerical jobs that might be handled by civilians instead. Civilianization became, in the 1960s, one of the main issues surrounding debates on police reform. It was perfectly obvious that many tasks in the police department could be handled by lesser paid civilians rather than cops. But this meant risking the admission of outsiders into the cops' exclusive club. After over twenty years of backing and filling about "going civilian" or abandoning that program, most police agencies remain predominantly staffed by cops. This domination by long-term insiders strengthens the isolation.

Cops usually spend about a quarter of a century at their jobs. It is a remarkably stable occupation. They come to stay. This makes the screening of applicants critical. For most of the entrants, being a cop is the focus of career aspirations. It will probably be the best job they've ever had or could ever get. Losing it makes other employment difficult and almost always leads to a real decline in earning power and status. Most cops come from economic levels that limit the choices available very strictly. They usually lack the skills or education that would make them marketable.

The police ladder, from rookie to chief, is almost invariably made up of cops at different stages in their careers. This ladder greatly strengthens the bond that holds them together.

It promotes the isolation and insularity of the agency and tempts everyone to adopt an "us-against-the-world" view that can cause many problems in the agency's performance.

Change and reform, in such circumstances, do not come easily.

Cops are welded together by dangerous experiences and shared secrets that produce a strong bonding effect. Theirs is an institution that, despite being on permanent public display, has successfully resisted intrusion and study.

In addition to the various financial benefits, cops find certain lighthearted aspects of the job enjoyable. They get to work outdoors and are usually subject to minimal supervision.

Entering cops are shocked by the contrast between their expectations of the job and the reality. They focus initially on fighting crime but soon discover that policing is mostly a service industry. About 80 percent of their work turns out to be responding to accidents, injuries, illnesses, and citizen emergencies that have nothing to do with crime. Before they decided to become cops, most people asked themselves whether they'd be tough enough, brave enough, strong enough, and hard enough for the job. They should have been asking themselves whether they liked helping people or not. Dealing with the fractious human beast on a daily, nonstop basis can be exasperating.

"Dealing with the fractious human beast on a daily, nonstop basis can be exasperating."

The importance of this disparity between reality and expectation suggests that employees may be entering the profession for the wrong reasons. Somehow, no one wants to publicize the unglamorous service dimension that is, far and away, the major part of the police job, maybe because it makes cops look too much like nurses or social workers and too little like the macho characters found in the fiery imaginations of youth.

The recruitment mystique sets the rookie up for a shocking discovery: Policing isn't much like what they've seen on television. Even though many of the recruits have links to the department through fathers, brothers, or relatives "in the job," they are mostly useful as encouragers and general prodders, rather than as divulgers of the profession's secrets. The rationale for not explaining the job clearly to rookies is that they'd never believe it anyway, so it's best to get them in and let them gradually find out what it's all about. It is one of the curiosities of the profession that cops always grouse about the job and counsel casual acquaintances against taking it, but they invariably encourage their relatives and loved ones to enter the department.

In most cities, recruits come from a blue-collar or civil-service family of workers who haven't quite made it into the middle class. They come from homes where the topic of college is rarely, if ever, brought up. The job becomes a path to middle-class security and respectability. The recruitment pool tends to represent a very specific slice of the socioeconomic-class pie.

Weeding Out the Unfit

The usual gauntlet begins with filling out an application, taking a written test, and submitting to a medical examination Then entering recruits must take a qualifying physical test of strength, coordination, agility, and mobility. All of these tests must be job-relevant because, in the past, they have served as artificial barriers to the entrance of women into the force. When the police had to prove that their daunting tests were really related to the everyday activities of cops on the street, they discovered that they couldn't. It was especially difficult to prove when so many beer-drinking cops lapsed into appalling physical shape soon after successfully entering and still managed to perform acceptably. However, there is ample room for legitimate doubt on this score. It is hard to believe that many of these out-of-shape hefties could rush up flights of stairs or chase fleeing felons. Because the departments didn't appear to be ready to fire their physical misfits, they were left with no argument for excluding women, however passionately they may have wanted to. In the end even the title *policeman* had to give way to the androgynous *police officer.*

Hiring Test

The really critical winnower, though, is the long and thorough background investigation. This inquiry typically results in a half-inch dossier of employment, school, military, and personal history. It is here that the agency really relies on weeding out the unfit, through discovery of behavior patterns in school, work, or personal life that presage failure in a job that requires optimal performance and superior personal characteristics. There is often a multiple-choice psychological screening test, although no one really expects these tests to identify the psychopaths. At best, they've proved occasionally useful ancillaries to the background check.

Some agencies use lie detectors, which actually measure reactive and physiological changes induced by our having been conditioned to tell the truth, thereby producing involuntary nervous reactions when we lie. The devices really measure such physiological changes as increased sweating, a quickening heartbeat, or an involuntary reaction of the nerves. Tying these to truths and lies is another matter altogether. The pattern of the questions is critical to measuring reactions to the known, and expert operators are essential to any hope of success. Even under the best of circumstances, these devices are not infallible. In fact, some consider them about as useful as witchcraft. The results of these tests have never been considered reliable enough to be admitted into a court of law as evidence.

A practice that has been gaining wider appeal recently is the use of drug testing. These tests have proved effective in weeding out drug-addicted candidates and even in discouraging many addicts from applying. Traces of marijuana can show up in urine samples as late as three weeks after use. Other illegal drugs vary in their duration in the system, but they all leave traces for at least a few days following the drug's use.

A wrong assumption made about the police is that they're not very adept at weeding out the palpably unfit at the entrance level. On the contrary, the thoroughness of the background investigation nearly guarantees that new recruits will be qualified for the job. The background investigators (other cops trained for that purpose) find out an enormous amount of information about a candidate's life. Those later found to be unfit are usually exposed because of a predilection for brutality. They tend to be veterans, shaped by the agency rather than by their genes or preentrance proclivities. Most of the brutes I encountered, in three police agencies, were probably formed and subtly encouraged by the agency's culture. The background check tends to exclude the feckless, the irresponsible, and those with poor or unstable school, work, or military records. So here we can see a clear illustration of the difference between people's illusion about the importance of identifying the psychologically unfit, on entrance, and the reality that the organization shapes these people, and all of its other members, into what they ultimately become.

> ### "Most of the brutes I encountered, in three police agencies, were probably formed . . . by the agency's culture."

In recent years, a great deal of energy has been spent on demands to screen out the potential brutes before they enter the police department. But this reasoning totally ignores the shaping nature of the institution itself. The brutes have not slipped through the agency's filter. Rather, they've been shaped by the organization's culture. The usual scenario goes something like this.

An act of brutality occurs, an investigation is launched, and the accused cop turns out to be some type of sadist. Predictably, demands for psychological screenings are made to identify others who may be potentially unfit for service. The odds are great that the officer was acculturated and shaped by the organization's own pressures and policies. An organization that condones, or subtly encourages, brutal measures will take normal employees and strengthen their aggressive instincts to the point where someone eventually goes over the line. Some may have had proclivities in that direction, in the way of aggressive youngsters recruited into any activity, but these tendencies could easily have been channeled into productive and positive pursuits by a more salubrious organizational climate.

The thumpers and thieves (the sadists and the thieving cops who practice ham-fisted methods or who would "take a hot stove") imitate the on-screen images they find so appealing. They are often tough, brave, and assertive cops. Yet they can also be sadistic leaders who set a tone that virtually coerces the timid majority into going along with them. Nobody wants to be called a wimp when the fur starts to fly. The organizational climate of a particular department is decided by how effectively the chief meets this challenge. His would not be the first department taken over by these kinds of tough characters. During the New York Police Department's Knapp Commission investigation in 1972, the distinction between these leaders and the rest of the herd was conveyed in references to "meat eaters" and "grass eaters."

If the organization blinks at charges of brutality and routinely exonerates accused cops, the rank and file will perceive this unwritten message and tailor their actions accordingly. In such a climate, even the reluctant recruit is carried along by the terrific pressures to conform to the expectations and actions of his or her peers. Although rarely comprising more than 1 or 2 percent of the force, the "meat eaters" can dictate prevailing attitudes, unless the chief moves quickly to keep them on a short leash. This is not easy.

Cops want the support of their commanders and their chief, and they are not forgiving if they don't get it in all circumstances. Right or wrong, they want the support of their bosses. This is, of course, unreasonable, but clubs tend to be clubby, and clubbiness breeds the sort of camaraderie that engenders the expectation of shared experience and overlooked misdeeds. The union becomes the instrument for the application of pressure on the chief to be a "regular guy," which really means joining the conspiracy of silence and secrecy about how cops really dispense justice.

"If the organization . . . routinely exonerates accused cops, the rank and file will perceive this unwritten message."

Surprisingly, pressure is often exerted to encourage the violence found in the more aggressive cops. Our societal belief in avenging angels and the pure justice they dispense dies hard. Shrill calls for law and order, to "clean up the mess" or to adopt "no-nonsense measures," are little more than thinly veiled invitations for the police to do whatever is needed to get the job done, without too much regard for constitutional limits. The drug hysteria, with the attendant shrieks for tough actions like roundups and sweeps, illustrates the point clearly. The police unions, eager to protect their members, often work to thwart the disciplinary process used to curb the excesses of police wrongdoers. The scared public can frequently be convinced by demagogues to sacrifice law in exchange for safety. Such trade-offs almost invariably ensure that they'll wind up with neither.

A Secret Society

So entering cops are, in a sense, admitted into a secret society where a code of loyalty, silence, secretiveness, and isolation reigns. They work around the clock and begin to socialize mostly with other cops, usually members of their own squad, thereby promoting even greater parochialism. Cops themselves reinforce organizational myths and rituals. They talk about good "stand-up" cops who don't turn in their buddies, about "assholes" and civilians and how to deal with them. There is a prescription for every situation.

Cops either possess or develop, as a result of role assignment (a not-to-be-underrated force), the courage to risk physical harm. They learn how to cope with moments of sheer terror that create urges in the rest of us to flee for our lives. Cops are physically brave and live with the absolute certainty that this is the prime value of their existence. *Coward* is such a powerful epithet that, even in a profession accustomed to the rawest language, it is a word that is used very sparingly.

On the other hand, cops seem to have no appreciation of the value of moral courage, if they are, indeed, even aware of its existence. Policing is not a profession that cherishes the iconoclast. It values conformity. Very rarely will a cop stand up and voice disagreement with colleagues on questions of police mythology. Assertions of commonly accepted truths—that the chief is a psycho or that the job sucks and that morale has never been lower and that they're all going to hell in a handbasket—are simply not challenged. Cops accept the myths circulating around them because resistance carries a risk of ostracism.

One of the theories that police work supports is that courage comes in many different forms, and that it is wise to think about what types matter the most in which circumstances. Bravery and cowardice, the *mater* and *magister* of police lore, do not succumb easily to compartmentalization. The cop who'll charge a murderous, knife-wielding brute wouldn't dream of contradicting another cop who asserts a commonly held opinion in a public setting. The citizen who throws herself across the gate of a munitions plant and goes to jail would be terrified at the prospect of a bar brawl. The person stoically facing certain death from some dread disease might blanch at either prospect. Courage has many dimensions, yet it is generally considered a single quality.

If cops are to develop the moral courage it takes to cleanse their agencies of corruption and brutality, they are going to have to learn that courage takes many forms, and that the type needed for such reforms is different from the street heroism they value so dearly.

"The ultimate betrayal is for one cop to fail to back up another."

Training recruits in the importance of moral courage, such as is so piously and consistently included in the widely ignored code of ethics that every police agency adopts as its credo, is as important as teaching the recruit to cope with street dangers, yet police training usually neglects this critical aspect. In fact, it might be held that the opposite message is being transmitted, that the thing to be is a "stand-up guy." The similarities of the value systems of the police culture and the underworld can be striking.

The cop's isolation begins early. Entering recruits, fresh and eager, approach the field with all the enthusiasm of breathless acolytes. They have come to serve humankind. They see themselves earning plenty of psychic income. The rookies are suffused with altruism and expectations of appreciation. The thrill of discovery is accompanied by an intense need to share new experiences. One's friends and relatives are the natural audience. Newly initiated recruits long to discuss the wonderful secrets they are now privy to. Cynical older cops look on with knowing glances and say nothing. The probationers will learn soon enough.

Rookies

Recruits are hired and soon discover that their role is to control fractious and rebellious souls who resent their very presence. Rather than appreciation, young cops encounter hostility and resistance. The need to preserve order and their own authority dominates every aspect of the job. Others are watching. It's a damnably difficult, slippery business, and rookies don't receive a lot of preparation, in terms of formal education or training. They see many of their colleagues escape into the "refuge" of the fire department, where the challenges are merely raging infernos. The appeal centers on the fact that firefighters have to deal only with objects (fires) whereas cops have to cope with troublesome people.

Chastened by the discovery that their ministrations are not welcome, and finding themselves challenged at every turn just to maintain control, young cops make another disappointing discovery. Nobody understands them. Not their friends nor their loved ones. Certainly not any outsiders, who laugh in all the wrong places, offer sympathy where condemnation is clearly demanded, and tend to look askance at what are demonstrably necessary measures to get the job done.

Cops are never told to be silent or to keep the agency's secrets. They never see an order upholding the code of silence that guides their working lives. There is no need to be explicit. The reactions, body language, whispered asides, and other rites of initiation convey what is expected. The reactions of those normally confided in reinforce the notion that the cop will be understood only within the ranks. One of the curious fallouts of this reality is that cops will not seek counsel from any outsiders. Every successful counseling program for the police is run only by cop counselors. Given the tensions of the job and the predilection toward alcoholism and other dysfunctional forms of escape, the need for these programs is obvious.

The tragedy is that society reinforces this seclusion and secrecy. Recruits have been entrusted with a secret, unmentionable mission in addition to explicit ones: They must keep the underclass under control, and society doesn't care to receive progress reports. Society is concerned with how well the police are performing when it is directly affected. It's the methods that society would rather not know about.

A disturbing discovery for recruits is that they need to deaden their feelings in order to perform the job well. Such an approach is essential if they are to deal with the broken bodies of children, handle smelly DOAs [dead on arrivals], and wallow in puke, gore, urine, brains, and offal with any degree of effectiveness. The trouble is that feelings cannot be turned on and off like tap water. Shutting them off means distancing oneself from all emotions, both good and bad, private and public.

"A disturbing discovery for recruits is that they need to deaden their feelings."

Conservatism accompanies the cop's development because conserving the mandated status quo is a cop's first duty. One day cops must arrest abortionists, and the next they are ordered to protect them and to arrest those who interfere with abortions. The same holds true for flag burners. The cop's role is to conserve, not to question. The adoption of a questioning or philosophical view might well get in the way of effective functioning. Yet the value of independent reasoning cannot be overstated, especially in a democracy. The cop has to be ready to shift and act, not to reflect or question. The dilemma is extended by the horrors produced in this century by people who just followed orders. But cops must enforce the law. Until their conscience is egregiously offended, and they are forced to quit, their only feasible alternative is to do what they're told.

Us and Them

The sense of "us and them" that develops between cops and the outside world helps to forge a bond between cops whose strength is fabled. It is called the *brotherhood in blue,* and it inspires a fierce and unquestioning loyalty to all cops, everywhere. It is widened by the dependence they have on each other for safety and backup. The response to a summons for help is the cop's life line. An "assist police officer" call is every cop's first priority. The ultimate betrayal is for one cop to fail to back up another. This is another method of pressuring conformity, as this support is withheld from the few organizational pariahs. . . .

Evidence of the extent of police insularity can be found in such simple exchanges as occur between two New York cops who establish that they're in the same organization through a series of oblique, coded questions. These messages will be understood only by other members. "Are you in the job?" is a common question. It seems to suggest that no other possible employment could be contemplated. And the answer can't be "The seventy-sixth precinct" but has to be "the seven six." Like most other secret societies, the cops have developed their own argot.

"The police do make mistakes but feel they can't afford to admit them."

The upper echelons of the police world are no more welcoming of public interference than the hardening young entrants. They don't want their actions to be probed too carefully. The police do make mistakes but feel that they can't afford to admit them. The stakes are too high. There are criminal and civil liabilities to consider. Cops, who depend on contrition and confessions from suspects, share a repugnance for admissions of guilt. Although they are contemptuous of such purgings, they are quick to recognize and exploit their value when dealing with suspects. The public is not terribly understanding of errors, although the possibility that they might be more tolerant than most chiefs expect seems at least plausible.

Cops are acculturated through actions and lore. They'll be told, by the senior cops who initiate them into the profession's rituals, that if questioned about the source of their wetness, the appropriate response is to deny it's raining. There is a common belief that even obvious facts can be beaten back by determined, hard-faced denials. Cops have seen too many repent of their soul-cleansing admissions of guilt in the dock to have any illusions about which is the better way, in the long run. They'll go to some lengths to avoid the same errors, even while continuing to cajole damaging statements from their targets. They've seen contrite murderers ease their minds with soul-clearing confessions, only to repudiate and challenge them weeks or months later during the trial. Cops exploit the criminal's instinct to unburden himself or herself at the emotional moment of arrest, but they also learn the lesson that such an outburst is almost invariably regretted later on, when the loss of freedom becomes the principal concern. This lesson strongly reinforces the cops' code of silence.

Although there is a good deal of formal training offered by police departments, a surprising amount continues to take place through the process of initiation conducted by senior officers. The use of field-training officers (FTOs), senior cops who are seen as models worth emulating, as formal tutors of recruits simply invests the practice with the blessing of official sanction.

Cynical Cops

A great deal of the cynicism created in cops can be seen in the time-hallowed advice given to the rookie by the "hair bag" senior cop, whose first words are usually held to be "Forget all the bullshit they gave you at the police academy, kid; I'm gonna show you how things really work here on the street." The use of FTOs is a way of trying to turn this inevitable and invariable practice into a positive. . . .

The cop, then, not only has enormous power but is likely to lack the philosophical, ethical, cultural, and intellectual base needed for its wise employment .

Economic Inequality Creates Police Brutality

Marc Cooper

About the Author: *Marc Cooper is West Coast correspondent for* The Village Voice, *a liberal weekly New York newspaper.*

The LAPD [Los Angeles Police Department] had been making nationwide prime time for decades before the Rodney King video exploded into the country's living rooms. *Dragnet, Adam 12, Starsky and Hutch, S.W.A.T.,* and even the doddering *Columbo* were based on the same department, now run by Chief Daryl Gates. But as three baseball teams' worth of cops, 21 of them LAPD, swarmed in and systematically fractured King's cranium, ankles, and arms, as they targeted his kidneys for dozens of blows from their two-foot-long solid aluminum Monadnock PR-24 batons, as they stomped and kicked him face down on the ground—while all the time the supervising officer took care not to break the two taser wires that had each carried a 50,000-volt charge into King's body and were now dug into him like harpoons—millions of horrified viewers may have wondered whatever happened to those two nice, clean-cut young men in Sears-Roebuck suits, Sergeant Joe Friday and his sidekick, Officer Frank Smith.

But for those of us who were raised and live in this city, at least for those among us who cared not to sleepwalk through the last 30 years, the Rodney King beating is not the aberration Chief Gates claims it is, no loopy, David Lynch-like spin-off of Jack Webb's old black-and-white series. No way. Indeed, the pictures of white LAPD

cops taking batting practice on King's black body are, for us, nothing but the outtakes from *Dragnet.*

Long before anyone had heard of Rodney King, our houses shook and dogs barked as squadrons of French-made LAPD helicopter gunships buzzed our neighborhoods. Thousands of our residential rooftops were painted with huge white numbers so the choppers could coordinate with computer-patrol cars on the ground. Infrared scopes mounted on the Aerospatiale helicopters could, after reading the heat signature of a single burning cigarette, guide the pilots to blind with 30-million-candle-power spotlights any lovers adventurous enough or tourists naive enough to attempt a midnight tryst on some of the most beautiful beaches in the world. . . .

"The pictures of white LAPD cops taking batting practice on King's black body are . . . nothing but the outtakes from *Dragnet.*"

As part of its "war" on crime—or maybe its "war" on drugs, or "war" on gangs—LAPD units routinely barricade off whole residential blocks, always in minority communities, and set up checkpoints to search and question every motorist and pedestrian unlucky enough to wander into the newly designated "narcotics enforcement area.". . .

Unlike the cops in many big American cities, the LAPD has yet to surrender, remaining as fixed and committed to its steely vision of law and order as were those two blue-eyed virtuous rookies on *Adam 12.* This is a department that not only regularly beats the stuffing out of wise-ass car-chase suspects, it also floods the county court's office with Latinos picked up for drinking beer on their own front porches (a violation of the city's open container statute). It's a force that, along with county and local police departments, not only has racked up hundreds of po-

Marc Cooper, "Dum Da Dum-Dum," *The Village Voice*, April 16, 1991. Reprinted with permission.

lice shootings in the last two decades, but every year takes the time to write more than 5000 jay-walking tickets in a city where the nearest cross-walk can be three blocks away. In a single day it can "jack up" and sweep as many as 1500 teenage "hoodlums" into holding cells and still have the energy to bust a ring of dart throwers caught making five-dollar bets *and* apprehend suburban housewife scofflaws who are feeding the jackpot kitty in their morning bowling league.

We are talking the Mother of All Police Departments. Relatively free of corruption, strikingly efficient and aggressive compared with other metro forces, the LAPD uses the firepower of a midsized modern army to pry open the nooks and crannies of what it sees as a rotting civilization. But it's a police force that, at least until the King tape became the most popular of America's Grimmest Home Videos, existed independent of any civilian or political control and scrutiny. Whereas the city annually paid out $11,000 in damage suits against the LAPD 20 years ago, in 1990 it shoveled over $11.3 *million* into the hands of brutalized citizens. Police misconduct lawyers report more than 600 calls a year arising from run-ins with the LAPD. This reputation is as far-flung as any cop show rerun: while living in Europe in the 1970s, I can remember reading a stern warning in a French travel guide that went something like this: "The LAPD should not be confused with the Bobbies. Do not approach them on the street to ask for information or directions. Call upon them only in case of emergency."

"The white minority . . . asks few questions of the 8300 cops charged with upholding civilization."

In a city that is increasingly cleaved between rich and poor, white and nonwhite, between Mercedes and '74 Chevies, between $30 million mini-mansions and $600-a-month roach-infested apartments, the white minority that continues to exercise a monopoly over political power (with a compliant black mayor in office) asks few questions of the 8300 cops charged with upholding civilization. The faceless, nonwhite, increasingly foreign-born, ever-more desperate underclass, in the wake of Reaganomics and the white-led taxpayers' revolt of Proposition 13, has been as much as abandoned by every arm of the state, be it local, regional, or national. Proposition 13 was a clear message that the only public service that would be freely offered to minority communities was a shit-kicking police department that would keep the lid on.

"The Rodney King beating is a watershed in the city's history," a Los Angeles area cop-turned-writer tells the *Voice*. "But not the way people think. A watershed not in revealing police brutality, but a historic turning point in the city's having to face the one problem it never does: race."

Officers Speak

In normal times, the LAPD operates under a code of silence. Reporters are viewed askance, as a mutant species akin to ACLU [American Civil Liberties Union] lawyers. And since the Rodney King beating became public, a siege mentality among the LAPD has almost hermetically sealed them off from the press. But after an ironclad shield of anonymity was hammered out and guaranteed through mutual friendships, three veteran LAPD officers agreed to "give their side of the story of what it means to be an L.A. cop" to the *Voice*.

The three officers I spoke with are highly representative of the guts-and-glue core of LAPD. All born to working-class families in Los Angeles, all white, all army veterans, all with more than 20 years on the job, all in their early to mid-forties, all members of an elite detail with city-wide jurisdiction, they are the typical "training officers"—the men who hone and shape incoming rookies, who in the privacy of the patrol car pass on the attitudes and rites from one generation of cop to the next, the men who will be there long after Gates leaves. For nearly three hours in the corner of a restaurant on the edge of downtown, for the first time since the Rodney King scandal unfolded, a group of LAPD officers spoke freely, for publication, with a reporter.

Jack: I feel sad about L.A. I feel we lost L.A.

Greg: We at least used to have the mystique of Hollywood. Now you go up to the boulevard and you got the whores, the female impersonators, every runaway in the world.

Jack: We've had an influx of tens of thousands of illegal aliens who contribute something to the economy, I guess, but also clog it up. Take North Hollywood. Five years ago it wasn't a bad place to live. Now there are 20 illegals on each corner waiting around for a job. This open border policy has got to go. We are getting all the world's rotten apples.

Greg: The hotel is full. Time to put out the no vacancy sign. Too many people here. Too many of the wrong people.

Doug: Yeah. You want to go downtown for a movie or play, OK. But getting there is the problem. I mean you're in the car, with your wife, and there are all these wetbacks everywhere peeing all over the buildings, drinking beer, throwing shit all around. To me L.A. is a place where I come to do a job and then go home where I can be safe.

"In white Los Angeles there is an inbred fear of the crowd."

Doug, Greg and Jack, as is the case with almost the entire LAPD, live not only outside of the city, but outside of Los Angeles County—as far as a two-hour commute each way.

Doug: I was raised like these two other guys here. Not from rich families. But you wanted something, you bought it, not stole it. The values we learned have turned to shit or are turning to shit because of the alien problem. They are going to ruin this city without a doubt. Economically, crime-wise, every which way. Two out of three people we stop are aliens. Drive 20 miles through this city and stop people at random, you won't find too

many who can even speak English.

The city the LAPD cruises has little to do with the bubble gum colors, snake-haired blonds on roller skates, and palm tree sensibilities of Steve Martin's *L.A. Story*. With the city limits spanning 450 square miles (only a seventh of the entire urbanized metro area) and crossed by over 500 miles of in-town freeway, the sunny, open public spaces of the past have been "containerized" into covered malls, corporate refuges, and upscale cultural enclaves. The cross-pollenization of races found in other big-city public transportation systems doesn't happen in L.A.—we have no such network.

In white Los Angeles there is an inbred fear of the crowd. Because the crowd, in a city where whites ceased to be a majority in the 1980s, is colored. And if it's colored, the city logic continues, it is poor. And finally, if poor, it must be dangerous.

White Fears

Whites have abandoned the city's world-class parks as Latino families came in to hold piñata parties. Dockweiler Beach, the only stretch of sand in L.A. county that permits open-fire barbecues, has been ceded to blacks and Latinos. White teenagers who live a straight-line 10-minute drive from the seashore will travel an extra 40 minutes to bask in the color-free sands of Malibu and Zuma. The 10 square blocks of restaurants and cinemas of Westwood "Village" adjacent to the affluent UCLA [University of California at Los Angeles] campus, the *only* pocket of Los Angeles with significant night-time foot traffic, is now considered a "rough" area because of the influx of black teens on the weekends.

Los Angeles, among 252 American cities analyzed by a University of Chicago study, was classified as "hyper-segregated." Segregation in this city is a function, however, not only of race and the centerless geography, but also of social class.

A new apartment complex in the suburban San Fernando Valley, one with a tenants waiting list, boasts that it is connected by an underground tunnel to the Sherman Oaks Galleria mall so "you never have to leave your apartment." From the airport tram stops to the art museum gardens, most of L.A.'s benches have been "bum-proofed," usually by making the seat round as a barrel, okay to sit on but impossible to lie on. Timed sprinkler systems scatter the city's 50,000 homeless from the few remaining public lawns as well as from the doorways of chi-chi commerce.

Deliberate Policies

"Los Angeles as a maker of deliberate policy has fewer available public lavatories than any major North American city," writes social historian Mike Davis in his *City of Quartz*. "On the advice of the LAPD, the Community Redevelopment Agency bulldozed the remaining public toilet in Skid Row. . . . The toiletless no-man's land east of Hill Street in Downtown is also barren of outside water sources for drinking or washing. A common sight these days is the homeless men—many of them young Salvadoran refugees—washing in and even drinking from the sewer effluent which flows down the concrete channel of the Los Angeles River."

"If you're not tucked away in a . . . security-gated condo complex, the cops want to know what you're doing out on the street."

In the flinty eyes of the LAPD and the economically secure minority that cowers behind it, not only open space and—God forbid—crowds have become criminalized, but so have individual pedestrians and rogue motorists. If you're not tucked away in a fluorescent-lit office or security-gated condo complex, the cops want to know what you're doing out on the street.

The overwhelming majority of LAPD officers are white. Most are first or second generation immigrants from the South and Midwest. They look at the city they police today and they see it as a formidable, threatening, unpredictable *foreign* land. They shake their heads in disbelief—and often in open disgust—at a city in which 60 percent of the kindergarten classes have Spanish as a first language; where the largest single racial group among UCLA freshmen are Asians; and where the most common name given to a male child born last year was "Jose."

Marc Cooper: What do you feel when you work in the South Central section of the city, where the population is mostly black and Latino?

Jack: Fear and excitement. Life down there is very cheap. People are dying there while we are sitting here talking. One police division out of 18 in the city has more murders per year than all of England. Life's cheap. So there's a good chance there you'll get in a gunfight, see some violence.

Greg: It's really us against them. Not against blacks, really. But there is a lot of crime down there. You look at the guy on the corner and you know he's not working, he's waiting to rip off a purse. You got the dope dealers there in their nice cars.

Jack: The feeling we get from down there is what anybody else gets. Except we wear the badge. What you feel against you is hate. They hate us.

Doug: The people committing the crimes hate us. And the good people don't understand us either. They don't understand what real life is about. They sit back and watch those [Rodney King beating] tapes and say, 'Isn't that just awful.' But is it really?

Jack: I'm not a sociologist, but the problem down there is no family structure. You see children having children with no fucking idea who the father is. In the black communities all the kids have different last names. All the mothers have six, eight kids and no fucking idea where they are. And they couldn't give a damn because they are too busy pumping out another kid. Picking up the government check. Every Cadillac and Mercedes you stop in the south end of town has food stamps in the glove box. They're on welfare and we're out here driving Volkswagens while they're driving Bentleys. I mean I saw a policeman dying in a car wreck once in the south end of town. Every resident and neighbor was out there while the paramedics were trying to give him CPR. But when he expired at the scene, the entire crowd cheered, clapped, whistled when they put the blanket over his head. This makes you cynical, bitter, makes you see life for what it is. Makes you see you are seen as the enemy down there. Makes you see maybe we really are an occupying force. When you clap when someone dies, to me that's not even a human being. You see the parents doing it and the kids watching and it makes you sick, pisses you off.

The South Central ghetto that runs the 20 miles from the civic center through Watts and Compton to dead-end at Los Angeles's garish postindustrial harbor has little, visually, in common with Harlem, Bed-Stuy, or even Boston's Roxbury. There's plenty of gang graffiti on the walls and fences, but behind those barriers are fairly well-kept rows of single-family homes, with green lawns and trimmed hedges, far from the tenebrous tenements of the East Coast.

The Jungle

True, South Central spreads itself out on a plain of dense metropolitan flatlands in a city where residential prestige is associated with canyons, hillsides, and beachfronts. But there are palms and gardens here, and even a few parks. One neighborhood, packed with postwar apartments backed by swimming pools set among banana trees and ferns, was lush enough to have been called "the Jungle."

But to the older L.A. police officers who grew up in the near-rural, all-white suburbs of the city, and to the recruits from Kansas lured to the force by $40,000 salaries, South Central is an exotic, harrowing, terrifying land inhabited by unruly natives.

Today the cops still call that street of apartments "the Jungle," but not for its now-tattered tropical landscape. The Jungle today is the capital of West Coast crack traffic. "It's 'the Jungle,'" as one cop told the *L.A. Times,* "because that's where the jungle bunnies live." Or, as the police wisecracked on the night of the Rodney King beating, *"Gorillas in the Mist."*

The economic devastation of this community,

its badge of segregation from mainstream Los Angeles, manifests itself in the so-called commercial district. Its main artery, Central Avenue, which in the '40s cradled a raucous music scene—till the LAPD cracked down on multiracial night clubs—and in the '60s housed the headquarters of the Black Panthers—till the LAPD inaugurated its SWAT team by dynamiting off the Panthers' roof in a 1969 shoot-up—is today a seemingly endless road to nowhere. The stores that aren't boarded up are imprisoned behind iron bars. Used appliance stores, dingy pawn shops, and, most of all, liquor marts—increasingly owned by Koreans—dominate.

Latinos have recently moved into what was a solidly black domain, attracting a few *panaderías* [bakeries] and *carnicerías* [butcher shops], but here there are none of the supermarkets, department stores, or strip malls that clutter and entice the rest of the city. Even gas stations are scarce. The handful of businesses that have truly valuable merchandise on the premises—auto parts stores and used car lots— are protected not only with bars, but also with the same coils of lethal razor wire used by Guatemalan oligarchs around the perimeter of their estates.

"The people committing the crimes hate us. And the good people don't understand us either."

Almost half the black families that live in the ghetto flatlands fall below the poverty line. On a per capita basis, *less* government money has been spent on social services and job training in this part of the city than on the affluent, white Westside. Mayor Tom Bradley has suffocated spending programs for youth recreation, allocating in 1987 only $30,000 for recreational equipment for 150 centers that supposedly serve tens of thousands of inner city kids. Youth unemployment hovers near 50 percent.

Against this background, along with the migration of well-paying manufacturing jobs to Mexico and Asia thanks to the "trickle-down" economic policies of conservative city, state, and national administrations, L.A.'s youth gang culture has grown into one of the most resilient in the Western Hemisphere. Estimates on youth gang membership in L.A. county range from a low of 10,000 to 10 times that amount—the most common figure being 70,000. What is certain is that an average of two gang-related murders a day take place in L.A. county.

L.A. Gangs

The Cain Street Crips favor aquamarine Dodgers caps. The Watts Grape Street Crips are into Lakers purple. The 118th Street East Coast Crips wax nostalgic in their Yankees hats. The Lime Avenue Bloods show off Celtics green.

The gang they have as common enemy wears dark blue: the select units of the LAPD division known as CRASH (Community Resources Against Street Hoodlums). After a Japanese-American woman (L.A.'s "most acceptable minority") was mistakenly killed by gunshots from a black gang in the predominantly white Westwood area in late 1988, cries for a crackdown on gangs issued forth from that neighborhood's liberal white city councilman.

Within weeks the LAPD, led by its CRASH division and under the banner of Operation Hammer, mounted full-scale retaliatory raids on the black community. In April 1988, a thousand extra cops were sent into South Central, and in a single night they rounded up 1453 black and Latino teenagers. Since then a state of siege has persisted in South Central, where each night— and often during the day—any teenager on the street is fair game for an LAPD roust, "jack-up," or bust. An astonishing total of more than 50,000 youths have been detained in Operation Hammer's ongoing maneuvers. And, much like the tactics I've seen used by General Pinochet's militarized police as they rampage through politically unreliable shantytowns in Chile, as much as 90 percent of the victims of Operation Hammer are released without charge—having been

arrested in the first place as an act of sheer intimidation.

"The black community is under siege from fallout of racism, gangs, drugs, and violence," says a 40-year-old black man I'll call William, an aide to an elected black official. "I *need* a protector. But if I'm walking down the street and see some gangbangers on the one side and an LAPD car on the other, I'm not really sure which group I'm more afraid of. But actually, I feel more threatened by the police. The gangs see me as a tall, powerfully built foe. To the cops, I'm one more nigger."

William, dressed in a three-piece suit, walks me through the Crenshaw Mall, the *only* full-scale enclosed mall in urban black America. Refurbished in the mid-'80s with city funds handed over to one of Mayor Bradley's white campaign contributors, the mall has an entire substation of the LAPD built into it. Even that was not enough to attract national retail chains, and today the shopping center is nearly empty.

"Almost half the black families that live in the ghetto flatlands fall below the poverty line."

"The LAPD now exercises authority to stop any black person in this community and subject him to any threat with total impunity," William continues. "I mostly get stopped in white neighborhoods, twice last year. Let me tell you, I have been hassled by cops so many times that when I get stopped now, I *shuffle, I shuck and jive!* Those dudes are asshole motherfuckers. They *want* you to give them a reason to kill you. I may be six foot five inches and 240 pounds, but when I get pulled over by the LAPD it is all 'Yes-suh, no-suh, how high you want me to jump-suh?'"

In the wake of the Watts riots and the black power movement, today's generation of black youth has assimilated rebellion. "It's an attitude that comes smack up against the torqued-down opportunities of Reaganomics," William argues.

"It means we are now engaged in a day-to-day confrontation with the power structure. A confrontation we don't have the power to win." Black youth, he says, "will no longer do stoop labor, it wants the same opportunities that other immigrant populations that have been here seven, eight, or nine generations have. Black folks no longer want to do what white folks want them to do to get ahead. We are not going to get up any more at 6 a.m. and put on a uniform for McDonald's. So how else do our youth achieve a sense of power without submitting to the rule of white society, other than by becoming outlaws? And that's where we meet the police."

Community Relations

The LAPD command does have an extensive community relations effort in South Central, ostensibly aimed at strengthening community-police cooperation and lowering tensions. But it's a program, William contends, that only further polarizes.

"The LAPD does a great PR [public relations] job here convincing black homeowners that it's 'you and me against them'—the no-good slime, the hoodlum gang members," William says angrily. "I go to these community block meetings and I sit and listen in horror as the white cops sit up there and openly and flagrantly recruit for right-wing politics. They speak about gang members not as our youth, but as dirty dogs, animals.

"They come to these homeowners and say it's the *liberal* politicians who keep our hands tied behind our backs, it's the *liberal* judges who put the punks back on the street, that the criminals have more rights than you do. And these older black folks are sitting there saying, yeah, we're terrified. And these cops go on inciting to right-wing politics while we who work for Democratic officials are sitting up on the stage next to them. The black community is never going to trust the cops wholly. But when you fall under siege you get in bed with them. It's that real fear of violence that allows the 'Local Militia' to come in here and proselytize for their right-wing politics."

Jack: Rodney King? Some dirty son of a bitch that was supposed to get two years and instead got six months. This whole thing shows you why people say it's Us Against Them. Suddenly, there's an opening to take shots at the police and now everyone and his brother is a fucking expert on the police. No one gives a shit about the police officers. Everyone in America is against them! Bury them! They're gone, dead, fucked! But everyone knows Rodney King. Why don't the newspapers run the criminal records of the two guys who were riding with him? Lengthy records, I'm sure. No one knows the name of Russ Custer, a cop blown away by an illegal alien. But they know Rodney King. That's what makes it Us Against Them. I hate to even say Rodney King's name.

Greg: We don't condone what happened out there, overkill. . . .

Jack: It was a tragedy.

Greg: Definite overkill.

Doug: From what I've seen on this job I would venture to say that King and his buddies that night did some crime and we just haven't found the victim yet. No doubt in my mind those guys weren't driving around just to be driving around at three o'clock in the morning. They were looking for a crime to do or coming back from one.

Jack: Too bad there's no audio portion on that tape. It's not as simple as it looks on tape.

"They teach us to make people do what you tell them. If they don't, you escalate."

Doug: I think King wasn't doing what he was being told to do. They teach us to make people do what you tell them. If they don't, you escalate. Like they took the choke-hold away from us because a few people died. If we had the choke-hold what you saw would have never happened.

Jack: That was the most humane way to put a guy out. You choke 'em out. Once you don't have that, your only option is to beat 'em. Maybe they beat him too long. According to the film, it looks like they did. Whatever. But if he's not complying with orders and he might have a gun or knife in his waistband or something, hey, you know. . . .

Cooper: What do you think was running through the minds of the Foothill division cops who chased and beat King?

Jack: You chase a guy at high speeds in the night like that, it's like someone has a gun to your head and says I'm gonna kill you. Then he presses the trigger and it's empty. You're still going to beat the shit out of him anyway because he scared you to death. Like Saddam Hussein scared the shit out of us with chemical weapons and even though it turned out he didn't use the gas, we still made him pay the price. Same with Rodney King. You got to chase him through red lights not knowing if you are going to crash and then he gets out of the car dancing and strutting, not acting normal. And you say, yep, PCP. This is what went through the officers' heads. I can't condone what they did, but I know what I would have felt after the chase myself. Sad part of it is some of those young cops are going to go to jail.

Fifty miles northwest of LAPD's downtown Parker Center slumbers the glorified desert truck stop known as Castaic. Home to Sergeant Stacey Koon, the supervising officer at the scene of the King beating and one of the four cops indicted on felony charges because of it. Numerous other LAPD officers live out here as well as in even more remote hamlets up the road toward Bakersfield. The mailing list of LAPD personnel is kept secret, for security reasons, but as many as 90 percent or more of the force is thought to live outside the city they are paid to police.

Where the Police Live

But in L.A. there are no equivalents of Queens or Yonkers. Rather, a one- or two-hour drive away, in the desert or mountains—not in suburbs nor even in what we have come to call "bedroom communities" but in that peculiarly Southern California-type cantonment known as a "housing development"—live most of the LAPD. Spiritless, soulless, prefabricated neighborhoods with no history, not even an immedi-

ate identity beyond the huge signs that announce: "3 Bedrooms—2 Baths—Security Gate— $119,000!"

"Cops expect everyone, including a stopped motorist, to be subservient."

Along a dusty half-mile stretch of access road along Interstate 5, the entirety of the Castaic business community sits as if at one big National Franchise Expo: a McDonald's, a 7-Eleven, a Del Taco, a Foster's Freeze, and two chain motels. A single strip mall is the only reminder of urban life, and it's an hour away down the highway. At its center is a CB Supply store with a faded Confederate Stars and Bars hanging over the doorway.

No sweat, really. Not much chance of any blacks living here. Or Latinos. Or Jews for that matter. On the hill above the mall are three residential developments, all Spielbergian tract homes on loan from the *E.T.* set, all identical, all the same sandstone color, most with a garage that serves as a Saturday workshop. There's an extraordinary number with small boats in the driveways (I counted 13 in a quarter mile).

This is cop utopia. No minorities, no gangs, no crime (except for an occasional trucker's dust-up at the Country-Girl Saloon), "a great place to raise kids," as they say. A perfectly ordered uniformity and predictability. A whole town of compliance, if you will. Safely distant from the dystopia of the daily beat—peopled by deviants, perverts, criminals, and aliens—desert towns like Castaic are a perfect incubator for the LAPD's closed police culture.

"The problem with the LAPD is they recruit from the outside. All cops hate the city. But when you come from the outside in the first place, you *never* stop hating it. Who can be surprised, then, that these guys all live as far away as they can?" says former NYPD [New York Police Department] narcotics officer Bob Leuci, the celebrated "Prince of the City."

Another ex-NYPD officer, Jim Fyfe, now a professor at American University and a national expert on law enforcement agencies, calls the LAPD a "closed society" of "rigid men of steel . . . a local variant of the FBI, with all of the same good and bad points. The LAPD is a national model for modern urban police departments, an aggressive, legalistic policing that allows the individual officer little personal discretion in the field. He merely follows an impersonal policy. That's why you can't talk your way out of a jam with the LAPD.

"Most LAPD cops wouldn't engage in the kind of beating you saw on the King tape," Fyfe continues. "Neither would they turn in a fellow cop. It's a fraternity in which no one can get through their career without breaking some law or another. So everyone is compromised. Combine that with an atmosphere of 'Us Against Them' and you get the mentality of a whole society apart, of a police department not *of* the city but *above* it."

Dehumanizing the Civilian

A certain dehumanization of the civilian, the potential enemy, festers inside the police culture. As American GIs went off to fight successive wars against "Gerries, Japs, Slopeheads, Gooks, and Ragheads," the LAPD's "soldiers" have carried on their war against "assholes."

You can see the first glimmers of it in the old reruns of Sergeant Friday who, already decades ago, was quick to demonstrate his Just-the-Facts-Ma'am impatience with his all-white interviewees; and though they were all either innocent victims of crime or witnesses to it, Sergeant Friday would grimace and strain to barely tolerate their jabbering tomfoolery. They were, after all, just civilians. Or, in the officially unofficial locker room lexicon of the boys in blue, mere "assholes."

"Burglars and rapists aren't necessarily 'assholes' in the eyes of the LAPD," says Fyfe. "An asshole is a person who does not accept whatever the police officer's definition is of any situa-

tion. Cops expect everyone, including a stopped motorist, to be subservient. Any challenge—or the mortal sin of talking back—and you become an 'asshole.' And 'assholes' are to be re-educated so they don't mouth off again. The real cases of brutality come in the cases of 'assholes.' Cops don't beat up burglars. I had a talk with a 25-year veteran of the LAPD who says he knows of no car chase that didn't end with the cops beating up the motorist once he was caught."

"The Anglo population has been circling its wagons in ever smaller . . . pockets of racial homogeneity."

Doug: Yeah, in Houston they call 'em turds. In New York I think it's shitbird. Here we call them 'assholes.'

Jack: A good officer can weed out an asshole from the common citizen, say a white guy is working in a black area. If he's treated nice by a black person he'll come on back to him overly nice, because it's so rare you get treated nice down there.

Doug: We treat people the way they treat us. Frankly there aren't a whole lot of cops who feel much compassion anymore for some guy just because he's in a shitty situation. You just say, 'Hey, another asshole.'

Doug: That's why like 98 percent of the guys live outside the city. Not just that housing is cheaper and that you want your kids out of the L.A. schools where there's so much violence. You don't want to go to the grocery store and be in the checkout line standing next to the same asshole you arrested the night before. You just want to get in your car and get away from the shit you've seen all day, from the city where everyone thinks we are the assholes!

Greg: I remember a class at the academy some 20-odd years ago where the instructor says, 'Within a few years, you guys, your only friends are gonna be cops.' Everyone laughs and says bullshit. But you know, he was right.

Jack: The businessmen don't like you, the poor Hispanic doesn't like you, the blacks don't like you. So you retreat into a cave full of policemen, where you are understood. Where you can sit around and say, 'Hey, I saw an asshole on the corner doing such and such,' and everyone knows what you're talking about.

Doug: That's right. When a guy walks into the bar you know he's an asshole, you just know it. And there are all the other assholes buying him a drink. It's a lot easier just to hang out with cops. . . .

Newcomers to L.A. tend to equate the Westside of the city with the "white" part of the metropolis. Though it's a cliché, being white in Los Angeles is every bit as much a state of mind as it is a place of residence. There are, indeed, a few all-white neighborhoods, and they are for the most part (but not exclusively) on the west side.

But the explosive growth of the city and the influx of immigrants from all social classes has hit like a blockbusting rain. The San Fernando Valley, for example, a 75 percent white refuge 10 years ago, today is 42 percent minority.

"As far as the white liberals are concerned, police abuse has never been a sexy issue."

As Angelenos of color, therefore, overflow the traditional boundaries of the ghettos and seep into historically white enclaves, the Anglo population has been circling its wagons in ever smaller, ever more checkerboard pockets of racial homogeneity. The white middle class, and more accurately, the middle class of all colors, hangs on to its identity—and to its property values—by subdividing, remapping, chopping, and splicing together wholly imaginary "communities." Their tools: simple two-by-five-foot blue-and-white "town" signs provided by the city Department of Transportation.

Allow this example: When too many Salvadorans and Mexicans moved into the Los Angeles neighborhood known as Canoga Park, the better-off, mostly white homeowners on the western fringe of the area petitioned their council member to allow them to secede and form a new "community" called West Hills. With one phone call from the council member's office, the new—better—community was born when a half dozen of the Department of Transportation signs were posted around the newly delineated perimeter. Now, since everyone involved still lives in the city of Los Angeles, nothing had really changed—except West Hills property values *doubled* overnight.

People Power

That's People Power, L.A.-style. White, affluent, militantly organized homeowners. And while, depending on their location, they might vote Democratic, and while on the Westside they are markedly "liberal," they are, nevertheless, pungently redolent of White Citizens Councils. These groups form the basis of support for the LAPD. . . .

"The Westside attitude tells you a lot about the essence of white Los Angeles," says a black adviser to a local state senator. "They like having a moderately liberal, relatively powerless black mayor who gives the city a face of dignity. But they also want a redneck, get-tough police chief who will kick butt. Not either/or, mind you. They want *both!*"

Greg: You want to fix this city? I say you start out with carpet-bombing, level some buildings, plow all this shit under and start all over again.

Jack: Christ, you'd drop a bomb on a community?

Doug: Oh yeah, there'd be some innocent people, but not that many. There's just some areas of L.A. that can't be saved.

A Lax Criminal Justice System Causes Police Brutality

Tom Kando

About the Author: *Tom Kando is a professor of sociology and criminal justice at California State University in Sacramento.*

Friedrich Nietzsche once wrote that the gravest threat to a society's survival is its unwillingness to control its criminals. To paraphrase a figure more widely known in our world, Michael Corleone, history teaches us that it is possible to murder anyone with impunity.

Both these sets of words are relevant in the discussion and investigation of police brutality in Los Angeles. There, a videotape of a beating of a black motorist by a group of police officers has touched off a Justice Department investigation. The beating itself was outrageous. The Justice Department is correct in perceiving this event as a "national" or "civil-rights" issue. But not, perhaps, a national civil rights issue in the sense that many are describing it.

To understand what is happening in Los Angeles, it is worthwhile to look at what is happening in the rest of the U.S. Take, for example, another California city—Sacramento. Sacramento has seen more than its share of crime. The early part of 1991 has been particularly disgraceful. A so-called thrill killer has murdered half a dozen people, and the total number of murders so far this year exceeds 23. The discovery of unidentifiable bodies is becoming commonplace, often reported only on the back page of the local newspapers. The murders are happening everywhere, including the most affluent neighborhoods.

The national clearance rate for murder has declined steadily since the l950s: Three decades ago, more than 95% of all murders led to an arrest. Today, the figure is less than 70% and going down. In Sacramento so far, fewer than 40% of all murders have led to an arrest.

Part of the reason for the increasing inability of law enforcement to solve murder cases is that the proportion of stranger-on-stranger murder is going up. Cases involving relatives, neighbors or acquaintances are easier to solve, of course.

However, the primary cause of our society's increasing lawlessness is the one to which Nietzsche alluded: Our correctional, criminal justice and political systems have simply lost the will to combat crime. In fact, they implement at every opportunity policies most likely to encourage crime.

Thus, the Sacramento thrill killer's mass-murderous spree has led to immediate calls in the state legislature for stricter gun control laws. It is useless to remind those folks that the two jurisdictions with the strictest gun control laws in the country—New York and Washington, D.C.—are also among those with the highest rates of murder and other violent crimes. Policy is increasingly dictated by ideological commitment rather than empirical facts.

> ## "Our correctional, criminal justice and political systems have simply lost the will to combat crime."

The thrill killer executed all his victims in fast-food and convenience stores located in middle-class neighborhoods. The victims were employees, and an occasional customer. An obvious and pragmatic response would be for every clerk, cashier and cook in such businesses to have ready access to a hand gun underneath the counter. But enabling citizens to protect themselves is not part of the professional criminological ideology.

Another way in which crime is encouraged is through the exclusionary rule. The definition and implementation of criminal justice policy is in the hands of politicians, judges, criminologists, academicians, Hollywood and media people, lawyers, parole agents and probation officers. With a few exceptions such as Harvard criminologist James Q. Wilson, a large majority among these professionals has, for many years, been much more occupied with the legal rights of defendants than with the plight of victims or the security of society. As a result, the typical policeman has long lost the motivation really to "go after" murderers and other violent criminals.

> ## "The more serious an offender's crime is, the more lavish are the resources . . . which society bestows upon him."

When my friends on the local police force stop a vehicle for a minor moving violation or a defective light, they routinely check the driver's license, his identity, whether the car is stolen and whether there is a warrant out for him. That's about it. They rarely try to find out where the individual is from, how long he has been in Sacramento, where he lives, works, etc. Yet it is through such inquisitiveness that most serious criminals are eventually apprehended. It is such inquisitiveness that was typical of citizen-police encounters in the past, and still is in Japan for example today. But most of my policemen friends no longer bother, since such fact finding is unlikely to lead to arrest or conviction, but instead more likely to their own punishment, reprimand or a lawsuit.

Another factor is the matter of reward and punishment, or simply put: justice. Every year, murderers such as the Sacramento thrill killer put a premature end to the lives of thousands upon thousands of innocent, hard-working, law-abiding citizens often putting them first through excruciating torture. One of this criminal's recent victims was a beautiful, promising, hard-working college girl. A few years ago, also in Sacramento, authorities discovered in another killer's apartment the remnants of the bodies of victims who had been partially eaten by the murderer!

Establishment Overruled Voters

It would be understandable if, in the face of such unspeakable evil, many would find slow torture a more appropriate punishment than swift and painless execution. But since the people of California are civilized, they simply voted to reinstate capital punishment in San Quentin's gas chamber. Yet, although capital punishment was approved twice by an overwhelming majority of the voters a decade ago, the criminal justice elite refuses to permit the state to execute anyone. Instead, each capital case is tried, appealed and suspended ad infinitum at an average cost of $8 million per case to the taxpayers.

During that endless process, every mass murderer becomes a celebrity, enjoying year after year free room and board, media coverage and the best legal services that the public can pay for. From Juan Corona to Salcido, from Charles Manson to Dorothy Puente, from David Chase to Dan White, and the dozens upon dozens of other killers and mass murderers, they have all learned the lesson that their crimes assured them of a spotlight on national television, a permanent place in history and the lasting attention of society. If this is not reward, what is?

The L.A. videotape case is still unfolding. The issues seem to be quite different from the ones in the cases discussed above. But they share the same surreal context, a context that will change if and when the citizenry wrestles back from the criminal justice professions and from opinion-makers the means to protect itself. Until then, the system will continue to reward criminals, endanger our lives and emasculate the police. An important principle which is supposed to guide criminal justice is that of proportionality, or just desserts, by which is meant a correspondence between the seriousness of a crime committed and the severity of the ensuing punishment. This principle is operative today, in a very perverted sense: The more serious an offender's crime is, the more lavish are the resources and the attention which society bestows upon him.

Police Officers' Need for Self-Defense Causes Police Brutality

Abraham N. Tennenbaum

About the Author: *Abraham N. Tennenbaum, a former police officer, is a researcher at the Institute of Criminal Justice and Criminology at the University of Maryland at College Park.*

The video recording of the brutal beating of a motorist by Los Angeles police officers caused the nation to ask how the police, who are sworn to abide by the law, can behave so violently.

The answers by well-meaning experts generally miss the main point: Police officers have to behave violently. Otherwise they won't survive, period.

Consider this small calculation. A police officer has to use force in only 1% of the cases in which he is involved. Assume that a serious injury to an officer occurs in 1% of those cases. Assume also that a police officer can recover from two serious injuries in the line of duty, but a third would force him to retire. Of 30,000 cases, only one would end with a police officer out of service. This is a very modest estimate if we take into account the nature of the work and the people with whom the police have to deal.

Assume that an officer encounters 10 citizens in one shift (and this is not unusual). We would have to predict that an average police officer will retire because of medical problems suffered on the job after about 10 years of duty.

Yet this rate of retirement doesn't happen, and the question is, why? Criminals are rarely

Abraham N. Tennenbaum, "Use of Force Is What Keeps Cops Alive," *Los Angeles Times,* May 8, 1991. Reprinted with permission.

pacifists, and police officers are rarely superhuman. The clue to the amazing survival of police officers is simple, if unpleasant: reliance on the use of force.

What behavior will get the maximum reaction from the police? There is almost universal agreement among the public: showing disrespect to an officer. And attacking a police officer can be suicide; a person would have to be certifiably crazy to attack an officer physically, because the perpetrator may not survive.

The public is absolutely right. Research shows that confronting a police officer is the worst strategy in any circumstance. The extent of the injury to the officer, if any, is not relevant. What is relevant is the fact that the person was crazy enough to attack a police officer.

It is not cruelty or excessive pride that makes the police respond with force; it is a means of survival. With this response available to them, the police create a climate in which no one will consider attacking them. Even serious criminals are careful to avoid encounters with the police. . . . If this climate were to disappear, police work would be prohibitively dangerous; no officer would survive for long.

> ## "Police officers have to behave violently. Otherwise they won't survive."

Here we face another unpleasant fact: Force is efficient. People confess, give evidence, cooperate and avoid committing crime because of fear. And fear of an immediate physical reaction by the police is much more effective than an abstract sanction by the court. We did not eliminate force and torture from our law books because they don't work but because they are unjust and inhuman. However, even an idealistic police officer will learn very quickly that many times he has no choice but to use force.

Moreover, the use of force does not always hurt the guilty. Every police officer knows that in violent demonstrations, those who get kicked the most are not the ones who throw the most stones, but those who run the slowest. If just a few officers have to confront a large, unruly crowd, the only effective strategy is to start beating people until the crowd disperses, otherwise there is a real chance that the crowd will turn into a dangerous mob. A good chief tries to avoid circumstances in which his officers are extremely outnumbered. But when it happens, there is no other choice but to use force.

Unfortunately, a culture of violence has many bad manifestations. When the use of force becomes legitimate, no one can predict exactly where it will stop, and no one can control it. The Rodney King incident is only one example of what can develop from such behavior.

However, anyone who criticizes the police should be prepared to offer viable alternatives—to explain precisely how the police can fulfill their role as crime-fighters without using force. Just complaining about police brutality is neither fair nor constructive.

"Just complaining about police brutality is neither fair nor constructive."

The public must recognize the reality of crime-fighting and give police officers better and more effective protection in their often thankless work.

Chapter 3

How Can Police Brutality Be Stopped?

Curbing Police Brutality: An Overview

Scott Armstrong and Daniel B. Wood

About the Authors: *Scott Armstrong and Daniel B. Wood are staff writers for* The Christian Science Monitor, *an international daily newspaper.*

Editor's note: One concern underlying much of the police brutality debate can be summarized in the question "Who polices the police?" Traditionally, police departments have policed themselves. Most police departments have internal affairs departments that investigate incidents of police brutality and other forms of misconduct, and officers found guilty are fired or otherwise punished by their superiors.

Some people have questioned whether these internal safeguards are adequate to investigate and punish officers guilty of brutality. Critics charge that the police may be hesitant to punish one of their own. In response to similar criticism, many U.S. cities have established citizen review boards that have the power to independently investigate allegations of police brutality. Their effectiveness, however, remains controversial. Some opponents contend that civilian review boards do not have enough independent power to police the police. Others question their competence, arguing that civilians cannot truly understand the police officer's perspective or the reasons for the split-second decisions police officers often must make.

*The viewpoints in this chapter give several opinions on how to stop police brutality. Some proposals focus on internal changes within police departments, while others emphasize greater involvement by the federal government and citizen review boards. The following arti-*cle by Christian Science Monitor *writers Scott Armstrong and Daniel B. Wood provides an excellent overview on the pros and cons of several proposed methods to stop police brutality.*

On a hot August night in 1988, 400 New York City police clashed with demonstrators for six hours in a melee that spread through the lower east side of Manhattan.

The skirmishes brought filings of complaints of 143 separate acts of abuse and brutality before the police department's Civilian Complaint Review Board (CCRB). Nearly three years later, some 14 officers have been found guilty of various offenses, and a half dozen others still await decision.

"The system didn't work," says the New York Civil Liberties Union.

"We feel the board does work," says New York police officer Robert Vilches.

"It would have been much worse without us," says Mary Burke Nicholas, CCRB chairperson.

From these "Tompkins Square Riots" to . . . the case of Los Angeles construction worker Rodney King, comes the enduring question: Who polices the police?

The answer, increasingly, is the public itself.

But in 15 major cities since 1983 and in 70 smaller towns over two decades, popular outrage has metamorphosed into what some call an equally unwieldy monster—the citizen review board. Its purpose is to turn the searchlight back into the precinct house.

"Who polices the police? The answer, increasingly, is the public itself."

In addition have come new efforts to examine police training, recruitment, and procedure. Integration of minorities into departments has also been a major focus, which experts say can be a powerful internal check on police abuse.

More than anything, however, experts say the key to curbing police misconduct lies in the tone set at the top—the central reason so much nationwide attention has focused on Los Angeles Police Chief Daryl Gates.

"All of these are just pieces of the puzzle," says Sam Walker, a criminologist at the University of Nebraska. "Each is essential for a truly accountable police structure that keeps itself out of problems."

Interest in civilian review boards, which grew out of the civil-rights movement of the 1960s, mushroomed in the 1980s as much because of concern about police violence as protecting the public pocketbook. Litigation and victim settlements cost time and money.

Though half of the nation's largest cities have such boards, several experts contend most are toothless—"public relations fronts for police departments," as Mr. Walker puts it.

To be effective, some scholars and police watchdog groups argue that complaint investigations should be handled entirely by civilians and that a nonpolice board or administrator review the probe and make recommendations for disciplinary action.

They maintain that probes conducted partly or fully by police—even if reviewed by civilians—aren't impartial.

In a 50-city survey, Mr. Walker identified Detroit, New Orleans, Washington, D.C., Cincinnati, and Baltimore as having the most independent boards. Omaha, Neb., and Phoenix are among the least independent.

Even civilian panels have problems, though: They're frequently underfunded and understaffed—and many police don't like them.

"Lawyers are judged by lawyers, doctors by doctors. We should be judged by our peers," says Joseph Mancini, a New York City police union representative.

"What we need are competent, professional civilian oversight mechanisms rather than merely representative ones," says Jerome Skolnick, a police expert at the University of California at Berkeley.

In Los Angeles, the civilian Police Commission that oversees the department has the power to take part in misconduct investigations, but critics say it hasn't done so in the past.

Some want the panel beefed up so it can play a more activist role, one local watchdog group even suggests appointing a special prosecutor. Recently reconstituted, the commission has move quickly to look into the King beating.

Other Ideas

Other ideas on the blotter to check police misconduct:

• Training and recruitment. Experts say there is a need for tighter screening of the people police departments hire to winnow out those who might be prone to violence or harbor ethnic stereotypes. Psychological testing—one method of doing it—is costly and controversial, however. "What kind of guy wants to wear a 20-pound belt of bullets, clubs, cuffs, and mace?" asks John Elliot, a criminologist at Trinity University in San Antonio. "By definition, you attract a personality predisposed to power and action."

Once in the academy, many of today's recruits are given several hours of "cultural awareness" training to enhance sensitivity to ethnic differences and other behavior they will encounter on the street. Some experts would like to see this kind of schooling increased and continued throughout an officer's career.

Cities such as Miami are sending all members of the force through such courses.

Part of San Francisco's core curriculum is to bring in gays, lesbians, blacks, and the homeless to talk to police. In line with a California law passed, the visitors interact with recruits in the field and prepare videotapes for senior officers.

"Experts say there is a need for tighter screening of the people police departments hire."

"Certainly cops need nuts and bolts on the law," says John Crew, director of the Police Practices Project, a San Francisco advocacy group.

"But they also need some feeling for the communities into which they are going."

Still, there are limits to tutorials. "It's pretty tough to change attitudes in four to six hours," says Cassandra Johnson, head of the National Organization of Black Law Enforcement Executives.

• Integration. Departments have made uneven progress in putting blacks, Hispanics, and other minorities in blue. Nudged by federal affirmative-action laws, police are doing better than many other American institutions, experts say, but some cities lag behind and not enough is being done to put minorities in top positions.

Affirmative Action

In a study of departments in the 50 largest US cities, the University of Nebraska's Walker found that 45 percent made "significant" progress between 1983 and 1988 in hiring black officers, while 17 percent reported a decline. Figures for Hispanics were similar: 42 percent increased, 11 percent declined. The number of women wearing badges is up nationwide.

Detroit, Atlanta, and Washington are among the best, the study says, while Cleveland, New York, and Baltimore are among the worst. Los Angeles has a higher percentage of blacks on the force than in the population at large, but fewer Hispanics.

"The L.A. beating is as good a case imaginable for the further integration of police departments," Mr. Elliot says, noting that a black presence among the white officers at the King beating may have mitigated it. Mr. King, a black, was beaten by a group of white officers in Los Angeles March 3, 1991.

Chief Gates said recently: "I've hired more blacks . . . Hispanics . . . women than any other chief in the history of the LAPD."

• Leadership. Experts concur that the moral and professional tone set at the top is of paramount importance in curbing excessive force.

In a culture as closed as the police, department brass not only determines day-to-day behavior but influences the kind of officers a force attracts.

To help foster the right atmosphere, many departments (among them Madison, Wis., and Houston, Tex.) have adopted explicit "value statements" guiding police behavior.

"The moral and professional tone set at the top is of paramount importance in curbing excessive force."

The old rules of conduct—"don't use more force than necessary"—are being replaced by policies that take into account community needs and human values.

As David Bayley, a New York criminologist, puts it: "The only people who will stop police brutality in the end are other cops."

How Can Police Brutality Be Stopped?

The Police Can Police Themselves

Strong Internal Leadership Can Stop Police Brutality
Internal Reforms Can Stop Police Brutality
Encouraging Contact Between the Police and the Community Can Stop Police Brutality
Prosecuting Police Perjury Will Stop Brutality
Using Police Foot Patrols Can Decrease Police Brutality

Strong Internal Leadership Can Stop Police Brutality

Donald B. Walker

About the Author: *Donald B. Walker is an assistant professor of criminal justice at Kent State University in Ohio.*

Police misconduct in general and police brutality as a specific form of that behavior are two of the most difficult issues in policing. The reason for this seems related to the citizens' perception of policing in American society. Citizens tend to divide into two camps with respect to contemporary policing. One camp, fearful of crime and disorder, views the police as the last remaining force standing between them and overwhelming chaos. They support any police actions against those they view as responsible for crime and disorder, and consider any criticisms of police conduct to be anti-police and therefore supportive of anarchy. The second camp views the police as brutal, oppressive agents of the state and tends to paint all police with the same brush. Any attempt to objectively examine police behavior becomes, from their point of view, merely further support for the establishment and the status quo. It is obvious that neither viewpoint accurately reflects the true relationship between the police and the community. Although crime levels and fear remain high, the police are only one among many social-control resources at hand. A critical analysis of their conduct is not evidence of an anti-police bias. And an acknowledgement that only a minority of po-

Donald B. Walker, "Police Brutality," in *The Encyclopedia of Police Science,* William G. Bailey, editor. New York: Garland Publishing, 1989. Reprinted with permission.

lice engage in illegal and extralegal behavior does not constitute an apology for police misconduct. It is evident, however, from daily newspaper accounts that police misconduct, particularly the excessive use of force, is a continuing problem straining the relationship between the police and the citizens they serve. A number of studies have documented police brutality, and certain cities (Philadelphia, Houston, Miami) have earned national reputations for the treatment their citizens receive at the hands of their police forces. The problem deserves the serious attention of scholars, police administrators, politicians, and citizens.

> ## "Police misconduct, particularly the excessive use of force, is a continuing problem."

Much of the difficulty in establishing the validity of a serious critique of police behavior lies in the historic and traditional definition of the police role as one of law enforcement. As long as the police are viewed as "crime fighters" and clichés such as "the war on crime" are used to describe the nature of their work, we will be encouraged to examine their performance only superficially. The definition of the police function supplied by Egon Bittner provides an alternative to the traditional approach. He argues that "it makes much more sense to say that the police are nothing else than a mechanism for the distribution of situationally justified force in society." He points out that this definition of the police function encompasses the wide range of police activities beyond merely enforcing laws. It reinforces the reality that police may use force to overcome resistance to their commands. Further, this definition focuses attention on the issue of police brutality because if, as he suggests, the authorized use of force is the core of the police function, then a critical understanding of how the police actually utilize force becomes a legitimate and necessary tool in evaluating police performance. One further point needs to be made before attempting to define police brutality: Force can be conceived of as both physical and verbal. The command of authority, properly expressed, makes the use of physical force unnecessary. The dichotomy of force into physical and verbal dimensions, while seemingly trivial, has important implications for the problem of police brutality. Generally, the concept of police brutality raises the specter of a police officer willy-nilly applying the nightstick or weighted flashlight to the skull or torso of a citizen. But it is important to remember that verbal abuse can do serious violence to a person's self-concept.

Defining Brutality

One of the most difficult tasks involved in discussing police brutality is defining the concept itself. Following Bittner's conception of force as being central to the police role, police brutality involves the unnecessary and unjustified use of force, either physical or verbal. Unfortunately, as Thomas Barker observes, the terms *unnecessary* and *unjustified* are themselves ambiguous and unclear. While the law provides the police with the mandate to use force to obtain compliance with their legal commands, it does little to establish boundaries between necessary and excessive force. Since the street milieu of the patrol officer presents numerous situations where the use of force is justified, each situation must be evaluated within its own context.

"The law . . . does little to establish boundaries between necessary and excessive force."

Probably the most widely known empirical study of police violence is the work of Albert Reiss, who studied police behavior in Washington, Boston, and Chicago with the aid of observers riding in police cars. His findings indicated an abuse rate of 41.9 per 1000 white citizens and 22.6 per 1000 black citizens. He concludes:

If one accepts these rates as reasonably reliable estimates of undue force against suspects, then there should be little doubt that in major metropolitan areas the sort of behavior commonly called "police brutality" is far from rare.

In evaluating Reiss's data, one should bear in mind that the incidents recorded as involving excessive or undue force occurred in the presence of observers. It is likely that Reiss's study underestimates rather than overestimates the occurrence of excessive force. Unfortunately, his data is twenty years old and has not been replicated. Richard J. Lundman concludes:

It is true that most defiant or deviant citizens are not assaulted by police. To this we can now add: It is also true that in absolute terms it appears that many cities contain relatively large numbers of citizens who have experienced needless police force.

Who are the most likely targets of police brutality? As L. Alex Swan points out:

Thus violence or rough behavior is used by the police against certain people and in certain communities. The police do not deny that they use violence against certain citizens; rather they defend it on the grounds of its effectiveness in dealing with what they define as violations and problems.

From the literature, a fairly consistent pattern emerges as to who these "certain people" are. Those who openly defy police authority, fail to demonstrate proper respect, resist arrest, or who fall into certain classes—drunks, street addicts, homeless people, or sexual deviates are the most likely recipients of police abuse. Historically, the black community has been the most critical of police abuse of force. The Report of the National Advisory Commission on Civil Disorders that investigated the wave of urban disturbances that occurred across the U.S. in 1967 concluded that tensions between the black communities and their police departments created by unresolved grievances over police practices were a significant factor in escalating these disorders. While racist behavior of individual police officers cannot be discounted as a factor, other factors affecting the black community and its citizens are probably more significant. The dispro-portionate distribution of black citizens in the poverty class brings them more into contact with police, relative to middle-class citizens, thus pro-viding more opportunity for police-citizen en-counters. Pervasive feelings of oppression by black citizens directed at police increase the like-lihood that these encounters will become hostile as a consequence of defiance or disrespect by the citizen. Lundman indicates:

> Because authority is so central to the police role, citizens who question or resist authority represent a very serious challenge to patrol officers. As a conse-quence, intense verbal coercion is used to establish police authority, and if that is not effective, physical force is used to elicit citizen acceptance of authority.

"Outside community controls of police practices . . . have failed."

Because authority is viewed by police as the key to their occupational success and self-es-teem, any challenge or disrespect to their com-mands can provoke excessive force. Police vio-lence is also directed against categories of per-sons evaluated by police as unworthy of legal safeguards. The administration of "street justice" in the form of beatings to sex offenders, drunks, or street junkies is a consequence of police per-ceptions of worth. As John Van Maanen ob-serves, police categorize their world into "suspi-cious persons," "know-nothings," and "assholes," the latter being the most likely targets of police brutality. He indicates:

> it is the asshole category which is most combined with moral meaning for the patrolman—establish-ing for him a stained or flawed identity to attribute to the citizen upon which he can justify his some-times malevolent acts.

Likely Targets

Identifying the likely targets and situations for the use of excessive force is not an adequate ex-planation for its occurrence. Obviously not all

defiant citizens are recipients of police brutality.

The conventional explanation of police bru-tality, the one most widely accepted by police themselves, is that it is perpetrated by the rela-tively few violent persons who become police of-ficers. In fact, police screening procedures are developed with an eye toward eliminating the maladjusted or flawed personalities from the ranks of police applicants. Some instances of po-lice brutality can be attributed to the pathologi-cal tendencies of some officers, but to approach the problem as an individual problem is to ig-nore the fact that police brutality has a long his-tory and has been endemic to a number of de-partments. An adequate explanation requires an institutional perspective and a focus on the role played by the police subculture and socialization into it. The values of the police subculture sup-port secrecy and in-group solidarity. The subcul-ture also provides a world view that categorizes citizens and furnishes rationalizations for the de-valuation of some groups. Overall, it creates a feeling of "us versus them." Finally, the domi-nance of white, working-class males in police work creates an atmosphere in which prejudice and racism remain entrenched. The values and norms of the police subculture are learned in the process of socialization into the occupation. Learning the values of the police subculture be-gins in the training academy through the infor-mal interaction between recruit and veteran in-structors. This process continues during the rookies' field training and is completed "on the streets" with the assignment of the new rookie to a veteran officer following completion of academy training. In short, the values and norms of the police subculture identify the tar-gets and situations where excessive force may be appropriate. The centrality of the use of force in the occupation combined with the constant awareness of the need to maintain authority and control provide the opportunities for its expres-sion. As William A. Westley notes:

> The policeman uses violence illegally because such usage is seen as just, acceptable, and, at times, expected by his colleague group and be-

cause it constitutes an effective means for solving problems in obtaining status and self-esteem which policemen as policemen have in common.

Police administrators and political leaders must begin to view the problem as an institutional one rather than an individual one rooted in the attitudes and behavior of "a few bad apples." Clearly the problem of excessive and unwarranted police violence is a form of organizational deviance described by Lundman. The role police administrators play in supporting organizational deviance is clear. In the case of police brutality, it is probably more informal through the lack of adequate and responsive action to citizen complaints than formal through encouraging illegal practices. The second step is to recognize from past experience that outside community controls of police practices—citizen review-boards, for example—have failed and are no more likely to succeed today than they were in the 1970s. Finally, to recognize the significant role that socialization into the police subculture plays is to understand the need for developing means of retarding the internalization of the negative elements by officers as they are assimilated into the police agency. In short, the primary responsibility for curbing police brutality rests with police administrators. Since the bulk of police violence is directed at essentially powerless people, the police hierarchy must take action to protect all of its constituents against police misconduct, not just those who are viewed as worthy. To accomplish this, police administrators must take all citizen complaints seriously, must initiate thorough and honest investigations of them, and must level meaningful sanctions against offending officers. Police-community relations programs must become more than public relations campaigns aimed at "selling" the existing product. The long-range benefit of these proposals will be the creation of an atmosphere that will weaken the support for police brutality within the police subculture itself.

Internal Reforms Can Stop Police Brutality

Gerald Williams

About the Author: *Gerald Williams is president of the Police Executive Research Forum (PERF), a professional organization of criminal justice officials.*

The beating of Rodney King by police officers in Los Angeles has focused the attention of this nation on the issue of the use of force by all police officers. I believe the overwhelming majority of police officers in America are dedicated men and women who strive to uphold the ideals of the Constitution. They do not abuse the authority granted them, including the authority to use force. They realize the actions of any officer—good or bad—reflects on each and every one of them. They were among the first to condemn the type of actions we witnessed against Rodney King.

The Police Executive Research Forum (PERF) is an organization of progressive police executives serving over 30 percent of the nation's population. As the President of PERF let me assure you we are committed to a professional level of policing with an emphasis on fairness, humanity and integrity.

All too often in recent years, incidents such as the videotape of the King beating have spawned enormous efforts at "spin control." There are those who will say that this incident has damaged the "image" of the police, and that steps must be taken immediately to repair that image. PERF takes a different view. We believe the King incident should be examined carefully; it should serve as a catalyst for self-examination for every

Gerald Williams, statement before the U.S. House of Representatives Subcommittee on Civil and Constitutional Rights, April 17, 1991. Public Domain.

city, large or small, every police or sheriff's department, and moreover for every man and woman who carries a badge. We must ask ourselves hard questions—are we fair? Are all our citizens well-served? Do we uphold the oaths we have taken to protect and to serve?

I believe the issues surrounding police use of force are many and complex. While there are no simple solutions, there are several steps which can, and must, be taken to minimize any chance of this type of breech of public trust from recurring.

Unfortunately in the past, many efforts at improving policing have been characterized by quick-fix solutions that amount to throwing dollars at problems with minimal success. My hope is that the horrible beating of Rodney King will not spawn such efforts, but rather will serve as an opportunity for government, police agencies, community groups and citizens to confront issues facing policing in America in the 90's. *Together* we can evaluate our agencies and the communities they serve. *Together* we will find problems, or rather challenges, to be met. *Together* we can work toward solutions, not quick-fix, band-aid solutions, but lasting system-wide changes that will improve the quality of life in our country. I would like to [discuss] with you some of the issues we must collectively confront.

"The issues surrounding police use of force are many and complex."

PERF has long endorsed a style of policing we call "Problem-Oriented Policing." This is a team approach in which the community and their police work together to carefully analyze problems and to develop and implement solutions tailored to those problems. This approach brings the police officer physically closer to the community. Working together to solve problems allows a strong bond to develop between the police and the community. This bond not only improves police effectiveness, it minimizes the necessity for the use of force by the police.

Accreditation: Leaders in our profession and our communities have identified the need for values and sound policies in police departments that can be integrated into every police activity by every member of the police agency. Many police departments have good rational policies on use of force. In fact, those departments seeking accreditation from the Commission on Accreditation for Law Enforcement Agencies are required to have such policies. PERF and three other national law enforcement organizations created the Commission for Accreditation of Law Enforcement Agencies (CALEA) to develop standards that address almost every aspect of police functions regarding administration, management and operations. Over 175 agencies have achieved accreditation status in the six years since CALEA's inception. I would challenge each of you to return to your home districts and inquire which of your law enforcement agencies is involved in the law enforcement accreditation process. And to go one step further, to encourage those not involved to examine the values of this national movement. Accreditation may not be a panacea for problems regarding police use of force, but it is a positive first step in the right direction.

Leadership: Listening, synthesizing, defining, articulating, directing: the role of the top police executive is key in identifying and accomplishing the goals of the police agency as expected by the community. Police executives must establish personal credibility with *all* segments of the community in order to be effective. Police executives must ensure standards of conduct are articulated both internally and externally. The community must know what behavior the Chief expects of officers. The community must believe their police executive will enforce the standards he or she has set. Police executives must articulate policy and procedure at the administrative and operational levels, being cognizant to address the police culture as well as the various community cultures.

Citizen Complaints: Law enforcement exists to protect the values of society as demanded by the Constitution. In order to be effective, the police must enjoy a good working relationship with their communities, predicated on feelings of mutual trust and understanding. To further these efforts, citizens must have faith an officer will investigate a complaint made against another officer in a fair and impartial manner. A model policy regarding the handling of citizen complaints was developed by PERF in 1981 and has been widely distributed to police departments throughout the country. Specific guidelines were set forth for the treatment of all parties involved in the complaint process, including the citizen and the officer or officers involved. The community as well as the officer should know and understand what constitutes unacceptable conduct and above all, the community must have a reasonable understanding of the procedures for investigating and adjudicating cases of police misconduct. The system for complaints must be easily understood by and accessible to all citizens.

Civilian Review Boards

There has been a renewed interest in civilian review boards to sit in judgment of police officials accused of improper actions. I believe this issue is better addressed on the local level, where the needs of each individual community are best assessed. The demand for civilian review boards is symbolic of the fear our citizens possess. The public fears violence from the criminal element, but many also fear the very people who are bound to protect them from that violence.

> **"The system for complaints must be easily understood by and accessible to all citizens."**

Research: There must be continuous, quality research and a national data collection effort if we are to truly understand the extent and severity of the police related problems facing our communities. In the past, in an effort to find the quick-fix, we have been too willing to simply throw money at the problem. We have funded too many short-sighted studies and programs. We must focus on research and studies that will provide genuine insight and alternatives on issues such as police use of force; relations between the police and the community; police race relations; recruitment, selection and training of officers; and myriad other factors that contribute to a quality police practice.

"Police departments should establish and articulate a preference for the use of negotiation skills rather than force in appropriate circumstances."

Race: It may seem to some that the ethnic diversity that created the unique culture of America is today tearing her apart. The police are no exception. There must be a frank discussion of racial issues internally and externally, as they relate to our police departments. We must confront in a much more direct way than many of us have in the past the issues of racism in our organizations and how it affects our interactions with individual citizens and the greater community. We need to establish an environment in which both male and female officers of all races and ethnic groups can talk about these issues in an open and honest way.

Drug war: As stated recently by the Executive Director of PERF, Darrel Stephens, "I cannot help but wonder what influence the so-called 'drug-war,' and the violence associated with it, has had on the way police officers conduct themselves on the streets. Many of our police agencies have switched to semi-automatic firearms over the past four or five years in an effort to try to match the firepower of drug dealers. In most cases, this change has come about with little or no debate in the community. Ten

years ago, I doubt that this type of change would have taken place without considerable public comment. In the name of the 'drug war' we have engaged in sweeps that have resulted in mass arrests in some of our urban areas. I have heard and read several stories about how citizens on the streets have applauded these actions. I have to wonder whether some police officers have misinterpreted this applause to mean it's okay to treat criminals any way the police want to—as long as they take criminals off the street. Have the messages that have been sent to our officers in fighting the 'drug war' been consistent and clear? In our justifiable concern of the increases in drug abuse, crime and violence, the noise generated by the 'get tough' rhetoric of our politicians and the applause from the community have become deafening. Have we failed to hear other important messages coming from the community? Where is their applause now?"

Training: How a law enforcement agency approaches training and the type of training provided must be carefully examined to insure it is reflective of the agency's values. Training must focus on developing a thinking police officer who is able to analyze situations and respond in an appropriate manner based on those values. Officers should receive training in the merits of and the use of negotiation as a primary tool in response to confrontation. When an officer can negotiate a solution he or she is less likely to utilize force as an immediate response to a crisis. Officers who employ communication and negotiation skills, rather than force, as a first resort are credited with reducing initial levels of tension during contacts. Expertise in the art of negotiation is not a natural talent. It should be a significant part of the training curriculum. Police departments should establish and articulate a preference for the use of negotiation skills rather than force in appropriate circumstances.

Necessary Steps

There is no simple answer to the problems raised by the LA incident, but there are steps that can be taken to minimize the chances that it will happen again. The values, policies and philosophy of a department must be carefully articulated by the police executive and supported by elected officials and community leaders. Then, a mechanism must be put in place to get the message to every member of the police department. Conduct that deviates from these values and policies must be dealt with immediately. The public must be encouraged to complain when appropriate and must assume its role in ensuring quality policing. Those officers who continue to uphold the high ideals of their agency and community should be rewarded and recognized.

"Police are not fighting a war. They are working to protect our public and enforce our laws."

The need to send a clear message to police officers cannot be overstated. Again the rhetoric that surrounds drug enforcement efforts exemplifies the mixed message we send our police. The "war on drugs" and the "arms race" we have waged with drug dealers reinforces the Rambo-like image of police officers. It is an image that professional departments discourage. The attitude that all is fair in war has exacerbated the misconception that police are an occupying army that should do whatever is necessary to apprehend criminals. This rhetoric has got to stop. Police are not fighting a war. They are working to protect our public and enforce our laws in an even-handed, professional manner. They are working to build communities. Yes, they must resort to force when confronted with a dangerous situation, but that force must be justified and reasonable.

Improved Policing

Some good will come of this tragic incident. For we now have the opportunity to reflect on the circumstances which led to this situation, and to move forward to a new era of improved policing in America. It is because of my commitment to professionalism in American policing and to strengthening the bonds between the community and their police that I am speaking to you today. Without the support of our communities, the police cannot hope to be effective. Without the support of the police, our communities cannot hope to be safe. By bringing police and community leaders together, encouraging research and debate, supporting law enforcement accreditation, revising the rhetoric that subtly affects our actions, and fostering strong national leadership, those of us at the Police Executive Research Forum hope to build a structure within which the police can protect and serve all citizens.

Encouraging Contact Between the Police and the Community Can Stop Police Brutality

Mark H. Moore

About the Author: *Mark H. Moore is Guggenheim professor of criminal justice at Harvard University's Kennedy School of Government.*

Four days before Rodney King was savagely beaten March 3, 1991, I publicly noted the achievements of [Los Angeles Police Chief] Daryl Gates in holding his officers to his own exacting standards of professionalism. Gates is not a different person now, nor is his department radically changed. I still admire them both.

Yet I cannot help but be troubled by my remarks. Whether that savage beating was a rare event or not, it must be witnessed. Lessons must be drawn.

The incident, I now believe, gives powerful evidence of the ultimate limitations of a certain ideal of policing that Daryl Gates and the Los Angeles Police Department [LAPD] have long exemplified and that has inspired police executives and guided police practices across the country. At the core of this ideal, which I call "professional crime-fighting," are two powerful values.

One is the value of professionalism. In the world of policing, professionalism is primarily concerned with creating a disciplined, highly

Mark H. Moore, "The Gulf Between 'Them' and 'Us,'" *Los Angeles Times,* April 5, 1991. Reprinted with permission.

trained, law-abiding and technically competent force. It has also meant keeping the police insulated from improper political influences, well away from local political machines. Finally, professionalism has been pursued through technical proficiency, expressed in such technologies as computerized crime analysis, automated fingerprint identification systems and the development of specialized units from SWAT [Special Weapons and Tactics] teams to narcotics task forces.

Gates has excelled at professionalism, and this approach is fine as far as it goes.

But there is another part of the Los Angeles idea: the focus on "crime-fighting" as the principal objective and dominant justification for the existence of the police force. A professional police department focuses its resources on the highest-priority task, which the police believe to be the control of the most serious crimes—robbery, rape, murder, assault. To attack those crimes effectively, police professionalism has insisted on the value of a mobile patrol force, able to respond immediately to calls for assistance. Thus police are always near when emergencies come, but sufficiently distant to preserve privacy and guard against the favoritism or prejudice that would follow from familiarity.

> ## "The end of controlling crime comes to dominate the legal means that the police are allowed to use."

Beneath this straightforward logic, the commitment to "crime-fighting" has a nastier edge. The end of controlling crime comes to dominate the legal means that the police are allowed to use; the criminals are transformed from sad and desperate people who get into fights or prey upon equally hopeless people for small economic rewards into well-armed, dangerous offenders. In this world, Dirty Harry becomes the hero of the law-enforcement community.

To a degree, the police are encouraged to think in these terms by a political rhetoric common among some chiefs of police, which also reflects the views of the officers themselves: The police are a "thin blue line" that protects the good people from the bad. If crime is rising, it is said to be because the recidivists the police arrested were allowed to walk and because the weak-kneed criminal-justice system exacted no real accountability. Such themes work well in external politics as well and may even have some truth to them.

A Tension

The problem is that, in the end, there is a profound tension between the ideal of professionalism and the nasty edge of crime-fighting. The effect of this tension is to create a hidden culture. Beneath the shiny surface of even the most professionalized police department is an undercurrent of cynicism. Street-level officers are often given mixed messages by their superiors: They are told to do whatever is necessary to get the job done, but not to get caught in any form of misconduct. This is less common in truly professionalized organizations like the LAPD. But in any case, officers know that if they do get caught, their supervisors will not back them. Thus, they band together to protect themselves not only from the criminal offenders but from the arbitrary demands and betrayals of management.

To a great degree, most of the time, the public colludes in this deal. When I was a member of a task force reviewing the Philadelphia Police Department, the task force was surprised to discover from a survey that most citizens thought their police department was performing well, despite the fact that they also thought that the officers slept on the job, were often rude, frequently took bribes and used unnecessary force.

The public seemed to think that if the police were going to do the hard job of dealing with crime and offenders, they had to be allowed to behave badly. This view was later articulated by one police officer who explained to me: "If you're going to have to shovel society's [garbage], you ought to be indulged a little bit."

The police eventually discover that this tacit deal with the community is as unreliable as their deal with management. When an incident occurs, as it inevitably will, and as it did in the case of Rodney King, the public turns on the police. Usually, scapegoats are sought and the cleansing power of improved training and discipline applied. Thus the police are reinforced in their cynicism and sense of isolation.

There is an alternative. The community and the police could decide that the ideal of professionalized crime-fighting embodies the wrong values and establishes the wrong relationships between the police and the community. The reasons for this are many.

By focusing on the instrumental goals of controlling serious crime, the police become too narrow in their objectives and too ruthless in their operational methods. They see only the worst parts of the community and form a view of human nature based on what they see. Law and democratic values become constraints on effective action rather than important ends.

By relying on motorized patrol and rapid response to calls for service, and by denigrating the importance of noncrime calls for service, such as neighborhood quarrels and the fears of the elderly, the police have limited their contacts with and their value to the communities they police.

> **"[The police] see only the worst parts of the community and form a view of human nature based on what they see."**

So, what seems to me important in responding to the beating of Rodney King is not more effective investigations of misconduct, or improved training, or closer supervision, though all those things may play a role. Instead, the Los Angeles community and its police department ought to return to a path that the LAPD once pioneered.

In the 1970s, the department experimented with "team policing," a vision of a police department broken into groups, each with a strong sense of responsibility and accountability to the people living within a small geographic area. The aim was to develop greater closeness with the community and a wider concern for the overall well-being of an area. The police department acknowledged its accountability to the citizens for the use of force as well as the other resources of the department.

"The values of mutual respect, restraint and civility must be the ultimate goals of those who guard a diverse, democratic society."

This vision still survives in Los Angeles in the form of "senior lead officers," who retain responsibilities for the quality of life in given geographic areas. Some of these officers, encouraged by superiors who see the value of promoting close relationships with local communities, are doing excellent police work. By concentrating on the problems that the communities nominate (rather than exclusively on serious crime) and by enlisting the cooperation of the communities (rather than going it alone), these officers are stilling fears and restoring hope in hard-pressed neighborhoods.

Ambivalent Commitment

Despite past successes, the department's commitment to this style of policing has remained ambivalent. When budgets tighten, officers are pulled from community assignments for citywide dispatching. And in the culture of the department, the rapid responders and crime-fighters enjoy higher status than the community-based "rubber gun" crowd.

It's a pity, for this kind of policing offers more to citizens than the narrowest kinds of professional crime-fighting. As my colleague David Kennedy, who has worked closely with some of Los Angeles' best senior lead officers, told me, "It is inconceivable to me that these officers could have beaten Rodney King in the way that the other officers did. They just think about citizens, even troublesome ones, much differently than the rapid responders.". . .

Whatever the path, the values of mutual respect, restraint and civility must be the ultimate goals of those who guard a diverse, democratic society.

Prosecuting Police Perjury Will Stop Brutality

Alan Dershowitz

About the Author: *Alan Dershowitz is a law professor at Harvard University and a well-known criminal defense attorney and author.*

The bad news is that several Los Angeles policemen repeatedly and mercilessly clubbed, kicked and beat a 25-year-old black man named Rodney G. King. The good news is that an amateur photographer named George Holliday videotaped the assault, and the videotape has been shown all around the world. But the other bad news is that the existence of the tape was made known before the policemen had testified under oath as to their version of what had transpired.

It does not take much imagination to speculate about what the policemen would have said had they been charged with brutality—or had King been accused of resisting arrest—and had they not known that their actions had been videotaped. I have read dozens of transcripts of such boilerplate police testimony; it almost always goes something like this:

"We attempted to place the perpetrator under arrest, sir, but he began to swing wildly at the officers. I tried to place him in handcuffs, sir, but he started to reach into his jacket for what I believed to be a weapon. When I grabbed his hands in order to prevent him from reaching for a weapon, he began to kick in every direction, hitting his legs against the side of the police car and other hard objects. At this point he fell to the ground and started to bang his head and

body against the pavement. We attempted to subdue him because we were concerned that he would hurt himself. He was strong and it took us several minutes to subdue him, sir. All of his injuries, and ours as well, were sustained as a result of his resistance and our efforts to subdue him."

The other arresting officers then parrot this testimony, and a knife is produced from the arrested person's pocket or the ground, in order to corroborate the tale.

The judge, upon hearing this story for the umpteenth time, generally shakes his head in knowing frustration, but accepts the officers' account as credible. As one prominent judge put it several years ago: "There are grounds for believing that 'the guardians of (our) security' sometimes give deliberately false testimony," but when police testimony is not "against the grain of human experience," the judge must believe it. Not surprisingly, many policemen—particularly the bad ones—have become experts at concocting stories that do not appear to be "against the grain of human experience." Yet they are as false as the testimony in the King case would surely have been had the police not been aware of the videotape. Any cops who would commit the crimes of assault and battery against a non-resisting citizen, would have little hesitation in later lying about it to protect their own careers.

> ## "Policemen would not lie so readily if they did not know that they could get away with it so easily."

The Los Angeles videotape had thus alerted the world to only half of a widespread problem. We have seen a few bad cops engaging in vicious vigilante injustice. But the other half of the problem—police perjury to cover up the first half of the problem—is still not sufficiently acknowledged.

Several years ago, I had an opportunity to expose an instance of police perjury by using an

Alan Dershowitz, "Legal System Should Stop Police Brutality," Manchester (N.H.) *Union Leader,* March 19, 1991. Reprinted with permission.

audio tape of which the policeman was unaware. Unbeknownst to the cop, my client had surreptitiously recorded several attempts by the policeman to turn my client into an informer by making both threats and promises. When I questioned the cop under oath, he denied having made either threats or promises. I then produced the tape, which proved he was lying. Nonetheless, the prosecutors and the trial judge claimed to believe the cop. Eventually, my client's conviction was reversed on appeal.

"A police badge is neither a license to commit assault nor to commit perjury."

But this case, and others since, have convinced me that the primary responsibility for the pervasiveness of police perjury lies squarely with those prosecutors who close their eyes to it and with those judges who pretend to believe it. Policemen would not lie so readily if they did not know that they could get away with it so easily. In the case in which my client recorded the policeman's threats and promises, the lying cop was promoted, despite the Court of Appeals finding that he had lied under oath.

A Small Minority

Police misconduct and perjury will continue until and unless the public begins to understand how dangerous it is to every one of us. The police know they can get away with virtually every other form of misconduct—because they can simply lie about what they did. A police badge is neither a license to commit assault nor to commit perjury. The vast majority of honest cops do neither. But the small minority who do both endanger all of our liberties. And the prosecutors and judges who encourage police perjury by their silent acquiescence are the real villains. They, above all, should know better. And they, more than anyone else, can do something about it.

Using Police Foot Patrols Can Decrease Police Brutality

Richard Lacayo

About the Author: *Richard Lacayo is a staff writer for* Time *magazine.*

While the Los Angeles Police Department [L.A.P.D.] has long relied on SWAT [Special Weapons and Tactics] teams and helicopters for high-tech law enforcement, police departments in many other cities are turning to methods that are decidedly low tech. Their weapons of choice? A good pair of walking shoes and a gift for small talk, coupled with rigorous training in the basics of policing.

Frustrated by the failure of standard methods to reduce crime, more than 300 cities and towns nationwide—including Boston, Houston and San Francisco—are adopting the concept of community policing. Through Community Patrol Officer Programs, these municipalities work to build rapport between police officers and the neighborhoods they patrol. "The message is: the beat cop is back," says New York City police commissioner Lee Brown. . . .

When police officers and the citizens of a neighborhood know each other, CPOP theory holds, it is more difficult for both criminals and cops to break the law. "Community policing is a deterrent to the improper use of force because it strengthens officers' relationships with the community," says Herman Goldstein, professor of criminal law at the University of Wisconsin. "The neighborhood support gives police a

greater sense of confidence and authority, which reduces their need for using force. If police officers feel they don't have the authority, the power, to handle a situation, they're more likely to resort to brute force." Referring to the L.A.P.D.'s beating of Rodney King, Goldstein says, "It's incomprehensible that a police officer imbued with community policing would engage in that type of behavior."

One typical CPOP officer is Donald Christy, 36, of Lansing, Mich. A little over a year ago, he was assigned to cover a nine-block area of the city. At first disheartened by the sight of crack houses and blighted streets, Christy took pains to get on a first-name basis with many of the area's 700 residents and learn what neighborhood problems concerned them most. Those conversations led him to recognize, he says, "that the good people far outnumbered the bad." Meanwhile, he organized a volunteer community cleanup, which filled 30 dumpsters with litter; arranged federal funding for floral plantings; and even held a contest to choose a name for the neighborhood: Sparrow Estates.

His unconventional approach to policing paid big dividends in terms of crime control. Residents began to give Christy tips that helped him drive away criminals. Indoor dealers found themselves evicted by absentee landlords. "You can walk around the block now without fear of being attacked," says Ralph Casler, a retired mechanic who has lived in the area for 30 years. Says Christy: "I haven't made an arrest in eight months."

"Community policing is a deterrent to the improper use of force."

The history of the beat cop has traveled full circle: once, he was nearly driven to extinction by a series of well-intended but ill-conceived reforms. Until the first decades of this century, police were all-purpose keepers of the peace. They ran lodging houses for the homeless, tracked down offensive smells, rounded up stray animals and kept the streetlamps supplied with oil. They also gained a reputation for taking payoffs and doling out a rough brand of curbside justice.

By the 1930s and '40s, reformers had refashioned police departments along more narrowly focused lines. Officers were trained to concentrate on apprehending criminals, especially for the most serious crimes such as murder, assault, robbery and rape. Other functions were handed off to city health and welfare departments or similar agencies. After World War II, patrol cars and two-way radios came into wider use. Police became a mobile force, cruising anonymously through neighborhoods they knew mostly as the staging ground for each night's disturbances.

The final reform was the all but universal adoption of the 911 system for emergency calls. With that, police were reduced to chasing from one crime scene to another, all the while consolidating the bleakest impression of the people they served. A recent study found that New York City police spend 90% of their time on the job attending to such calls; they once spent just 50%. That leaves almost no time for anything else.

Though the reforms were designed to make police better crime fighters, it was the law of unintended consequences that they wound up enforcing most effectively. Many academic experts believe the changes fostered conditions that contributed to the sharply higher crime rates of the past three decades. A spate of scholarly studies has demonstrated that the offenses to quality of life that police now routinely overlook—such things as loud radios, graffiti and aggressive panhandling—create an atmosphere in which more serious crime is likely to occur. Those petty disturbances are the ones that trouble and frighten ordinary citizens the most. In turn, their fear acts like an acid to disintegrate neighborhood ties. It leads citizens to shun the streets and abdicate responsibility for conditions outside their doors. That invites a dismal cycle of deteriorating conditions, more fear—and more crime.

Accordingly, CPOP cops try to discourage crimes before they happen by maintaining—or creating—stable neighborhoods. That requires them to learn which local problems are of greatest concern to residents, and help them find solutions. "Police lost the most valuable thing we had, which is contact with people," says Washington police chief Isaac Fulwood. "We really got away from basic common-sense approaches." In a city where the murder rate soared 10% last year, partly owing to drugs, Fulwood has established community-policing pilot programs in two crime-ridden districts. In addition to a lawbook, patrol officers now have access to a fat directory of government services.

"We deal with broken playground equipment and potholes just as we do with crime," says David Couper, chief of police in Madison, Wis., which has committed its entire force of 310 officers to the community-policing concept. Officer Joe Balles, who patrols the city's low-income Broadway-Simpson neighborhood, hands out a business card with the phone number of the answering machine in his office. At the end of every day he has a tape full of pleas for assistance, messages from tipsters and calls from people who just wanted to chat with their cop.

"A recent study found that New York City police spend 90% of their time . . . attending to [911] calls."

"The police here are more on top of things then they've ever been," he boasts. Balles may act as point man with the bureaucracy to get streetlights for a dark alley, or arrange marital counseling for a household that accounts for repeated 911 calls when the couple starts fighting. Defusing situations like that can be highly cost effective. In many cities, more than 60% of emergency calls are generated by just 10% of the households.

Community police may also use unconventional means to combat more serious crimes. When drug dealers in Houston turned a bank of pay phones outside a convenience store into their personal business office, a patrolman got the phones removed. In the same city, a deserted apartment complex where dealers flourished was finally boarded up after a community cop tracked down and harangued the property's bankruptcy trustee.

Whether CPOP can actually drive down the crime rate is still unproven. The most thorough study of its effectiveness, a 1981 examination of an experimental foot-patrol program in Newark, found that it did not decrease crime. It did pay off, however, in psychological well-being. The visible presence of so many patrolmen made people feel safer and better disposed toward the police.

More recently, though, other cities have reported lower crime rates in specific neighborhoods where the CPOP approach has been given a try. On Madison's south side, property crime was reduced 14% between 1987 and 1989. A west Houston neighborhood recorded a 38% drop in serious crime over a six-month period in 1988. But the neighboring Houston area reported increases in crime, which suggests that community policing simply relocated the problem.

One big difficulty for police departments is finding the time and resources to make community policing work. Though some CPOP cops are assigned full time to the job, many cities are trying to rely largely on patrol-car officers' doubling as community police. But the frequency of 911 calls means that their time for closeup patrolling is limited. Houston's Neighborhood Oriented Policing program, known as NOP, is sometimes referred to derisively by police themselves as Nobody on Patrol.

Because the 911 system can never be abandoned—woe to the mayor of any city in which the police cannot be summoned quickly during a break-in—many departments are looking at ways to cut down on the number of calls. In the Denver suburb of Aurora, where only about a fourth of an estimated 190,000 calls each year are for real emergencies, police operators perform "911 triage." Where appropriate, they direct nonemergency callers to other city agencies. Police officers take the less urgent crime reports over the phone.

"We've ingrained the mentality that a stolen bike will bring an officer to your doorstep quickly," says Aurora division chief Ronald Sloan. "That has to change."

Community policing is reshaping police forces themselves. Some police academies are revamping their curriculums to train cadets in social-service skills. To dispel the impression in minority neighborhoods that police are a white army of occupation, many CPOP plans require increased hiring of minority officers. . . .

"Community policing is reshaping police forces themselves."

Among the people who don't want to see cops back on the beat are many of the cops themselves. Middle-level department brass are suspicious of plans that make patrol officers more independent. Many of the rank-and-file personnel also scoff at anything that smacks of social work. "There's an unfounded fear that it detracts from the macho image and takes the fun out of putting the bad guys in jail," says Carolyn Robison, a Tulsa police major. A lot of officers just don't like walking. For years, being assigned to the beat was a standard way to punish officers.

The most daunting aspect of CPOP may be that it so dramatically expands the idea of what it means to be a police officer. "This is a radical notion for police," says University of Wisconsin's Goldstein, "that they have 30 or 40 tools at their disposal to bring to bear upon complex problems." But after so many years of getting mixed results from just a few tools—handcuffs, a billy club and a gun—many police are ready for a change. And so are most of the citizens they serve.

How Can Police Brutality Be Stopped?

Civilians Must Police the Police

Civilian Review Boards Can Reduce Police Brutality
Stricter Laws Can Stop Brutality
Both Federal and Local Reforms Are Needed to Stop Police Brutality
Sting Operations by Private Investigators Can Deter Police Brutality

Civilian Review Boards Can Reduce Police Brutality

Debra Carillo

About the Author: *Debra Carillo is a public defender and former police officer.*

Had Rodney King not had the benefit of videotape, you wouldn't know his name today. I know this because I'm a deputy public defender for the County of Orange, with dozens of clients who have been victims of police brutality, with only their word against the officers' word. This isn't just a Los Angeles problem.

Ah, you say, here's another liberal defense lawyer jumping on the Rodney King bandwagon. Right and wrong. Yes, I am another liberal, proud to safeguard the constitutional rights of all citizens.

I am also an ex-cop.

My first great disillusionment in law enforcement was an unforgettable moment in the Orange County Sheriff's Training Academy. A crusty investigator was teaching us about probable cause—suspicious criminal activity that justifies police contact with a citizen. One of the recruits was having trouble grasping the concept. Exasperated, the investigator leaned forward conspiratorially. With melodramatic flair, he whipped a ball-point pen from his pocket and held it between his fingers, rotating his outstretched arm slowly for all to see: "*This* is probable cause." He explained that what mattered was how the officer described what happened. He was teaching a creative-writing course in law-enforcement fiction.

On the street, I was shocked by the attitude of

Debra Carillo, "Can Brutalizers Care for Justice?" *Los Angeles Times*, March 31, 1991. Reprinted with permission.

a small percentage of officers. They were the zealots, frequently arresting people for resisting arrest and for assault on a police officer. Curiously, it always appeared to be the arrestee who came out on the short end of the nightstick. Even more curiously, these people were often arrested for only one or both of these charges. Why were they apprehended in the first place?

Other officers, in the majority, were able to work a 20-year career without a single arrest for either of these charges.

Too often, defendants would arrive at the station with an officer gleefully recounting how he had slammed on his brakes so that the handcuffed and helpless "dirtbag" would have his face "waffled" by the metal grille separating the patrol unit's front and back seats. Gang-in-blue officers have the luxury of selecting their victims: almost always male, poorly educated, frequently with some sort of criminal history and a member of a minority group.

Newport Beach officers gained notoriety in the early 1980s for their efforts to keep Newport Beach "clean." One of their unwritten codes was NIN: "(Negro) in Newport." Officers would stop the cars of blacks on a pretext and strongly encourage them to leave the city. The radio chatter would describe the incident as "November-India-November."

"The police must be policed."

Ah, but I digress. If Rodney King had been my client, without benefit of videotape, there would be a thick stack of protective police reports by the officers who witnessed the beating, neatly justifying and minimizing the brutal actions of their brethren. As reflected by the casual attitude of the onlooking officers, jovial post-event radio colloquy and supervisorial participation, what occurred was standard operating procedure for a certain cadre of the LAPD's [Los Angeles Police Department's] less-than-finest.

I have worked as a criminal defense attorney

for Orange County for nearly three years and I have dealt with officers from 12 police agencies. In that time, I have handled dozens of cases in which my clients told me of outrageous police brutality. The best they can expect, if their injuries are serious, is to have their cases dismissed, often after several days in jail and perhaps loss of their job. Often enough, only the charge of assaulting the officer will be dropped, in exchange for a guilty plea to the underlying charge. Of course, my clients have the option of fighting the case, but to do that they almost always must remain in custody. Judges are reluctant to release someone accused of attacking a police officer.

"Injured and harassed citizens must have access to a fair tribunal so they can report . . . without fear of reprisal."

If the victim perseveres, he is entitled to a hearing in which the judge reviews the disciplinary history of the accused officer. But in order for there to be a history of brutality, complaints must have been registered with, yes, the police department responsible for the brutality.

The good, the bad and the ugly of society are represented in the ranks of law enforcement, and being a police officer is a tough, often dangerous job. Still, the vast majority of officers never behave as those officers did; they are as outraged as the rest of us by the King affair. But can you expect them to snitch on their brethren? Would you want one of your colleagues to be responsible for your life as a back-up officer if you had reported him for violence and he despised you for it? Would you report someone who may have saved your life in the past?

Policing the Police

The police must be policed. What this takes is civilian review and civilian governance for every department. Injured and harassed citizens must have access to a fair tribunal so they can report intimidation without fear of reprisal or further intimidation. This means a permanent, independent, elected citizen review board with disciplinary powers, not just a free-wheeling blue-ribbon appointed commission. The board must have free access to evidence, including police audio tapes.

Fair and neutral review of police actions will restore the honor and integrity of the majority of officers and will save millions of tax dollars that we'll otherwise keep paying out in settlements to brutality victims who somehow prove their cases.

Stricter Laws Can Stop Brutality

David L. Llewellyn Jr.

About the Author: David L. Llewellyn Jr. is president and special counsel of the Western Center for Law and Religious Freedom, a public interest law firm based in Sacramento, California that provides legal support for activist organizations, churches, and citizens.

The Los Angeles police department has an official policy and practice relating to the use of "pain compliance techniques" which authorize the infliction of "excruciating pain" and injury on passive, non-threatening civil rights protestors, particularly right-to-life demonstrators.

In Los Angeles, hundreds of similarly passive and non-threatening sit-in demonstrators blocking the entrance to abortion clinics have been arrested by use of brutal "pain compliance techniques," including "nunchucks" [nunchakus], a martial arts weapon which the LAPD has used only against right-to-life demonstrators and not other civil rights protestors or criminal suspects in general.

Nunchucks consist of two rods of metal or wood connected by a length of wire or rope. Nunchucks are so dangerous that mere possession of one is a felony under California law.

LAPD officers use nunchucks for the purpose of producing "excruciating pain." The description of the pain as "excruciating" is the term the LAPD sergeant responsible for supervising the use of nunchucks against right-to-life demonstrators used in his sworn declaration.

The police twist the nunchucks wire around the arm or wrist of a passive demonstrator and

David L. Llewellyn Jr., statement before the U.S. House of Representatives Subcommittee on Civil and Constitutional Rights, April 17, 1991. Public Domain.

torque down hard. In the course of producing the excruciating pain that the police seek, their nunchucks and pain compliance techniques also have produced broken bones, permanent nerve and ligament damage, a miscarriage, and innumerable injuries requiring surgery and other medical attention and requiring months to heal. . . .

Police use of brutal "pain compliance techniques," particularly the use of nunchucks, against passive, non-threatening civil rights demonstrators should be prohibited by law.

Intentionally inflicting pain when it is not necessary to effect arrest is excessive force and unreasonable seizure in violation of the Fourth Amendment. Pain properly may be an unintended or incidental event in a lawful arrest, but a policy like that of the LAPD which authorizes unnecessary, intentional infliction of pain should be unlawful.

"Pain compliance techniques" provide police with standardless discretion to hurt or injure people. Police policies that permit the use of weapons such as nunchucks on passive, non-threatening demonstrators are overbroad and unconstitutionally vague. They are an open invitation for the use of excessive force.

> ## "Police use of brutal 'pain compliance techniques' . . . should be prohibited by law."

Labeling the intentional infliction of force to induce pain as "pain compliance" is dangerously misleading.

"Compliance" merely describes the goal for use of force to inflict pain. It provides no standards to regulate the degree of force or pain. "Pain compliance" is an arbitrary and subjective process that violates the "objective reasonableness test" for the use of force in effecting arrest under the U.S. Supreme Court decision in *Graham v. Connor*. Even though a police officer subjectively may be motivated to inflict pain only for the purpose of inducing compliance, the law looks objectively at the actions used to inflict the pain and the circumstances of the arrest. Under *Graham v. Connor* the law looks at four factors. (1) The severity of the crime—in the case of civil rights sit-in demonstrators it is simple trespassing. (2) The threat of safety of officers and others—the class of plaintiffs in the *John* case constitutes no threat whatsoever. (3) Actively resisting arrest—the right-to-life plaintiffs in *John* were passive and non-resisting. (4) Attempting to evade arrest by flight—clearly not applicable.

"The use of nunchucks and other pain compliance techniques causes some people to comply but many people to break."

The "pain compliance" policy and practice of the LAPD was declared by the trial court at the preliminary injunction hearing to be: "Whatever force is necessary to overcome resistance." This standard, if not found to be unconstitutional by the courts, must be made unlawful by the legislature. The "force necessary to overcome resistance" was the standard of the inquisition. When a policy fails to require the termination of force and pain when they produce injury without compliance, that policy is an authorization for torture.

If a demonstrator is willing to endure force and pain past the point of injury, does that justify the police inflicting such pain and injury? The LAPD policy cannot tell police officers how much force and pain will be necessary to obtain compliance. The policy is ever-increasing force and pain until compliance is achieved. The policy provides no upward limits on the pain to be induced.

Police officers do not know when or even whether their infliction of force and pain will result in compliance or in injury. The policy does not require the termination of force even after

injury has occurred.

People's ability to endure physical force and to tolerate pain varies widely. The use of nunchucks and other pain compliance techniques causes some people to comply but many people to break. The police do not know how much pain it will take to break the will of a passive demonstrator. The police do not know whether any amount of pain will be sufficient.

Even a conscientious police officer cannot know in advance who will comply before breaking. Even a conscientious police officer cannot know how much pain actually is being inflicted. Even a conscientious police officer cannot know when such pain compliance techniques will produce temporary or permanent injury.

But an unscrupulous police officer can induce pain to teach people a lesson, pain to intimidate and silence civil rights protests, pain to vent passion or prejudice, pain to punish. An unscrupulous officer could even induce pain for the sake of pain.

Under the current LAPD policy that fails to acknowledge any degree of pain as excessive, even pain produced by force beyond the point of injury, there is no limit on the pain or injury that an LAPD officer may produce without violating department policies and procedures. In short, there are no objective limits in the LAPD "pain compliance techniques" and, as such, they represent rule by the force of weapons rather than the force of law.

Pain Counter-Productive

The pain induced by the use of nunchucks can be so intense that it is counter-productive. Many demonstrators have reported that the pain was so severe that they lost the ability either to comply or to communicate their desire to comply. The force and pain effectively disable the demonstrators due to reduced blood circulation, nerve interference, nausea, muscle failure, loss of feeling, total focusing of the mind and body on the areas of excruciating pain, shock, fear of further injury, surges in blood flow and nerve activity due to pressure and release, even loss of consciousness. Some demonstrators could not control their muscles. Some could not stand. Some could not speak. Some could not even think. The pain so overwhelmed them that compliance with the demands of the police became impossible. Some demonstrators reported that they became willing to comply, to do anything to stop the pain, but that they were physically disabled from compliance by the pain itself.

On the other hand, some demonstrators would not comply despite the pain, and thus the pain produced no effect except torture.

Devices intended by the police to inflict "excruciating pain" ought to be unlawful. Inflicting excruciating pain on a convicted felon would constitute cruel and unusual punishment. Certainly the law ought to prevent the infliction of such pain on people merely being arrested for trespass.

Passive Resistance

The LAPD contends that they must balance the rights of the public and the businesses being blocked against the pain being inflicted on the demonstrators. But this is an illusory argument. The rights of the public and the businesses will be vindicated in any event. The demonstrators will be removed. The only issue is whether they will be removed with or without brutal force and "pain compliance."

The LAPD also asserts that the use of nunchucks makes arrests easier for the police because they need fewer officers and they do not have to carry passive demonstrators. In actuality, however, videotapes show at least two officers accompanying each arrestee, whether the arrestee is walking voluntarily or being lifted and carried by officers squeezing nunchucks. Certainly to some degree the threat and actuality of excruciating pain inflicted by the police increases the probability of voluntary compliance in some people. But excruciating pain and risk of injury cannot be justified simply to make the job of the police easier.

Before June 1989, when nunchucks were introduced by the LAPD, police had managed to arrest demonstrators safely and effectively for the past 70 years or more without institutionalized brutality. Moreover, the right-to-life demonstrators against whom the LAPD has used nunchucks are among the most docile people who will ever be arrested. Nunchucks and barbarous "pain compliance" tactics cannot be justified.

"Devices intended by the police to inflict 'excruciating pain' ought to be unlawful."

In the lunch counter sit-ins and similar civil rights demonstrations beginning in 1957 and continuing through the early 1960's in the South, police used excessive force in the form of water cannons, billy clubs and police dogs, and the nation condemned their brutality. In the huge sit-in demonstrations at the University of California at Berkeley in 1966, the police carried the demonstrators away, without brutality. The only difference now is that the issue is not racial equality, academic freedom, or freedom of speech, but the right to life.

One reason that some right-to-life demonstrators remain passive and motionless when approached by police in their sit-in demonstrations is to symbolize the passive helplessness of unborn children in abortions. Their very passivity is a form of symbolic speech.

The lessons from past generations of civil rights activism must not be forgotten today nor denied to demonstrators because of the ideology of their cause.

Using Pain as Punishment

Pain compliance techniques, particularly the use of nunchucks, give the appearance to the public that the police are not merely arresting demonstrators but are punishing them. An LAPD captain, in a sworn declaration in the *John* case, justified the use of nunchucks by stating that: "Some [demonstrators] appear as a young child **welcoming punishment** for past transgressions." (Emphasis added.)

In practice, the LAPD use of pain does appear to be a form of extra-judicial punishment. If we want to use pain as punishment: if, for example, we want to reintroduce public whipping as a punishment for crime and to sentence civil rights demonstrators to 39 lashes in the public square; let us do so by laws adopted by legislatures and let us inflict these punishments on people after they are convicted of their crimes. But at least let us advocate pain as punishment honestly, without the present hypocrisy of averting our gaze and shrugging when we hear of police inflicting pain intentionally in the course of an otherwise peaceful arrest.

Federal law should prohibit law enforcement officers from using "pain compliance" techniques against people whose conduct is passive and non-threatening. . . .

If a Department of Animal Control used pain-inducing techniques on dogs or coyotes like those used by the LAPD, when other means were available, they would be universally excoriated as inhumane.

"The lessons from past generations of civil rights activism must not be forgotten today."

The Los Angeles police department policy authorizes inhumane treatment of human beings, and not even criminals but the most conscientious and non-threatening class of people imaginable, people who have put their bodies on the line because of their belief in the sanctity of life.

Let them be arrested. Let them be carted off to jail. But do not let them be put into the hands of police officers who have been taught that it is acceptable to break their bodies in order to break their wills.

Both Federal and Local Reforms Are Needed to Stop Police Brutality

American Civil Liberties Union

About the Author: The American Civil Liberties Union is a national organization that works to defend Americans' civil liberties established by the U.S. Constitution. It has litigated hundreds of cases concerning police brutality.

"It can't happen here, it can't happen here," has been the familiar refrain of officials around the country in the wake of the shocking video of the Rodney King beating in Los Angeles. It's tempting to think that there is something fundamentally different about the police force in Los Angeles that allowed this incident to occur.

Yet while police departments vary in practices, make-up and attitude from locality to locality and from state to state, there are common themes that need to be addressed in every community before the public is asked to believe that brutality and abuse are not problems in their own local police agency.

Police abuse has neither a single cause nor a single cure. It's not "just" an issue of racism or a lack of training or poor leadership, although all of these can be extremely important factors. If the focus is on one of these issues to the exclusion of the rest, the impact on the overall problem will be minimal. Only a comprehensive approach addressing at least the following five key areas can bring lasting results.

The common strain underlying all of these areas is the need for greater openness on issues of local police misconduct. Too often walls of secrecy hide not only incidents of brutality but also inadequate responses to these incidents. The public has a right to be shown how thoroughly allegations of misconduct are investigated. Controversial or dangerous tactics should be publicly debated and evaluated instead of left just to police insiders. Since taxpayers often must cover the tab for police misconduct in the form of litigation settlements and awards, they should have oversight and control over systems that can effectively manage the risk of liability while providing for safer, more professional and more effective policing. Finally, the isolation pervasive in the internal culture of many police departments must be broken down in order to minimize the "us vs. them" attitude that complicates the difficult role of police officers and contributes to an atmosphere where abuse is tolerated.

"Police abuse has neither a single cause nor a single cure."

Before anyone claims "it can't happen here," they should first address the following five questions:

(1) Is the mission of police officers realistically defined and understood?

(2) Is there effective leadership that sets an unmistakable tone in words and deeds that abuse and brutality will not be accepted?

(3) Does the police department truly reflect the diversity of the community in which it operates?

(4) Are the department's policies and training programs established openly and designed to comprehensively deter, identify and remedy incidents of police abuse?

(5) Is there an open, independent and credible system of accountability that will ensure that violations of policies and standards will be appropriately handled?

American Civil Liberties Union, *On the Line: Police Brutality and Its Remedies*, April 1991 pamphlet. Reprinted with permission.

Police abuse is caused, in part, by unrealistic and inappropriate expectations of what police officers can and cannot accomplish. Police departments are society's institutions of last resort. Severe societal problems are often left to local law enforcement whether or not they involve criminal justice issues and whether or not police officers have the tools, training and expertise to effectively address them.

"Police chiefs . . . set the tone for their departments in their statements, deeds and attitudes."

For example, in many communities there are increasing demands on police officers to roust homeless people from public places where they are viewed as unsightly or bad for business. Even though poverty and homelessness are not crimes, the implicit messages to some police officers is that they should "do whatever it takes" to protect certain neighborhoods from the depressing sight of poor people. We should not be surprised that officers who are asked to confront people who may have committed no criminal act at all will sometimes cross the line into inappropriate, illegal or abusive behavior.

In some communities, the sheer volume of violent criminal activity can be overwhelming for police officers who are asked to somehow protect the public and to prevent the lawlessness. In some officers, the inevitable frustration can play itself out in incidents of violence and brutality.

When "war" is declared on drugs, the implicit message is "win at all costs." Basic standards of reasonable force and probable cause become mere luxuries. "Wars" are the most extreme exercises in "us vs. them" and necessarily involve the labelling of entire groups of people as "enemies" whether or not they have individually engaged in any wrongful acts. The result can be tactics and actions that are disturbingly racist. "Wars" inevitably involve "collateral damage" on innocent civilians that must be tolerated for the greater cause. Applying these concepts to domestic policing is not only frightening and dangerous, it is ultimately counterproductive.

In 1989, the ACLU brought together 100 criminal justice experts, including police administrators, prosecutors, political officials, and others in a unique three-day conference entitled, "Confronting Crime: New Directions." Three major themes emerged from that conference. First, crime will decrease only after we address the underlying causes of crime—unemployment, poverty and lack of educational opportunities. Second, effective law enforcement is not inconsistent with respect for constitutional rights. And third, community groups and police departments must work cooperatively both on fighting crime and on quality of life issues.

Broader discussion and acknowledgment of these themes on both a local and national level can bring a healthy dose of realism to the expectations we place on police. Police simply will never be able to prevent and solve the enormous problem of crime by themselves. If police officers shoulder the entire burden of fighting crime, the overwhelming scope of the problem will lead to "anything goes" tactics born from frustration and desperation.

Leadership

Even with an appropriate and realistic mission defined for police in a community, actions of officers carrying out that mission can be heavily influenced by the leadership of their department. Police chiefs and administrators set the tone for their departments in their statements, deeds and attitudes towards the communities they serve.

If a chief of police shows contempt for the legitimate concerns of certain communities, the actions of his or her officers will most likely mirror that contempt. If a chief of police is disrespectful or racist in his or her comments about individuals or certain groups of people, the officers may mimic their chief's disdain. In short, it's difficult to have a professional police department led by an unprofessional chief of police.

When incidents of brutality, misconduct or racism occur, the chief's immediate reaction to these incidents will have a great impact on whether the incident will be repeated in the future. A chief that seems more concerned with protecting the department's image than with identifying and disciplining the wrongdoer can send the message that getting caught is a worse sin than the underlying misconduct. In contrast, a willingness to publicly and thoroughly examine even the most embarrassing and damaging incident will demonstrate to both the public and the officers a serious commitment to avoiding the same mistakes in the future.

"Police policies should be subject to public review and debate instead of being . . . the sole province of police insiders."

If the misconduct or policy/training/supervision failure is clear, it must be immediately condemned and addressed. In other incidents where the facts will become apparent only after a more lengthy investigation, the chief must refrain from comments that seem to excuse the conduct before the investigation is even complete. Any sign that abuse will be tolerated or rationalized or covered-up will erode public confidence in the department and encourage future misconduct.

Police departments should reflect as much as possible the ethnic, racial and gender diversity of the communities they serve. A fully-integrated police department will not be immune to problems of brutality. No one would suggest that Latino police officers, for example, will never abuse Latino civilians. However, the lingering problem of local police departments that remain disproportionately white and male, either throughout the department or in the supervisory ranks, is a contributing factor to police abuse in two ways.

First, the dangerous "us vs. them" mentality can be exacerbated in departments, shifts or assignments where officers are not exposed to co-workers and supervisors from different cultural backgrounds. Opening up the profession of policing to people of varied backgrounds and experiences can, over a period of time, lessen the gap between the internal culture and values of a police department and the external culture and value systems of the communities in which they operate.

Second, persistent resistance to affirmative action can heighten tensions within a police department. Tension over racism or equal opportunities in the station house can bubble over into frustration and abuse on the street.

Policy standards reinforced by training programs are often viewed as the most important weapons against police abuse. Many departments adequately cover at least the "basics" on topics like reasonable force, probable cause or use of firearms. However, policies and training programs need to be continuously and openly re-evaluated to ensure they are effective, up-to-date and not inconsistent with the values and priorities of the local community.

Police policies should be subject to public review and debate instead of being viewed as the sole province of police insiders. Open policy-making not only allows police officials to take advantage of community input, it also provides an opportunity for police officials to publicly explain why certain tactics or procedures may be necessary. Local police departments should have little interest in policies or practices that cannot withstand public scrutiny.

Cooperative Solutions

Open and inclusive policy-making can also bring creativity and cooperative solutions to persistent controversies. For example, the San Francisco Police Department faced nearly a decade of lawsuits and problems related to crowd control and use of force against demonstrators. In the wake of the Dolores Huerta incident, a special task force was appointed in 1990 to conduct a comprehensive review of the department's crowd control policies. With active participation from the local ACLU, the police union, department officials and legal and community groups, the result was a new manual that provided clearer and explicit restrictions on the use of force and stronger protections for free expression. While some problems remain, complaints of brutality during demonstrations have decreased dramatically in the nine months the manual has been in effect.

"Internal peer pressure and fear are powerful deterrents to police officers reporting brutality."

The following examples illustrate how going beyond the "basics" in other policy and training areas can help prevent abusive behavior.

Tracking the use of force: Policies governing use of force typically define when force is appropriate and set standards for particular types and degrees of force. However, the use of force should be the exception rather than the rule. Policies should also require a written report any time certain types of force are employed (batons, stun guns, mace, etc.). These use of force reports should, in turn, be evaluated on a case-by-case basis and as part of an ongoing program aimed at spotting problems and patterns. If a particular officer or watch is using force disproportionately often, further inquiries can be made before a tragic incident or lawsuit results. Also, this systematic tracking can help identify particular policy or training problems that are causing force to be used in circumstances when it could be avoided.

Breaking the "code of silence": Internal peer pressure and fear are powerful deterrents to police officers reporting brutality committed by fellow officers. A simple policy requirement that officers report any misconduct they observe will have little effect by itself. A procedure must be developed that realistically allows the reporting to actually take place. Just as it might be inap-

propriate to require a racial or sexual harassment victim to follow the chain of command if the commanding officer has engaged in or tolerated the harassment, a workable procedure must protect the officer reporting the abuse from reprisals from supervisors or other officers. Specialized training should be created to reinforce the importance of exposing violent behavior by other officers and to explicitly describe how incidents can be reported. Finally, as with any policy, failure to report significant misconduct must result in disciplinary sanctions.

Avoiding and de-escalating violence: Since officers must be provided weapons and taught how to use them, they should also be taught special skills that will help them de-escalate situations and avert, whenever possible, situations where force may be necessary. Police officers routinely find themselves in extremely dangerous situations and their acts of bravery are appropriately rewarded. However, some acts of bravery are needlessly risky to themselves and others and should be discouraged rather than encouraged. Officers are trained extensively on that "moment of truth" where they must make a split second decision whether or not to fire their weapon. Techniques that can help lessen the likelihood of ever reaching that moment of truth should also be taught.

Community Relations

Community sensitivity training: Community-police tensions can be reduced by providing training on issues of special significance in particular communities. For example, the ACLU of Georgia worked with the Atlanta Police Department to address concerns of the gay and lesbian community by providing regular sensitivity training at the police academy and regularly meeting with community leaders. The Northern California ACLU recruited homeless activists and individuals in San Francisco to create a special training video and a police academy presentation on homeless issues.

Even model policies aimed at curbing police abuse will have little impact if they are not enforced. The ability to hold officers to policy standards is largely dependent on civilian witnesses and victims of misconduct being willing to actually file complaints. Only a tiny fraction of brutality incidents will be captured on videotape or reported by police officers.

However, civilian cooperation will remain elusive if the public does not have confidence in the police department's process for investigating misconduct complaints. There are two factors that are crucial to the credibility of any investigative system: the degree of openness in the system and the presence or absence of an independent civilian review mechanism.

Openness: Too often police complaint procedures seem designed as though only the department and accused officer have any legitimate interest in the process. Both the public's interest in evaluating the effectiveness of their complaint system and the complainant's interest in learning how their own complaint is handled are undermined by a fundamental lack of openness. Once a complaint is filed, people are often asked, in effect, to blindly accept that it will be handled appropriately.

The Blanket of Secrecy

The blanket of secrecy that covers many complaint processes leaves even the complainants in the dark about the results of their own cases. This secrecy hides both inadequate investigations and inadequate disciplinary responses to serious acts of misconduct.

Police officers have legitimate privacy interests about personal information regarding, for example, their off-duty conduct, their home addresses or family relations. However, when an on-duty officer is alleged to have brutalized a member of the public in public and the taxpayers may be required to pay not only that officer's salary but also any settlement or award that results from the incident, the public and complainant should have the right to basic information about the investigation of that event.

Only a small percentage of police misconduct cases are sustained. It is important to be able to show to the complainant and the public that all cases are fully and fairly investigated and that the evidence supports the conclusion that no misconduct occurred. Such information enhances public confidence in both the department and its complaint system. As for the sustained cases, secrecy about the investigation and results prevents other officers in the department from determining whether or not their fellow officer is being "scapegoated" and prevents the public from evaluating whether or not the discipline is appropriate for the offense.

"The lack of independent civilian involvement in the police complaint process . . . undercuts the credibility of many systems."

In the absence of particularly sensitive issues (for example, rape or sexual harassment allegations) at the conclusion of an investigation three types of basic information about the complaint should be available to both the complainant and the public: (1) the finding; (2) the investigative or disposition report reviewing the investigation and analyzing the evidence; and (3) the specific disciplinary action that resulted, if any.

Civilian Review Boards and Agencies: The lack of independent civilian involvement in the police complaint process also undercuts the credibility of many systems. Internal affairs processes that involve the police policing themselves are viewed by the public with great skepticism. From a complainant's perspective, the idea of taking your complaint to the very police department that may have brutalized you and/or accused you of criminal conduct is particularly intimidating. Civilian review boards or agencies created to independently investigate complaints, therefore, can help overcome public skepticism and encourage community cooperation.

Of the 25 largest U.S. cities, 13 now have some official civilian oversight board or agency monitoring their police department. Many of these were created in the last five years. The trend towards civilian oversight has been fueled by concerns about misconduct and by fiscal concerns. In an era of scarce government resources, it is particularly important that localities attempt to minimize their risk of liability for police abuse by identifying problem officers or tactics in a timely fashion. A civilian review system that enjoys public confidence is better able to provide this early warning system than less credible internal affairs processes.

Police opponents to civilian review continue to argue that only police officers can fairly review the actions of other officers. But in places like San Diego County, Indianapolis, Minneapolis and Long Beach where new civilian review systems have recently been created, these arguments are no longer persuasive. With appropriate training, civilian investigators and board members can perform their oversight function objectively and with a high degree of professionalism.

There is increasing recognition that since we give police officers unique powers to make arrests and use force, civilian oversight of how they exercise those powers is particularly important. Just as systems of independent checks and balances serve to curb abuses of power in other government institutions, civilian review serves this same function with local police departments.

Models of Civilian Oversight

There are several models of civilian oversight. Civilian review boards are typically panels of appointed members that review allegations of police abuse in a hearing format. Civilian oversight agencies, in contrast, use trained professional civilian investigators to probe misconduct allegations by collecting evidence and interviewing witnesses before or instead of a hearing. Some civilian systems review cases as "appeals" after a police investigation. Others require all cases to be originally investigated by the civilian system. Some handle all types of complaints and others only certain categories.

Regardless of the particular model, civilian oversight systems do not by themselves solve police abuse problems. Many systems lack adequate authority, independence or staffing to be effective. Even strong models of civilian review need ongoing commitment and backing from local officials to overcome resistance from police officers who often continue to oppose the agencies or boards even after their creation.

"Civilian oversight systems do not by themselves solve police abuse problems."

However, the presence of certain key components greatly enhances the effectiveness and credibility of particular civilian review systems:

(1) Independence. While the ultimate power to discipline officers should reside with the police chief or his superiors, there must be independent civil review. Civilian review boards must be fully empowered to investigate, conduct hearings, subpoena witnesses and report their findings and recommendations on misconduct complaints to the public.

(2) Investigatory Power. Merely auditing or reviewing how police internal affairs systems handle complaints is not as effective as independently investigating and issuing findings on complaints.

(3) Mandatory Police Cooperation. Either through legal mandate or subpoena power, civilian oversight systems must have complete access to police witnesses and documents.

(4) Adequate Funding. A civilian review system should not be a lower budgetary priority than a police internal affairs system merely because it is comprised of civilians.

(5) Hearings. Whether conducted by a board or individual hearing officers, a hearing component provides an important tool for solving difficult credibility questions and greatly enhances public confidence in the system.

(6) Reflect Diversity of Community. As a body

designed to represent the public, civilian review systems should be broadly representative of the communities they serve.

(7) Policy Recommendations. In addition to holding officers accountable, civilian oversight can help spot problem policies and tactics and provide a forum for developing reforms.

(8) Statistical Analysis. Public statistical reports can detail trends in allegations and early warning systems can identify individual officers who receive an unusually high number of complaints.

(9) Separate Offices. If the civilian oversight system is housed at police headquarters and if complaints may not be filed at non-police locations, community confidence and the perception of independence can suffer.

(10) Role in Discipline. The findings of the civilian review system must have a meaningful impact on whether and how much discipline results in particular cases. If the findings are routinely ignored, the civilian oversight system will soon lose public confidence.

The problem of police abuse is primarily a local problem which must be addressed in each local area. However, the federal government also has an obligation to protect people from abuse by local police. The federal government should be playing a more active role in this effort. Some recommendations toward that end are presented in the next section.

The Federal Response

The federal government's response to the problem of police abuse by local law enforcement agencies has been largely indifferent and not effective. The Justice Department has not fully exercised the power it has in this area. The President has failed until the King incident to take the problem seriously, and that indifference has led to a less than forthright response. At the same time, the Justice Department lacks a key power: the legal authority to bring civil enforcement actions to challenge patterns and practices of police abuse in violation of federally protected civil rights when there are no other effective means of redress.

The Justice Department should more aggressively exercise its existing authority under the provisions of 18 U.S.C. §§ 241 and 242 to prosecute law enforcement officers for federal criminal civil rights violations. Congress should give the Justice Department additional authority to deal effectively with patterns and practices of police abuse. Congress should also condition the receipt of federal funds on the institution of local reforms that would deal more effectively at the local level with the police abuse described in this report. It should also consider making it easier for private citizens to sue for damages.

"The federal government's response to the problem of police abuse . . . has been largely indifferent."

The Justice Department has the power to bring federal criminal civil rights prosecutions under 18 U.S.C. §§ 241 and 242. These Reconstruction era civil rights statutes provide for criminal penalties for willful violations of federally protected civil rights and conspiracies to violate these rights. The statutes provide for penalties of up to ten years imprisonment for violations, or any term of years if death results. These statutes, however, have been narrowly interpreted by the Supreme Court, making prosecution difficult.

Since 1985, the Department of Justice has received approximately 8,000 complaints of criminal civil rights violations by local police each year. It is clear that these complaints represent only a fraction of the police abuse in the nation each year. One police abuse referral agency, the Police Misconduct Lawyer Referral Service, recorded more than 2,500 police abuse complaints in 1990 in the Los Angeles area alone. Complaints to the Justice Department have declined by 20% since 1981, at a time when complaints about police abuse appear to have increased nationally.

The Justice Department conducts an investigation in fewer than half the cases brought to its attention each year. Moreover, attorneys familiar with the FBI [Federal Bureau of Investigation] investigative process believe that the majority of investigations are cursory. The FBI does little more than accumulate the local police reports, which themselves may be unreliable, as the Rodney King incident graphically illustrates. The ACLU is aware of a number of cases of severe police abuse where the Justice Department failed to undertake even a cursory investigation into brutality allegations from lawyers representing the victims.

Out of the approximately 3,000 complaints that are investigated in a year, only about 50 cases are presented to a grand jury for possible indictments. That translates into prosecutions in little more than one half of one percent of the complaints received by the Department of Justice. Moreover, a significant number of those charged under the criminal civil rights statutes are prison guards not law enforcement officers. In 1990, only 35 law enforcement officers nationwide were charged with criminal civil rights violations.

"The Justice Department should play a more aggressive role in enforcing federal criminal sanctions against law enforcement officials."

The Justice Department should play a more aggressive role in enforcing federal criminal sanctions against law enforcement officials who violate civil rights. While the Justice Department activities have broadened in scope over the past decade, the resources devoted to the investigation and prosecution of criminal civil rights violations have not increased. The Justice Department cannot undertake serious investigations of police abuse if it does not allocate sufficient resources to this vital task.

Local U.S. attorneys' officers should be encouraged to bring such actions on their own initiative, instead of being restricted by internal department guidelines as they are now. A more aggressive enforcement posture, based on independent FBI investigations into police abuse allegations would send a much needed message that federally protected civil rights cannot be ignored.

Finally, Congress should consider amending or supplementing 18 U.S.C. §§ 241 and 242 in order to facilitate prosecution of law enforcement excesses while maintaining the due process rights of accused officers.

The Absence of Authority

The absence of authority for the Justice Department to undertake pattern and practice lawsuits where police abuse is widespread in a community is a fundamental problem that Congress must correct. If the Justice Department had such authority it could seek federal court relief that would address broader patterns and practices of police abuse and prevent incidents like the Rodney King incident, instead of focussing exclusively on the narrower range of abuses involving criminal wrongdoing by officers.

The Justice Department has a unique and vital role to play in this area because of limits on the ability of private litigants to challenge such practices and the inability of internal disciplinary systems or local prosecutors to restrain police misconduct effectively.

Existing Supreme Court cases severely limit the ability of private litigants to address these problems through private civil rights suits under 42 U.S.C. § 1983. These cases prevent most private pattern and practice police abuse suits from being brought because no individual or class of plaintiffs has standing in federal court.

This principle is illustrated most vividly in *City of Los Angeles v. Lyons,* an ACLU case challenging the use of chokeholds by the LAPD [Los Angeles Police Department]. Since 1978, 27 people, most of them African Americans, have died as a result of LAPD chokeholds. Most of these deaths occurred before 1982 Police Commission restrictions on the use of the practice. In *Lyons*, the Supreme Court found that the plaintiff, who had previously been choked unconscious, had no standing to challenge the practice because he could not demonstrate that he was likely to be choked again. As a result no one had the ability to bring a lawsuit to stop this deadly practice. The Lyons principle prevents private civil rights plaintiffs from obtaining truly effective relief to put a stop to even the most egregious of police practices.

Previously in 1976, in *Rizzo v. Goode*, the Supreme Court overturned a district court injunction which sought to remedy a pervasive pattern of abuse in Philadelphia in the context of a lawsuit by private groups and individuals using federal civil rights law to remedy these abuses. The burdens of *Rizzo* and *Lyons* make it nearly impossible for private litigants to put an end to the most pervasive patterns of police abuse by means of federal civil rights suits. Moreover, lawsuits seeking damages may result in monetary awards to individuals, but these awards have not always been effective tools to prevent future abuses.

"The Justice Department must also maintain national data about police abuse complaints."

In the 1970's, after private litigation was thwarted in *Rizzo*, the Justice Department embarked on an eight-month investigation into complaints of police abuse in Philadelphia and filed a pattern and practice suit challenging the widespread abuses discovered in the course of this investigation. But in *United States v. City of Philadelphia*, 644 F.2d 187 (3d Cir. 1980), the Court of Appeals for the Third Circuit found that the Justice Department lacked the authority to bring such pattern and practice suits in the absence of specific statutory authority.

The Justice Department has been given this authority in many areas involving constitutional and civil rights, including the rights of prisoners under the Civil Rights of Institutionalized Persons Act; voting rights under Title VI of the Civil Rights Act of 1960; public accommodations, under Title II, prohibitions on segregation in jails, under Title III, and rights against employment discrimination, under Title VII, of the Civil Rights Act of 1964. But the Justice Department does not have the same authority to protect people from a pattern and practice of police abuse.

The Justice Department must be given this authority and it should be provided with the resources to exercise it.

Other Federal Responses

Congress should also consider changes to 42 U.S.C. §1983, the basic civil rights statute relied upon by private litigants to redress violations of civil rights, so that §1983 can become an even more effective weapon against police abuse.

In recent cases, the Supreme Court has erected unnecessary barriers to imposing liability on municipalities whose police departments violate constitutional rights. For instance, a city is not liable for actions of its officers unless it is proved the misconduct was done pursuant to an established custom or policy of the city. Moreover, recovery against individual officers is often barred by immunity doctrines created by the courts. Legislation is needed to remove these barriers and make state and local governments fully responsible for the unconstitutional actions of their police departments.

Another needed reform would be to permit federal courts to award punitive damages against cities that have policies and practices of police abuse. In 1981, the Supreme Court decided that punitive damages could not be awarded under §1983 in even the most egregious cases of municipal wrongdoing. The availability of punitive damages against state and local governments who tolerate or encourage police abuse would be an important tool in the struggle to eradicate these abuses.

The federal government should also condition the receipt of federal funds by state and local government on the undertaking of needed reforms by local law enforcement agencies. . . .

Federal technical assistance should be made available to aid local law enforcement agencies with inadequate policies and procedures.

Federal law should require that local law enforcement officers be accountable to the public through adequate systems for the consideration of civilian complaints and internal discipline. . . .

The Justice Department must also maintain national data about police abuse complaints and the local responses to such complaints, just as the Justice Department maintains crime statistics. The American people should have information about the patterns of police abuse and the response to this abuse at the local and national level. This information is also vital to Congress' oversight function.

The persistence of police brutality cannot be viewed in historical isolation. The problem did not begin with the Rodney King incident in Los Angeles in March 1991. Nor will it end there. In truth, police brutality has always been with us. All of us must acknowledge that. The question is how to remedy it.

First and foremost, we must recognize that police abuse is fundamentally a local problem. It is here reform must begin. Police chiefs and administrators bear primary responsibility for developing and implementing proper and workable procedures and standards of performance and accountability. They must also ensure that their police are well trained so that they do not perform as an occupying army that views citizens as aliens or enemies, but rather that they act as a community resource working in conjunction with other social resources to eradicate citizen problems. Crime is not the exclusive responsibility of the police.

The federal government should also con-

tribute significantly to preventing police abuse in two ways: The Justice Department can prosecute egregious cases where individual officers have violated the civil rights of citizens, and it can file "pattern and practice" lawsuits to enjoin police abuse where it is systematic. This latter authority would require additional congressional legislation.

"Police abuse is fundamentally a local problem."

Third, politicians and public officials should declare a moratorium on the use of "war" as a metaphor for solving complicated social problems.

Finally, federal and state lawmakers must devise and fund social, economic and education programs that address the root causes of the problems that afflict our cities and act as a catalyst for the crime all of us wish to prevent.

Ending police brutality is a difficult task facing us at this particular time in our history. For the past decade, the Supreme Court has undermined a number of safeguards guaranteed by the Bill of Rights. At the same time, successive administrations under Presidents Reagan and Bush have advocated expansion of police powers, often at the expense of the constitutional rights of the accused. Those developments, taken together, have set the wrong tone and sent the wrong signal.

Pattern of Brutality

Our communities cannot simply ignore those signals or the past pattern of police brutality and its causes, for the problem will only worsen. The means to correct the problem are well known. What is needed now is the political will to implement them.

Sting Operations by Private Investigators Can Deter Police Brutality

Gene Stone

About the Author: *Gene Stone is a writer for* People Weekly, *a general-interest magazine.*

Two-thirty A.M. Prairie Avenue, Lennox, Calif., outside Los Angeles. Private detective Don Jackson and a friend are driving an aging Pontiac through the streets when, suddenly, lights flash and sirens howl. State Highway Patrolman Kevin Koko pulls them over, accusing Jackson's friend of driving erratically. He has not been, and when Jackson disagrees, Koko tells him he will have to take a sobriety test. Jackson refuses.

After a brief argument, Koko abruptly returns to his car without issuing a citation to the two black men. Thinking about the incident later, Jackson says he believes Koko suddenly recognized him and chose not to force a showdown in court. Don Jackson is no ordinary citizen. Earlier, his face was posted in police stations all over the Los Angeles area following an ugly occurrence in Long Beach, just 20 miles south. Jackson had been pulled over there too. And that time the encounter escalated into violence: A police officer allegedly threw Jackson against a plate glass window, which shattered around his head.

That confrontation made the evening news because Jackson, 31, was being videotaped not only by his partners, David Lynn, 38, and Joe Travers, 32, but by an NBC news team they'd tipped off about a possible incident. Such "stings," in fact, are part of the operating procedure for the Jackson Lynn Travers agency, which bills itself as the only public-interest private detective agency in the country. JLT specializes in exposing police brutality, particularly against minorities. Both the agency's mission and its tactics have become increasingly controversial since the Long Beach episode.

"They are heroes," says California State Assemblywoman Maxine Waters from L.A. "No one ever documented racism in the police before." Not surprisingly, the police take a more jaundiced view of their motives. "These stings are theatrics designed for the men's personal advantage. Nothing good comes out of this for anyone except them," says Mike Tracy, president of the Long Beach Police Officers Association. "There are examples of police misconduct, but there are more viable ways to expose it."

The Lennox police refused to comment publicly on the episode there—which was also videotaped—but the next day, an internal memo from Sheriff Sherman Block said that the driver's "actions were consistent with those of a person driving under the influence," adding that Jackson's clothing was "similar to gang clothing." (Jackson had been wearing a dark sweater and a baseball cap.) The memo urged officers to be alert to the possibility of such "artificial" incidents in the future.

"A police officer allegedly threw Jackson against a plate glass window. . . . That confrontation made the evening news."

In fact, JLT, acting on complaints of police brutality in the Los Angeles area, has conducted four such stings in the past two years, incurring three incidents of what they describe as "harassment" (being stopped by police without reason), including the violence in Long Beach. Even before viewing the Long Beach videotape, Los Angeles Chief of Police Daryl F. Gates called it "a crazy, crazy, stupid, idiotic act." Long Beach Mayor Ernie Kell was more restrained. "Perhaps our police overreacted," he said. "I don't think Mr. Jackson was malicious, but he knew the right buttons to push. We have 680 policemen—maybe one or two overreact. I don't think that what Don Jackson does is the best way to weed them out." Nevertheless, two Long Beach officers are facing charges as a result of the incident—one for assault, both for writing a false report—and the city has brought in an outside investigator to examine charges of police brutality.

"They turn their videos over to lawyers representing victims of police brutality."

When a town is targeted (often through L.A.'s Police Misconduct Referral Board, where Lynn volunteers), Jackson rides through the streets at night in an old car, while Lynn and Travers follow with a minicam. They turn their videos over to lawyers representing victims of police brutality or to community groups. Some of these clients can pay, but 80 percent of JLT's work is *pro bono*. (They also earn lecture fees and are paid as expert witnesses.)

"We don't do this for money. We didn't even *want* to do this," says Jackson. "It was shoved down our throats by our lives." Travers and Jackson are both ex-policemen, and Lynn is an ex-Marine who served in Vietnam but was given a hasty honorable discharge after organizing a series of nonviolent protests against what he perceived as racial injustices. ("Black soldiers were victims," he says. "They were given all the dangerous missions.") Since then, he has been a full-time activist for causes including nuclear disarmament and opposition to apartheid. Unmarried, he lives in a Latino neighborhood near downtown L.A.

Joe Travers also served in the armed forces before joining the Hawthorne Police Department in 1981. But during training, Travers says he witnessed repeated acts of police brutality. He complained and was eventually asked to leave the force. That scenario was repeated in 1987, when Travers signed on with the city's Rapid Transit District Police. When he complained about other officers' treatment of minorities, says Travers, it was he who lost his job once again. Married, with a 10-month-old son, Travers has since sued, and the FBI [Federal Bureau of Investigations] is investigating his charges of civil rights violations by the RTD force. (RTD refuses to comment on Travers's suit.)

Don Jackson's father, Woodrow, served 28 years with the L.A. County Sheriff's Office. But he never told his children of the racism he encountered on the force, so Jackson was surprised when he joined the police himself in 1980. "The officers told me things like 'black women liked being raped,'" he says. Worse were the regular instances of brutality he claims to have seen—and refused to participate in. "The other officers got down on me for not blowing people away," he says.

Jackson was promoted to sergeant in 1986, but the trouble continued. Then in April 1987, Jackson's father was stopped while driving in middle-class Pomona and allegedly beaten by police—even though he was carrying his deputy sheriff's badge at the time. "It broke me for good," says Jackson. "I couldn't stay on the force anymore." He was placed on administrative leave and recently began receiving a $2,200-a-month pension for a stress-related disability.

Investigating the Police

Eventually, Jackson, Lynn and Travers got to know each other through their activities with various police watchdog groups. Travers had a private detective's license, so the three decided to begin investigating the police because, says Lynn, "no one else would stand up—we felt we had no choice." Adds Travers: "The fact that we've all been on the other side is a real strength."

In 1989 the three formed the Jackson Lynn Travers agency and decided that involving the media would help bring them clients. That has not made JLT very popular. Inglewood Councilman Garland Hardeman, a friend of Jackson's who is also an LAPD training officer, claims he recently saw a photo of Jackson with a bloody arrow through his head on a police bulletin board. "They hate him," he says. "They're just waiting for him to make a mistake so they can harm him."

"Travers says he received several death threats."

Jackson claims they've already tried. "I've been run off the road by cops trying to intimidate me," he says. Lynn attests that someone recently broke into his office and ransacked his desk. And Travers says he received several death threats when his wife was pregnant.

Still, the JLT partners believe that only a small percentage of officers are guilty of using excessive force. Nor do they necessarily fault these officers. Police training, they say, neglects civil rights. Moreover, says Jackson, "they never teach you how to get along with people, or how to back down. Training teaches you to be a clone. How to take orders and never snitch."

Minor Celebrities

Since Long Beach, Jackson, Lynn and Travers have become minor celebrities, with local television appearances, front-page newspaper stories and a benefit, featuring Jesse Jackson and Dionne Warwick, which raised money to support JLT's work. A criminal-procedures course at Harvard Law School is even using their sting tapes in class. Too well known now to carry on their work in Southern California, the self-proclaimed "people's detectives" have decided to take their show on the road, perhaps to New York City. In the L.A. area, at least, they've made their point. Clay Bryant, the Vice Mayor of Pomona—where Jackson's father was allegedly assaulted—said, "I've asked Don Jackson to come up with a proposal to develop a more sensitive approach for our police department. I hope we can bring him in. I think he's brilliant. He exposes the flaws in the system."

Appendix: A Police Brutality Case Study

On July 26, 1985, an 18-year-old male in San Diego, California, was arrested for indecent exposure and illegal drug use. Brian D., one of the arresting officers, wrote the following in his arrest report:

Officer Walter P. and myself responded to a call of a indecent exposure. When we arrived we were told by witnesses the subject was sitting on the stairs. We approached the subject from behind and observed him unbutton his pants and start to fondle his genitals. The subject then jumped up and started to walk east through the apartment complex. He attempted to climb up to the second story window by pulling off the screen on the first floor window and using it for leverage (this was done on one of the apartments located on the south side of the apartment complex.)

The subject then turned around and started to walk towards us. We backed off, but when the subject spotted us, I ordered him to his knees. He dropped to his knees and put his hands behind his back. I placed my handcuffs on the subject while Walter P. covered me.

Once the handcuffs were on the subject he started to fight us. We called for additional help and restrained the subject. Once cover arrived, I hog-tied the subject and he was further restrained by additional officers. The subject was placed into a marked police car and transported to the western sub-station.

Additional Information: During the course of the fight, before additional help arrived, both Walter P. and myself had to use our PR-24 batons on the subject to restrain him. This was done by blows to his upper torso on the back of

Source: Civil Service Commission of the city of San Diego, August 7, 1986.

the subject. The subject acted in an irrational and crazy manner. He uttered comments that at times didn't make any sense. It appeared that the male was under the influence of an unknown drug.

The incident, however, was not over. A person who happened to witness the arrest complained to the police department that one of the officers had used unnecessary brutality. The allegations prompted an internal investigation by the San Diego Police Department. Reprinted here are excerpts from documents resulting from that investigation.

While no one incident can be said to be typical of all police brutality cases, the following documents do give an interesting example of one such incident and one police department's response. It shows some of the steps police departments take to investigate events, and also shows the importance of citizen action in initiating complaints and serving as witnesses. Names have been changed to protect privacy.

Sergeant Peter K. of the San Diego Police Department, Internal Affairs Division, began his investigation July 29, 1985, three days after the incident and after a witness, Ronald L., filed a complaint with the San Diego Police Department. After reviewing Ronald L.'s written complaint and the arrest report from the incident, Peter K. interviewed Ronald L. on July 30. Peter K. wrote down the results of the interview as follows:

Interview of Ronald L. On July 30, 1985, at 0850 hours, I interviewed Ronald L. regarding an incident that occurred on July 26, 1985, at his apartment complex.

"The subject acted in an irrational and crazy manner."

Ronald L. said an unknown man, approximately nineteen years old, was running through the apartment complex looking for a friend or maybe his apartment. He said the man was disoriented and appeared to be under the influence of some type of drug. Ronald L. said someone must have called the Police Department.

Ronald L. said he was made aware of the incident by his wife who was visiting at an apartment that the man had attempted to enter. Ronald L. said he went to the area near that apartment and saw two officers with a man lying face down on the ground. He said one officer was an Hispanic male [Walter P.] and the other, a Caucasian male [Brian D.]. He said the Caucasian officer had his knee on the man's back and was jabbing him in his kidneys with a baton.

"The kick was so hard it 'sounded like a watermelon being dropped.'"

Ronald L. said he heard the Caucasian officer saying, "Bend your knees, fucker," repeatedly. Ronald L. said other officers arrived and started to lift the man from the ground to put him in a police car. Ronald L. said as the man was lifted, he saw the Hispanic officer kick the man in the face with his right foot. He said the kick was so hard it "sounded like a watermelon being dropped."

Ronald L. said a lady, who also saw the officer kick the man, yelled out that it was not necessary to kick the man and said, "I wish I had your badge number, I would report you." Ronald L. said the officer said, "Shut up," and turned his badge around on his shirt so the number could not be read. The other officers kept telling everyone to stay back. Ronald L. said the officers put the man in a police car and drove away.

Next, Peter K. interviewed Sharon T., a neighbor who had also witnessed the incident.

Interview of Sharon T. On July 31, 1985, at 1151 hours, I interviewed Sharon T. regarding an arrest that was made by Officers Brian D. and Walter P. on July 26, 1985, in the apartment complex.

Sharon T. said she was closing the upstairs bedroom window of her apartment when she saw two women standing on the grass below watching someone on the ground with seven or eight officers on top of him. The man appeared to be angry. The officers were trying to handcuff him.

Sharon T. said she told her husband what she saw and they went outside to watch. She said the officers handcuffed the man. She said she saw one of the officers kick the man in the face after he was handcuffed and on the ground.

Sharon T. said a woman known as "Debbie" yelled, "Hey, cool it. What are you doing? I wish I had your badge number; I'd report you." Sharon T. said the officer just turned and walked away. She said another officer yelled back, "what if he was doing to you what he was trying to do to her," as he pointed at another woman in the crowd. She said it appeared that the officers were attempting to protect the officer who kicked the man.

Peter K. interviewed several other civilians who had witnessed the incident. On August 1, he interviewed Patricia L., the wife of the person who originally filed the complaint.

Interview of Patricia L. On August 1, 1985, at 1212 hours, I interviewed Patricia L. regarding the arrest of Jason B. on July 26, 1985.

Patricia L. said she was talking with her sister-in-law, when she heard several loud banging noises. She said it sounded like someone banging something against a car. She said they went outside to see what was causing the noise and saw a group of people gathered nearby. Several people were motioning to them to stay back.

An Intruder

Patricia L. said a young man, eighteen or nineteen years old, with long blond hair, ran up to them and stood staring at them as though he was lost. She said he took a seat on a nearby staircase. She said she and her sister-in-law went back inside her sister-in-law's apartment. The man tried to get into the apartment, prompting Patricia L. to call her husband at their apartment on the telephone.

Patricia L. said two police cars arrived at about the time her husband came to the apartment. She said the police officers had the man on the ground and were telling him to bend his knees. She said the police officers were hitting the man in his back as the man swore at the police officers. She said additional officers arrived and eventually eight officers were there.

No Apparent Reason

Patricia L. said the officers were trying to handcuff the man's hands to his feet. She said the man stopped swearing and said, "I'm sorry, I'm sorry, I didn't mean it." She said the man was face down on the ground with his hands and feet bound when an officer walked over and kicked the man in his head. She said she did not know which officer kicked the man but she saw an officer kick the man for no apparent reason. She said the officers were also hitting the man in his back during the struggle. She said that, suddenly, the man did not move anymore. She said she was not sure if he was unconscious or under the influence of drugs.

Patricia L. said the officers took the man to the police car. One officer told them that in his condition, the man could kill someone. She said the crowd left and so did the police officers.

After talking to civilian witnesses, Peter K. then began interviewing police officers who were at the scene. First he questioned Brian D., the officer who wrote the original arrest report and the partner of Walter P., the accused officer.

Interview of Officer Brian D. On August 6, 1985, at 0726 hours, I interviewed Officer Brian D., regarding the arrest of Jason B. on July 26, 1985.

Officer Brian D. said he and Officer Walter P. responded to a radio call regarding some type of disturbance. He said when they arrived, they were directed to the suspect's location by several people in the apartment complex. He said the suspect was lying on the sidewalk near a stairway. The people said the suspect had jumped into cars and was trying to get into people's houses.

Officer Brian D. said the suspect had started to disrobe when he and Walter P. arrived. He said he immediately thought the suspect was on some type of drug. He said they backed off and watched the suspect for a while. He said the sus-pect tried to climb up to a second story window. He said he requested cover. The suspect walked around the corner and saw them, at which time Brian D. said he ordered the suspect to the ground.

Officer Brian D. said the suspect got on his knees and put his hands behind his back. He said they handcuffed the suspect. He said the suspect started to fight just as the handcuffs were applied. He said they fought the suspect for about two minutes before other officers arrived and the cordcuff was applied.

Officer Brian D. said he was told what happened regarding Officer Walter P. kicking the suspect. He stated Walter P. said he just pushed the suspect's face with his boot because the suspect spat at Walter P. Brian D. said his head was turned at the time as he was "catching his breath." The other officers told Brian D., "Hey, get your partner out of here, man, and tell him to knock it off." Brian D. said he did not see Walter P. kick the suspect but "everybody" told him that it had happened. Brian D. said there were at least six officers present at the time and he was certain that some of them had to have seen Walter P. kick the suspect.

"He was hitting the suspect with his baton to get him to 'loosen up.'"

Brian D. was asked, "How much fighting can this guy do when he's already in handcuffs?" Brian D. said, "He was giving us a ride like a bucking bronco. He was stiff and rigid as a board, and just kicking up and down. We were fighting just to get his legs cranked up so we could cordcuff him." Brian D. said they (six or more officers) could not just drag the suspect over and put him in a police car. Brian D. said the suspect weighed about one hundred sixty pounds.

Brian D. said he was hitting the suspect with his baton to get him to "loosen up." He said he was hitting him in the back area and in the back of his legs to get him to bend his legs. He admits to yelling, "Bend your fucking knees," at the suspect.

Officer Brian D. said he heard the lady tell Walter P. that it was not necessary for him to kick the suspect. He said the lady came up from behind them and started saying, "Hey, that's not cool. We want to know, what's your name?" Brian D. said he knew something had happened. He said he did not know if Walter P. ever told the lady his name.

Peter K. then interviewed several other police officers involved in the incident. Excerpted here are accounts of interviews from three of the officers, Robert W., Stephen R., and Charles N.

Interview of Officer Robert W. On August 14, 1985, at 0518 hours, I interviewed Officer Robert W. regarding the arrest of Jason B. on July 26, 1985.

Officer Robert W. told me he received a radio call because of a "mental case" possibly on drugs. He said this person was running around "terrorizing" the neighborhood. He said he did not remember any of the other specifics of the call.

Officer Robert W. said Officers Brian D. and Walter P. were the first to arrive. Shortly after their arrival Robert W. said he remembers a "cover now" call being broadcast. He said when he arrived, Brian D. and Walter P. had the suspect handcuffed and face down on the grass. One officer was pinning the neck and shoulders of the suspect while Officer Brian D. was attempting to apply the cordcuff to the suspect's legs.

Afraid of PCP

Officer Robert W. said he assisted Brian D. with the suspect's legs. He said the suspect displayed remarkable strength. He said he thought the suspect was under the influence of phencyclidine (PCP). Robert W. said the suspect was able to straighten his legs while he was lying on them. Finally, they were successful in applying the cordcuff.

Robert W. said there were several officers present besides the three officers who actively engaged in the struggle. He said there were at least six officers there at that time. He said they stood up and were trying to catch their breath. Robert W. said he turned on his flashlight to check the suspect for any obvious injuries. He said another officer also used a flashlight to check the suspect.

"He thought the suspect was under the influence of PCP."

Robert W. said Officer Walter P. told the officer to turn off the flashlight. He said as soon as the flashlight was off, Officer Walter P. kicked the suspect in the head. A woman who was standing twenty to twenty-five feet to Walter P.'s rear said, "Hey, that's not cool," as soon as Walter P. kicked the man. The woman said he should not have done that. Robert W. said a bystander told the woman that the officers were just doing their jobs. Robert W. said he told Walter P. to get away from the scene because Walter P. was obviously upset.

Robert W. said the woman contacted Walter P. as Walter P. walked toward the police cars. He said they talked but it was not a heated conversation because he could not hear their voices. He said he thought the woman just wanted Walter P.'s name.

Robert W. said it was determined that he and Officer Stephen R. would transport the suspect because they were third watch units. He said they put the suspect in Officer Charles N.'s car.

Robert W. said he walked around and talked to some of the citizens who said the suspect walked into their homes. He said he was the last officer to leave the scene.

Robert W. said he was questioned by Sergeant C. about the incident. He said he told the sergeant that he saw Walter P. kick the suspect.

Robert W. said the suspect had a "mouse" on his face (right eye) that he could have suffered when kicked by Walter P. He said he thought Walter P. kicked the suspect in the head.

Interview of Officer Stephen R. On August 14, 1985, at 0554 hours, I interviewed Officer Stephen R. regarding the incident that occurred on July 26, 1985.

Officer Stephen R. said he went to the site of the incident to what he thought, according to the radio broadcast, was a man under the influence of phencyclidine (PCP). Stephen R. said he was walking up to the scene when a "Code-4" was broadcast.

Officer Stephen R. said he walked up to the scene because he was assigned to third watch and he was aware that second watch officers were present. (It was near shift change.) Stephen R. said he saw Jason B. face down, "hogtied" and handcuffed. He said he asked if Jason B. "was PCP or what." Someone replied, "Yeah, they think he's PCP."

"He could not speculate as to how the suspect got the lump under his eye."

Stephen R. said he turned and looked to see if there was any other third watch unit present so he could let the second watch units go. He said he heard a woman scream, "There's no need to do that, there's no need to do that." He said the woman was pointing at Officer Walter P. and saying, "What's his name? What's his name?" Stephen R. said he heard a man tell the woman to "just leave the officers alone, they were just doing their jobs and that the guy asked for it."

Stephen R. said he volunteered to assist Officer Robert W. with transporting the subject to jail.

Stephen R. said he did not witness any part of the struggle and stated the man was already handcuffed when he arrived. He said he did not notice if the suspect suffered any injuries. I showed Stephen R. a booking photograph of Ja-

son B. depicting some minor swelling around the right eye. Stephen R. said it was the first time he noticed the lump. He said the suspect was face down most of the time until they arrived at the Central Station.

Stephen R. said he and Robert W. removed the cordcuff leg restraint from the suspect at the Central Station. He said the suspect started "going crazy, but he seemed to mellow out."

Stephen R. said he could not speculate as to how the suspect got the lump under his eye. He said he did not see Walter P. kick the suspect, but he heard the woman say "there was no need for him to do that." Stephen R. said he did not attempt to find out what it was the woman was referring to.

Interview of Officer Charles N. On August 15, 1985, at 1525 hours, I interviewed Officer Charles N. regarding the incident that occurred on July 26, 1985.

Officer Charles N. said he and his partner, Officer Keith F., were on a "stakeout" for a homicide suspect at Doctor's Hospital when an "expedite cover call" was broadcast. He said he covered the call and assisted with handcuffing a PCP (Phencyclidine) suspect. He said two officers had the suspect down on the grass between the buildings when he arrived. He said they were wrestling around with the suspect and he walked over and put his knees on the suspect's back to hold him down.

Cops' Testimony

Officer Charles N. said there were four officers wrestling with the suspect until they got the handcuffs applied. He said additional officers had arrived and assisted with applying the cordcuff restraint. Charles N. said he used his weight to hold the suspect on the ground while the other officers handcuffed him. He said the suspect was fighting with the officers throughout the struggle. He said judging from the suspect's strength and the amount of resistance the suspect demonstrated, he felt the suspect was under the influence of PCP. Charles N. emphasized that he weighs in excess of two hundred forty pounds and with the weight of the other officers on him, the suspect was still attempting to get up.

Officer Charles N. said he did not see any officer hit the suspect with a baton. He said he did not hear any officer use obscene language directed at the suspect. He said he did not remember seeing any officer with a baton. He said he did not notice any signs of injury to the suspect. I showed Charles N. a booking photograph of the suspect and asked him to describe the picture. Charles N. responded, "He's got a mouse under his eye." Charles N. was asked how he thought the suspect got the "mouse." Charles N. replied, "Somebody hit him in the eye." Charles N. would only say it was possible that one particular officer was responsible for the suspect's eye injury. He said he did not know who that officer was. Charles N. denies seeing Walter P. kick the suspect.

"When the officer kicked the man, his head went up off the ground."

Officer Charles N. said the officers all stood up after the handcuffs and cordcuff restraint were applied. He said he was not looking at Walter P. or the suspect when he heard a woman scream, "Hey, that's uncalled for." Charles N. said he assumed that was probably what the woman was referring to. He said he was standing close to Walter P. but did not see him kick the subject.

Officer Charles N. said he saw an officer turn on a flashlight to check the suspect. He said he told the officer not to use the light. He said he thought light activated PCP people. He said he did not know who that officer was as there were eight to ten officers present at the time.

Officer Charles N. said they put the suspect in his police car because it was the largest vehicle there. He said he and his partner drove the sus-

pect to the Western Area Station. Charles N. said two officers from third watch got into their car and transported the suspect to jail. He said during the transportation to the Western Station the suspect kept saying, "Give me a gun, I'll kill somebody," and that he "wanted to rape a bunch of women."

The last person Peter K. interviewed was civilian Debra S., the "Debbie" mentioned by previous witnesses.

Interview of Debra S. On August 18, 1985, at 1049 hours, I interviewed Debra S. regarding the arrest of Jason B. on July 26, 1985.

Debra S. said she was getting ready for bed when she heard a loud banging noise. She said she went downstairs and saw that a man had kicked his way into one of the nearby apartments. She said the man was running around banging on doors and fences. She said he jumped the fence and went into the swimming pool. She said she called the Police Department.

Debra S. said everybody in the apartment complex was following the man around and observing what he was doing. She said she stopped a police car with two officers in it. The officers told her they were already on a call that they were going to take care of first. She said that within a few minutes another police car came to their location.

Debra S. said the two officers got out of their car and went toward the man. She said the man saw the officers and just got on his knees and put his hands behind him. She said the man surrendered to the officers. She said she walked away and did not see what happened to start the fight. She said she was told later that the man just started fighting. She said she heard the commotion as she walked away and went back to see what was happening.

Confronting the Officer

Debra S. said the officers had the man on the ground and were hitting him with a baton in the back and on the back of his legs. She said the officers were pulling the man's hair. She said they struggled with the man for about five minutes before they got him handcuffed. She said that, by this time, there were about eight officers present.

Debra S. said that when the officers went to pick up the man to put him in a police car, the Mexican officer kicked the man in the head as hard as he could. She said she got upset. She said she could not identify the officer because he hid his badge. She said she told the officer, "That was wrong and it was uncalled for." She said she started crying and got close to the officers as she spoke directly to him. She said the officer "behaved like a little child" and said, "Well, he was hitting me first." Debra S. said one of the neighbors grabbed her by the arm and pulled her away from the officers. She said she could not get the number of the car the officer was driving.

"Hey, there's too many civilians around to be doing that stuff."

After Debra S. gave her account of the incident I asked her a series of questions to clarify what she had told me. Debra S. said she could not remember which officer was pulling the man's hair. She said she was certain that the man was handcuffed and that the officers were trying to bend his legs up to secure them to his hands.

Debra S. said the man was yelling that he was "Mad Max" and could not feel any pain. She said she heard one officer saying, "Oh, you feel no pain," as he hit the man with a baton. She said she thought it was the Mexican officer who was sitting on the man and hitting him. She said she heard the officers saying, "Bend your fucking knees."

Debra S. said there was one officer whom she thought saw the officer kick the man. She said, "When I got into the Mexican guy's face, the one, I don't know, he could have been a sergeant or something, maybe, he was walking with

him and he had his arm around the Mexican guy. And he says, 'Hey, there's too many civilians around to be doing that stuff.'"

Reporting Brutality

Debra S. iterated that when the officer kicked the man, his head went up off the ground. She said she heard the noise caused by the impact. She said it made her "sick to her stomach." She said it was "uncalled for" and she said, "I want your name or your badge number. I'm gonna report this." She said the officer said, "Go ahead and report it. I'll give this guy your address so he can come and you guys can get together and report me." She said the officer did not give her his name; instead, he avoided her.

Debra S. said she had come face-to-face with the man before the officers arrived and he had no injuries at that time.

Sergeant Peter K. interviewed these and other people in the course of his investigation. Walter P., the accused officer, did not talk to Peter K. on advice of his attorney. On August 26, 1985, Peter K. wrote up his final report and recommendations. The excerpts reprinted here have been edited for length and to avoid repetition.

On July 26, 1985, at 2249 hours, officers from the Western Area Command were dispatched regarding a disturbance involving a man who walked into an apartment uninvited, sat down, and unzipped his trousers. The request for the police was made by Bill J. who said the man looked like he was under the influence of some type of drug. Bill J. described the man as a white male with long brown hair, a dirty face, wearing blue jeans, a dark t-shirt, and no shoes. He also told the operator that the man had been beating on a truck and breaking down a fence. Bill J. said the man took a swing at another man who was assisting in removing the man from a neighbor's apartment.

Officers Brian D. and Walter P., Unit 612-K, went to the apartment complex in response to a broadcast of an indecent exposure dispatch. The suspect, Jason B., had attracted the attention of numerous people in the complex who witnessed the encounter with the officers.

Jason B. was trying to climb the wall to a second story apartment from the ground when he noticed the officers on the scene. Officer Brian D. ordered Jason B. to the ground. Jason B. complied by dropping to his knees and putting his hands behind him. The officers approached Jason B. and were handcuffing him when a struggle began. Officer Walter P. called for additional officers, resulting in at least eight officers arriving at the scene.

During the struggle with Jason B. the officers decided to apply the cordcuff leg restraint. Officer Brian D. was observed by witnesses as he repeatedly hit Jason B. in the back with his baton. Brian D. was heard saying, "Bend your fucking knees!" as he hit Jason B. who was lying face down on the ground. Jason B. was screaming obscenities at the officers and saying that he was "Mad Max" and could feel no pain. A witness said each time Jason B. said he could feel no pain, an officer, believed to be Walter P., would respond, "Oh, you feel no pain," as he hit Jason B..

The Investigation

On July 29, 1985, I received a Complaint Control Form filed by Ronald L. for investigation. Ronald L.'s complaint read:

Two officers, one Caucasian and one Hispanic, had a guy face down and handcuffed. After he was hogtied, several officers arrived. When everyone started to lift the guy, the Hispanic cop kicked him in the face. . . .

On August 5, 1985, I spoke with Jason B.'s mother. The telephone number Jason B. gave to the officers at the time of his arrest is his mother's work number.

Afraid to File Complaint

She said Jason B. did not file a complaint because he was afraid. She said she was afraid for him to complain because the police officers might try to get back at him. She said Jason B. was badly beaten by the officers. She said that based on the advice of their attorney, Jason B.

would not talk to me. I convinced her to have Jason B. meet with me after conferring with their attorney since it was I who had contacted him in the interest of investigating a complaint filed on his behalf by a witness. . . .

On August 6, 1985, at 1320 hours, I interviewed Jason B. regarding his arrest. He said he was walking through the apartment complex when he was contacted by police officers. He said the officers were probably called because he had been hitting on people's doors. He said he was not fighting with anyone.

"I didn't resist arrest. They had me."

Jason B. said he was put on the ground by the officers. He said they were kicking and hitting him. He said he was knocked unconscious. He said he never fought back because he was handcuffed. He said he had bruises on his ribs and scratch marks. He said his eye was "almost gone." He described his eye as being swollen closed with discoloration around it. He said he had bruises and bumps on his head. He said he still did not have any feeling in his right thumb from being handcuffed too tightly.

Jason B. said he did not resist when the officers arrested him. He said when the officers had him on the ground he was screaming and yelling at them because they were kicking him. He said, "I didn't resist arrest. They had me. If I resisted; how can you resist arrest and they got you down on the ground."

On August 6, 1985, I contacted the Narcotics Laboratory and ordered a comprehensive drug test of Jason B.'s blood sample. On August 14, 1985, I was advised by the Narcotics Unit that the blood test was negative and that a report was pending. The test did not include a check for cocaine or amphetamines. I asked that a test for cocaine and amphetamines be conducted.

On August 12, 1985, I received Jason B.'s booking photograph. The photograph showed that he had a "mouse" under his right eye when he was transported to County Jail. . . .

Did Not See Incident

On August 15, 1985, at 1502 hours, I interviewed Officer Keith F. Officer Keith F. said he and his partner, Officer Charles N., were traveling along when they were stopped by a woman carrying a stick. The woman said a man was trying to get inside her apartment. Keith F. said at that time the radio was dispatching another unit to handle the incident. The dispatcher told them to continue on to Doctor's Hospital to "Code-5" a homicide suspect. Keith F. said they returned after about four or five minutes because a "cover now" call was broadcast.

When they arrived, Officers Brian D. and Walter P. were wrestling with the suspect. There were several other officers present at this time. Keith F. said he and Charles N. helped control the suspect until he was handcuffed and the cordcuff was applied. Keith F. was unsure if the suspect was handcuffed before or after he arrived. He said they put the cordcuff on the suspect because he was acting violent. He said the suspect was kicking around and he (Keith F.) held one leg until the cordcuff was applied.

"Officer Walter P. stated he did not wish to talk to me."

Keith F. said he did not see any officer hit the suspect, nor did he hear any officer use coarse language directed at the suspect. Keith F. said he had no knowledge that the suspect was injured. Keith F. said he did not see Walter P. kick the man. He said he did not hear the woman yell at Walter P. about his treatment of the man. Keith F. denies any knowledge that Officer Walter P. kicked the man.

On August 18, 1985, at 0903 hours, I interviewed Officer John H. He said when he arrived on the scene he saw a group of officers on a grassy area. He said the officers had broadcast a "Code-4." He said he continued up to the scene to see what was going on. John H. said he saw a man lying face down on the ground with the cordcuff applied. He said there were officers around the suspect and people near the apartments in front of the officers. He said it appeared there was nothing going on so he turned around and started walking away.

John H. said he heard a female voice yell, "That wasn't necessary." He then heard numerous people yelling and screaming. John H. said he heard several officers say, "I'm getting out of here." He said he went back to the car and left without asking why everyone was leaving. John H. said he later heard that someone had kicked the man. He said he "just heard it in the locker room." John H. said he did not know who said the man had been kicked; he said he "just heard it." He said he did not know that it was Officer Walter P. whom the officers were saying had kicked the suspect. John H. said he did not hear the officers on the scene tell Officer Brian D. to get Walter P. away from the scene. . . .

On August 19, 1985, I interviewed Officer Walter P. in the presence of his attorney. Officer Walter P. was advised of his constitutional rights in compliance with Miranda versus Arizona. Based on the advice of his attorney, Officer Walter P. stated he did not wish to talk to me.

Based on the information developed during this investigation I request that Officer Walter P. be charged with violation of §245(a) of the State Penal Code in that he committed an assault on the person of Jason B. with force likely to produce great bodily injury.

I also request that Officer Walter P. be charged with violation of §149 of the State Penal Code in that he assaulted Jason B. under the color of authority without lawful necessity.

The Appeal

Based on this and on previous incidents, Walter P. was fired from the San Diego Police Department effective October 1, 1985. He appealed his firing to the Civil Service Commission of San Diego, and was granted his right to a hearing.

*The appeal was heard over several hearings begin-
ning May 29, 1986. The Civil Service Commission reviewed all the documents reprinted here, as well as additional oral and written testimony about the incident,
including testimony from Walter P. The Commission
decided to uphold the dismissal. Excerpts from the findings and conclusions are reprinted below. In these proceedings Walter P. is referred to as the Appellant, and
representatives of the San Diego Police Department are
referred to as the Appointing Authority.*

The matter of the appeal of Walter P., Police
Officer II, from an order effective October 1,
1985, terminating his services as an employee of
the City of San Diego Police Department was
heard before the Civil Service Commission of
the City of San Diego at 9:00 a.m. on May 29,
June 11, June 12, and at 8:00 a.m. on July 3,
1986. . . .

The Commission, having held said hearing
and having heard testimony pursuant thereto,
and having received evidence both oral and doc-
umentary, and after hearing arguments by the
respective sides, now makes its findings and conclusions as follows. . . .

Findings

1. Testimony and evidence revealed that at approximately 11:00 p.m. on July 26, 1985, the Appellant and his partner, Officer Brian D., were
dispatched to an apartment complex in response to a disturbance call involving a male suspect who was reportedly exhibiting lewd behavior and was attempting to unlawfully enter private residences. Shortly after their arrival at the
scene, the Appellant and Officer Brian D. observed the suspect, who was later identified as Jason B., displaying lewd behavior and subsequently attempting to enter a residence through
a window. Believing Jason B. to be under the influence of PCP, the Appellant requested that
cover units be dispatched to the scene, after
which time he and Officer Brian D. confronted
Jason B.

2. Testimony revealed that when the Appellant and Officer Brian D. confronted Jason B.,
he was cooperative and willingly complied with
their order to put his hands behind his back and
voluntarily knelt on the ground in between the
two officers. As Officer Brian D. was in the process of handcuffing him, Jason B. suddenly and
unexplainably stood up. The Appellant, unsure
if the handcuffs had been completely secured,
grabbed Jason B. by the upper torso, after which
a struggle ensued between Jason B. and the two
officers which resulted in the officers falling to
the ground on top of Jason B. Testimony revealed that while on the ground, Jason B. continued to struggle with the two officers, and was
yelling obscenities and unintelligible comments.
Testimony further revealed that Jason B. was resisting the officers' efforts to subdue him. Testimony and evidence revealed that within a short
period of time, approximately 6-8 other officers
arrived at the scene, some of whom assisted the
Appellant and Officer Brian D. in placing Jason
B. in a cordcuff restraint. Testimony and evidence revealed that once Jason B. was fully under control, face down on the ground with the
handcuffs and cordcuff restraint secured, the officers stepped back for a moment to catch their
breaths prior to carrying Jason B. to the patrol
vehicle. Inconsistent testimony was provided regarding the actions of the Appellant prior to Jason B. being carried to the patrol vehicle.

"The force with which the Ap-
pellant kicked Jason B. created a
'thud' sound."

---

3. Testimony provided by Officer Robert W.
revealed that after the other officers had
stepped away from Jason B., he used his flashlight to examine Jason B. to determine if he had
sustained any injuries during the struggle. Officer Robert W. testified that he observed no
bruises on or sign of injury to Jason B.'s face at
this time. Officer Robert W. further testified that
shortly thereafter, another officer, using his
flashlight, started to examine Jason B. for injuries when the Appellant directed him to turn

off the flashlight. According to testimony provided by Officer Robert W., within a few seconds after the officer turned off his flashlight the Appellant, who was standing next to Jason B.'s head, kicked Jason B. in the head area. Officer Robert W. testified that the force with which the Appellant kicked Jason B. created a "thud" sound.

4. Ronald L., a citizen who observed the entire contact between Jason B. and the officers, testified that as the officers were picking Jason B. up to carry him to the patrol vehicle, he clearly observed the Appellant step up to Jason B. and forcefully kick him in the face area. Ronald L. testified that the force with which the Appellant kicked Jason B. caused Jason B.'s head to "snap" and resembled the sound of a watermelon being dropped to the ground. . . .

5. Testimony provided by Jason B. revealed that he had earlier in the day ingested five papers of LSD and that his recollection of some of the evening's events was somewhat unclear. Jason B. testified that he did clearly remember being kicked in the face while being lifted off the ground, from which he sustained injury to his right eye area. Jason B. further testified that after being kicked, he lost consciousness which he did not regain until after being placed in the patrol vehicle.

"A review of the Appellant's performance history revealed . . . incidents of misconduct."

---

6. Testimony provided by the Appellant revealed that after Jason B. was fully handcuffed and cordcuffed, he was face down on the ground with his head next to the Appellant. The Appellant testified that shortly after the other officers stepped back, Jason B. rolled onto his side and started expectorating at him. When Jason B. did not comply with his order to "knock it off", the Appellant shoved his foot across Jason B.'s

face to restrain his actions. The Appellant testified that his action did not cause Jason B. to lose consciousness, but that it did cause him to stop expectorating. The Appellant further testified that he considered his action to be justified and proper as the desired effect of such action was achieved.

7. Testimony provided by several of the officers who were at the scene revealed that they did not observe the Appellant kick Jason B. Testimony provided by the aforementioned officer revealed, however, that their attention was not focused on the Appellant and Jason B. during the entire incident.

8. Inconsistent testimony was presented regarding whether Jason B. was expectorating during the incident, as well as regarding his actions while being carried to the patrol vehicle. Considerable corroborated testimony revealed that after the Appellant's foot made contact with Jason B.'s head, a female watching the incident along with several other citizens yelled to the Appellant something to the effect of "Hey, that's not cool—you can't do that." Testimony revealed that none of the officers spoke with the female to determine the basis for her remark.

9. Testimony and evidence revealed that Jason B. was transported to county jail by Officer Robert W. and when "booked" into the jail facility, his right eye area was bruised and swollen.

10. Testimony and evidence subsequently revealed that Ronald L. filed a complaint against the Appellant alleging the use of excessive force which led to the investigation and subsequent termination of the Appellant.

11. The Appointing Authority testified that officers are not expected to allow themselves to be expectorated at or on and offered several lawful and acceptable methods which would have been available to the Appellant to prevent its occurrence. The Appointing Authority further testified that the Appellant's actions in kicking Jason B. while he was fully restrained and under the complete control of several officers, in spite of his contention that Jason B. was expectorating at him, was a blatant, willful act of excessive and

unnecessary force, constituted a serious violation of department policies, and warranted considerable discipline. To determine the appropriate degree of discipline to be administered to the Appellant for his misconduct in the Jason B. incident, the Appointing Authority reviewed and considered the Appellant's performance and disciplinary history with the San Diego Police Department.

12. A review of the Appellant's performance history revealed the following incidents of misconduct and related discipline:

a) On September 4, 1985, the Appellant received a written reprimand for violation of Department Instructions regarding transporting prisoners.

b) On May 17, 1985, the Appellant was counselled regarding his failure to adhere to department procedures pertaining to detaining and transporting subjects in police vehicles.

c) On March 7, 1985, the Appellant received a five-day suspension and disciplinary transfer for poor judgment and conduct unbecoming an officer by becoming involved in a verbal and physical altercation with a female citizen and for absenting himself from his assigned beat area without prior supervisorial approval.

"Termination of the Appellant was fully justified."

---

d) The Appellant received an "Improvement Needed" performance evaluation for the period of February 28, 1984–February 28, 1985 wherein his performance was rated as Improvement Needed in the categories of officer safety/self-covering, attitude towards police work, relations with police personnel and citizens, demeanor, personal appearance, acceptance by others and leadership ability, and as Unsatisfactory in the categories of judgment and knowledge of department guidelines.

e) On April 17, 1984, the Appellant received a written reprimand for conduct unbecoming an officer by becoming involved in an off-duty confrontation with his ex-wife.

f) On October 14, 1983, the Appellant received a Supplemental Employee Performance Report for unsatisfactory performance. The report cited three supervisors' investigations that sustained complaints for discourtesy, unbecoming conduct, unlawful arrest and disregard for established Department Rules and Regulations. . . .

13. After a thorough review of all testimony and evidence and consideration of the motivation and credibility of all witnesses, the Commission finds that sufficient evidence was presented to prove that the Appellant intentionally and forcefully shoved his foot across Jason B.'s face, causing injury thereto, and that such action was unjustifiable and constituted unnecessary and excessive force as Jason B. was fully restrained, defenseless and under the complete control and authority of at least eight police officers. The Commission finds that such egregious misconduct warrants considerable discipline.

14. Based on a thorough review of all testimony and evidence regarding the Appellant's performance and disciplinary history, the Commission finds that the Appellant has demonstrated an unwillingness and inability to adhere to and comply with Department Rules and Regulations, exhibited a trend of offensive conduct toward the public, and apparently has failed to benefit from the considerable efforts extended by the Police Department to correct such behavior. Based on the severity of the Appellant's misconduct in the Jason B. incident, aggravated by his past performance and disciplinary record, the Commission concludes that termination of the Appellant was fully justified and warranted.

This case study does not directly answer the broader questions addressed in this book, such as the frequency of police brutality, its causes, and whether police reforms are necessary. What it attempts to do instead is portray one example of police brutality and the steps taken by authorities to determine the truth.

Bibliography

Books

Geoffrey P. Alpert and Roger G. Dunham — *Policing Urban America*. Prospect Heights, IL: Waveland Press, 1988.

Anthony V. Bouza — *The Police Mystique: An Insider's Look at Cops, Crime, and the Criminal Justice System*. New York: Plenum Press, 1990.

Bill Clede — *Police Nonlethal Force Manual*. Harrisburg, PA: Stackpole Books, 1987.

Edwin J. DeLattre — *Character and Cops*. Washington, DC: American Enterprise Institute for Public Policy Research, 1989.

Frank Donner — *Protectors of Privilege: Red Squads and Police Repression in Urban America*. Berkeley: University of California Press, 1990.

Larry Miller and Michael Braswell — *Human Relations and Police Work*. Prospect Heights, IL: Waveland Press, 1988.

Malcom K. Sparrow, Mark H. Moore, and David M. Kennedy — *Beyond 911: A New Era for Policing*. New York: Basic Books, 1990.

Periodicals

James N. Baker — "Los Angeles Aftershocks," *Newsweek*, April 1, 1991.

Michael Biggs — "Non-Lethal Weapons: A Tool for Law Enforcement," *Journal of Contemporary Criminal Justice*, February 1990. Available from Department of Criminal Justice, California State University, Long Beach, 1250 Bellflower Blvd., Long Beach, CA 90840.

Katherine Bishop — "Police Attacks: Hard Crimes to Uncover, Let Alone Stop," *The New York Times*, March 24, 1991.

Anthony Bouza — "Pressures from Overclass Exacerbate Police Brutality," *In These Times*, April 24-30, 1991.

William F. Buckley Jr. — "L.A. Law," *National Review*, April 29, 1991.

Christianity Today — "L.A. Cop: Robert Vernon," April 29, 1991.

CJ the Americas — "Violence Between Police and Public Declines," April/May 1991. Available from *CJ the Americas*, 1333 S. Wabash, PO Box 53, Chicago, IL 60605.

Alexander Cockburn — "In the Shadow of Rodney King," *The Nation*, April 15, 1991.

Alexander Cockburn — "State-of-Siege Mindset Adds to L.A. Police Violence," *In These Times*, April 17-23, 1991.

Miriam Davidson — "The Mexican Border War," *The Nation*, November 12, 1990.

Keith Ellison and Chris Nisan — "Battling the Rise in Police Brutality," *Forward Motion*, June 1989. Available from PO Box 1884, Jamaica Plain, MA 02130.

Michael Ervin — "Police Torture Comes to Light," *The Progressive*, June 1991.

Don Feder — "Double Standard on Police Brutality," *Conservative Chronicle*, April 10, 1991. Available from PO Box 11297, Des Moines, IL 50340-1297.

Gilbert Geis and Arnold Binder — "Non-Lethal Weapons: The Potential and the Pitfalls," *Journal of Contemporary Criminal Justice*, February 1990.

Geoffrey Taylor Gibbs — "L.A. Cops, Taped in the Act," *The New York Times*, March 12, 1991.

Rick Henderson — "L.A., Lawless," *Reason*, May 1991.

Jesse Jackson — "In the Camera's Eye," *Liberal Opinion Week*, March 25, 1991.

	Available from PO Box 468, Vinton, IA 52349.
John Leo	"The Abortion Protesters and the Police," *U.S. News & World Report,* August 6, 1990.
Gerald Lynch	"Cops and College," *America,* April 4, 1987.
John F. McManus	"No Civilian Review Boards," *The New American,* March 14, 1988.
Joe Maxwell	"YFC Worker Claims Police Harass Street Youth," *Christianity Today,* February 19, 1990.
Harold Meyerson	"Gatesgate," *The New Republic,* June 10, 1991.
Peter Michelmore	"New Cop in Town," *Reader's Digest,* March 1990.
Kim Neely	"Protesters, Police Clash," *Rolling Stone,* February 21, 1991.
Hugh Pearson	"White America Still Treats Blacks Like Slaves of Yore," *National Catholic Reporter,* April 19, 1991.
Alex Prud'homme	"Police Brutality!" *Time,* March 25, 1991.
William Raspberry	"The American Ideal and the American Reality," *Liberal Opinion Week,* March 25, 1991.
Paul Reidinger	"Necessary Roughness," *ABA Journal,* August 1990.
Kayne B. Robinson	"The New Police Peril: Civilian Review Boards," *American Rifleman,* May 1991.
Norman Siegel	"Policing the Police," *The New York Times,* March 23, 1991.
Richard Starr	"Good Cops Must Restore Image," *Insight,* April 8, 1991.
John Taliaferro and Andrew Murr	"After Police Brutality: L.A.'s Identity Crisis," *Newsweek,* May 20, 1991.
Bill Turque	"Brutality on the Beat," *Newsweek,* March 25, 1991.
Jonathan Walters	"Dirty Harry, Meet Officer Nice Guy," *Governing,* December 1990. Available from Congressional Quarterly Inc., 1414 22nd St. NW, Washington, DC 20037.
Gordon Witkin	"Cops Under Fire," *U.S. News & World Report,* December 3, 1990.
Susan Yocum	"Why It Happened: An L.A. Cop's View," *Newsweek,* March 25, 1991.

Organizations
to Contact

The editors have compiled the following list of organizations that are concerned with the issues debated in this book. All of them have publications or information available for interested readers. The descriptions are derived from materials provided by the organizations. This list was compiled upon the date of publication. Names and phone numbers of organizations are subject to change.

American Civil Liberties Union (ACLU)
132 W. 43rd St.
New York, NY 10036
(212) 944-9800

The ACLU is a national organization that works to defend Americans' civil liberties guaranteed in the U.S. Constitution. It provides legal assistance for victims of police brutality. The union publishes the quarterly newsletter *Civil Liberties* and various pamphlets and position papers, including *On the Line,* a policy report on police brutality.

International Law Enforcement Stress Association (ILESA)
PO Box 3360
Plymouth, MA 02361
(508) 747-5746

ILESA is an international organization concerned with reducing the job-related stress of police officers and other criminal justice professionals. It publishes *Police Stress,* a quarterly journal.

National Association for the Advancement of Colored People (NAACP)
4805 Mt. Hope Dr.
Baltimore, MD 21215
(301) 481-4100

The NAACP is one of the oldest and largest civil rights organizations in the nation. It produces research and documentation on police brutality and provides legal services for victims of brutality. It publishes the magazine *Crisis.*

National Association of Chiefs of Police (NACOP)
3801 Biscayne Blvd.
Miami, FL 33137
(305) 891-1700

NACOP is a professional organization of police chiefs and law-enforcement officers. It regularly surveys its members on criminal justice matters, including police misconduct. It publishes books and the periodicals *Chiefs of Police Magazine* and *Criminal Investigator.*

National Institute of Justice (NIJ)
U.S. Department of Justice
PO Box 6000
Rockville, MD 20850
(800) 535-8811

The NIJ supports research concerning crime and the criminal justice system. It publishes and distributes reports, books, and bibliographies through the National Criminal Justice Reference Service, an international clearinghouse of criminal justice information.

Police Executive Research Forum (PERF)
2300 M St. NW, Suite 910
Washington, DC 20037
(202) 466-7820

PERF is an organization of police executives that seeks to stimulate public understanding and discussion of important criminal justice issues. It publishes newsletters and reports on a variety of issues, including police brutality and civilian review boards.

Police Foundation
1001 2nd St. NW, Suite 200
Washington, DC 20037
(202) 833-1460

The foundation conducts research projects on police practices and aims to improve the quality of police personnel. It publishes *Police Manager,* a quarterly journal.

Police Misconduct Lawyer Referral Service (PMLRS)
633 S. Shatto Pl.
Los Angeles, CA 90005
(213) 387-3435

PMLRS provides legal consultations and assistance for victims of police brutality. It publishes statistics and reports on police brutality and the pamphlet *Remedies for Police Misconduct Abuse of Power and Brutality.*

Index